D0286017

EXTRAORDINARY CHILD

DISCARDED
WILLIAMS COLLEGE LIBRARIES

A publication of the
SCHOOL OF HAWAIIAN
ASIAN & PACIFIC STUDIES
University of Hawai'i

EXTRAORDINARY CHILD

Poems from a South Indian Devotional Genre

. . .

PAULA RICHMAN

SHAPS Library of Translations
UNIVERSITY OF HAWAI'I PRESS
HONOLULU

© 1997 School of Hawaiian, Asian & Pacific Studies
All rights reserved
Printed in the United States of America

02 01 00 99 98 97 5 4 3 2 1

Library of Congress Cataloging-in-Publication Data
Extraordinary child : poems from a South Indian devotional genre. /
Paula Richman.
p. cm. — (SHAPS library of translations)
ISBN 0-8248-1063-5 (pbk. : alk. paper)
1. Piḷḷaittamiḻ. 2. Devotional poetry, Tamil—Translations into English. 3. Devotional poetry, Tamil—History and criticism. 4. Tamil language—Grammar. I. Richman, Paula. II. Series.
PL4758.65.E5E97 1997
894.8'111009382945432—dc21 96-40072
CIP

"Wannaplay?" by June Goodwin,
© 1995 by June Goodwin.

University of Hawai'i Press books are printed
on acid-free paper and meet the guidelines for permanence
and durability of the Council on Library Resources

Designed by Trina Stahl

In Memory of Dr. Ku. Paramasivam

teacher, scholar, and lover of Tamil poetry

(1933–1992)

CONTENTS

ILLUSTRATIONS AND TABLES

FIGURES

TABLES

PREFACE

The Design of the Book

THIS BOOK SETS out the distinctive features of the pillaittamil: a genre of Tamil devotional poetry to an extraordinary deity or person, addressed in the form of a child. The book provides resources to transform the reader into a person equipped to savor well-crafted pillaittamil poetry from several religious communities. We know how connoisseurs of calligraphy immerse themselves in the subject matter and techniques of the artistic tradition in order to develop the discernment to appreciate pieces of calligraphy they encounter. In a similar manner, Part One of this book initiates the reader into the pillaittamil tradition. Chapter 1 explains the distinctive subject matter of a pillaittamil and its highly conventionalized poetic structure. Chapter 2 displays the aesthetic of poetic virtuosity upon which the genre rests by looking closely at one standard component of a pillaittamil: the moon verse.

This book also reveals the range of poetry found in the genre. Part Two is designed like an embroidery sampler. There the reader will find a wide-ranging and carefully selected anthology of verses translated from diverse pillaittamils. The anthology facilitates judicious poetic tasting for readers who do not know Tamil, as well as for Tamil readers who want to see pillaittamil poetry in a fresh light, through the lens of translation.

More specifically, Part Two provides the reader with selections from six pillaittamils, varied in their historical context and ideological affiliation. From each one-hundred-verse poem, I have selected and translated a set of outstanding verses. Since the majority of all pillaittamils come from the Śaivite community, three chapters deal with their texts: a fifteenth-century poem to a god (chapter 3), a seventeenth-century poem to a goddess (chapter 4), and a nineteenth-century poem to a saint (chapter 5). The following chapter focuses upon an early pillaittamil to the Prophet Muhammad (chapter 6), while another centers on the life and writings of an author who recently published a pillaittamil to Baby Jesus (chapter 7). Part Two closes with an examination of two pillaittamils written as part of the Tamil Culture movement in the 1980s (chapter 8).

In Part Three I conclude with some reflections on presuppositions and consequences of the pillaittamil genre's poetic structure. This section contains some observations about male poets' use of a maternal voice, the social dynamics of praise, and the political implications of poets from diverse religious communities writing in the same genre. This book is, to my knowledge, the first comprehensive critical treatment of the pillaittamil genre as a whole and the first set of translations to include pillaittamils from multiple religious traditions. The closing remarks, therefore, are intended to encourage continuing conversation about the nature and meanings of pillaittamils.

Acknowledgments

THIS PROJECT INVOLVED several phases of research, for which I have been fortunate to receive funding at key junctures. A senior fellowship from the American Institute for Indian Studies in 1984–1985 enabled me to locate and study major pillaittamils. A National Endowment for the Humanities Fellowship for College Teachers allowed me to develop my translations and explore the historical development of the genre. In 1990–1991 I returned to India with an American Institute of Indian Studies grant to examine the composition, performance, and publication history of the genre, as well as to interview living pillaittamil poets. I am grateful to Oberlin College for the sabbatical that enabled me to complete this book.

I appreciate the aid given to me by the library staff at the following institutions: the Dr. U. V. Swaminathaiyer Library in Thiruvanmiyur, the Theosophical Society Library in Adyar, the Maraimalai Adigal Library and the University of Madras Library in Madras, the Tamil University Library and Sarasvati Mahal Library in Tanjore, the Tamil Sangam Library and American College Library in Madurai, the India Office Library and Oriental Manuscripts Division of the British Museum as well as the School for Oriental and African Studies Library in London, and the University of Chicago's Regenstein Library.

I am most indebted to Ku. Paramasivam, whose vast knowledge of the poetic complexities and religious nuances of Tamil literature aided me greatly in untangling the many complex poems I encountered. This book is dedicated to his memory and the many gifts of Tamil instruction that he bestowed upon a generation of Tamil scholars. I thank V. S. Rajam for her reference grammar, to which I have had recourse on many occasions, and for her conversations about grammatical, syntactic, and semantic issues in response to textual queries. My translations are indebted to A. K. Ramanujan, who created, *ex nihilo,* a set of poetic strategies to respond to the complexities of rendering Tamil into unstilted English and whose work set the standards for translation from Tamil. He also insisted that this book be short, so it would suggest the richness of the genre rather than sate the reader with too much. As always, Wendy Doniger's insightful reading of the manuscript revealed new avenues of exploration. David Shulman commented upon some of my earliest translations and critiqued my later ones; I appreciate his sensitivity to the many linguistic registers of Tamil poetry and to the tropes and poetics of the pillaittamil genre. George L. Hart reviewed the manuscript for the press, making helpful suggestions. To Prema Nandakumar, I owe special gratitude for her encouragement of this project.

Because poetry by Muslim writers has long been marginalized in the study of the Tamil literary tradition, I am particularly grateful to M. R. M. Abdul Rahim, book publisher, and to M. Syed Mohamed Hasan, for helping me locate key texts, as well as to S. Fathima and Nayinar Muhammad. Invaluable aid came from Dr. M. M. Uwise, whose pioneering scholarship on Tamil Islamic texts was matched by his generosity in sharing that knowledge.

I appreciate the suggestions of many who read sections of the book: Marcia Colish, Frank Conlon, Norman Cutler, Charles Hallisey, Alf Hiltebeitel, Seth Houston, Katherine Linehan, James Lindholm, Patricia Mathews, Indira Peterson, Martha Selby, Tony K. Stewart, Sandra Zagarell, and Abbie Ziffren. Also helpful were the thoughtful comments at talks given at the Research Triangle South

Asia Colloquium in Raleigh, the Advanced Centre for Historical Studies at Aligarh University, the Conference on Religion in South India in Austin, the South Asia Seminar at the University of Virginia, the panel on Language, Genre, and Discourses of Plurality at the Association for Asian Studies in Washington, D.C., and the Department of History of Religions at Uppsala University, Sweden. Thanks also go to poets Aruḷ Cellaturai and Mu. Singaravelu, who took the time to give such thorough answers to my many questions. At Oberlin I am deeply indebted to Terri Mitchell and Thelma Roush, who typed many versions of the manuscript and dealt with innumerable computer complications.

I am grateful for the help of two extraordinary readers. As a referee for the press, John Stratton Hawley read the manuscript with a care that most people reserve for their own translations, coupled with an ability to suggest fruitful ways in which I could make the poetry more accessible to non-Tamil speakers. Michael H. Fisher encouraged me from the beginning of this project to its end and read several versions of each chapter. As always, he has been my toughest critic and greatest support. All of these people have enriched the book in many ways; I alone am responsible for any errors that remain.

Transliteration Policy

BECAUSE MY GOAL was to translate pillaittamil poetry into English, rather than some kind of scholarly hybrid English-Tamil, the translations contain minimal transliteration and diacritical marks, except for the names of deities. Notes at the bottom of the page are limited to information necessary for the nonspecialist reader to understand the nuances of the poetry. The fine points of the analysis addressed to Tamil specialists appear in the endnotes.

When transliterating, I use the standard *Tamil Lexicon* system. After the first mention, I have done away with diacritical marks and italics for a couple of core terms that recur often throughout the book, such as "pillaittamil" and "talelo" (a lullaby refrain). I employ modern standard spellings for place names in English, such as Madurai. I use the familiar Anglicized spelling for terms that have passed into general usage in Tamilnadu in that form, such as "Sangam" and "Chola." When an author has consistently used an Anglicized version of his or her name in English publications, I use that form rather than a Tamil transliteration. (For example, I use E. V. Ramasami, rather than Ī. Vē. Rāmacāmi.)

Translation Terminology

"POEM" REFERS TO the entire pillaittamil, "paruvam" refers to one of the ten sections of a pillaittamil, and "verse" refers to a single, self-contained poetic unit (of which there are usually about one hundred in a pillaittamil). The term "refrain" indicates the short phrase repeated twice at the verse's end, which identifies the verse as belonging to a particular section of the poem. For each verse translated in Part Two of the book, I give the verse number within the poem, followed by the number within the paruvam (section).

PART ONE

HOW TO READ A PILLAITTAMIL

1. *The God of Beginnings.* Drawing by Prafullah Mohanti
(original in the collection of the author; photograph by Joseph Romano).

CHAPTER ONE

EXTRAORDINARY CHILD

THE SOUTH INDIAN devotional poetry called the pillaittamil is a genre built of multiples: multiple verses, multiple sections, multiple poems, and multiple religious affiliations. This genre always contains a particular sequence of poetry found again and again, but never in quite the same way. In a pillaittamil, the poet assumes a maternal voice to praise an extraordinary being (deity, prophet, saint, or hero), envisioning him or her in the form of a baby. The pillaittamil moves through ten sequenced sections, each of which usually contains ten verses, adding up to one hundred (or slightly more) verses. What has made this genre so attractive for nearly eight hundred years? In A. K. Ramanujan's description of patterns within Tamil literary tradition, he notes that often "poems do not come singly, but in sequences often arranged in tens, hundreds, and thousands." Such genres bring together poets and audiences "sharing motifs, images, and structures, yet playing variations that individuate each poem. Every poem resonates with the absent presences of others that sound with it,"[1] says Ramanujan, in words that aptly describe pillaittamil poetry.

This book sketches the ways in which the pillaittamil genre produced a corpus of diverse and sophisticated poetry over many centuries. Approximately sixty-nine million people, located primarily in the modern state of Tamilnadu, South India, speak Tamil as their mother tongue.[2] The Tamil language possesses an unbroken poetic tradition whose origins lie in the first centuries of this millennium; the first extant pillaittamil dates from the twelfth century, and pillaittamils continue to be written today. The religious pluralism of the pillaittamil tradition reflects the religious pluralism of the Tamil-speaking population. Although the genre began within the Tamil Hindu literary tradition, later Muslim and Christian poets have adopted it as well.[3] Now poets also write pillaittamils in praise of political figures and movie stars.

The genre demands adherence to specific—and highly stylized—poetic conventions. Despite such potentially stultifying restrictions, more than two hundred and fifty pillaittamils have been written.[4] In other words, poets have composed thousands of distinctive pillaittamil verses of vivid variety. Pillaittamil poets have written in different historical periods, belonged to diverse religious communities, sought varied forms of patronage, and addressed several kinds of audiences. The genre's apparently rigid conventions seem to have nurtured literary invention and communities of pillaittamil connoisseurs sensitive to the nuances of poetic creativity.

Praising the Child and Depicting Domesticity

THE IDEA OF venerating a deity in the form of a child has a long history in Hindu literature. For example, one influential Sanskrit bhakti (devotional) text lists five relationships through which devotees can relate to their chosen deity:

1. as one humble before the supreme deity
2. as a slave serving a master
3. as a friend
4. as a lover
5. as a parent caring for a child.[5]

This last relationship, which tradition labels *vātsalya,* emphasizes the affection of a parent toward an adored offspring.[6] The first relationship, viewing one's chosen deity as one's master, emphasizes the distance between the human and the divine, foregrounding the remote power of the deity. In contrast, viewing the deity as a baby emphasizes the nearness and intimacy of the human to the divine, foregrounding the accessibility of the deity.

The pillaittamil genre can be viewed as an elaboration of this parental mode of worship that developed (initially) in the Hindu Tamil literary tradition. The name of the genre, a compound of *piḷḷai* and *tamiḻ,* testifies to the centrality of the subject of childhood. *Piḷḷai* means "child" or "baby," so the title can be understood and translated simultaneously as "Tamil [poetry] *for* a child" and "Tamil [poetry] *to* a child."[7] Although poets envision, address themselves to, and praise an extraordinary child, they also praise the grown child's powerful and salvific acts. Each verse of a pillaittamil juxtaposes praise of this baby with praise of this adult. Thus, pillaittamils can express closeness to one's chosen deity, conceived of as accessible and responsive to devotion, while simultaneously praising the adult deity's awesome and miraculous powers.

Pillaittamil writers do more than adopt the role of parent; they take on a specifically maternal voice. And yet, with only one partial and recent exception, all known pillaittamil poets have been men.[8] The male poets' use of the maternal voice, as gender was culturally constructed in Tamil society during the period when the pillaittamil genre crystallized, remains one of the genre's most intriguing features. This poetic use of a female persona—more specifically a maternal persona—is not unique in the history of Tamil literature. In classical Tamil love poetry (beginning ca. first to third centuries C.E.), writers adopted a maternal persona to write poems about a mother's worries as her daughter set out to follow her beloved across the harsh desert. Also akin in emotional tone was the poet's adoption of the persona of the child's nursemaid, who watched over the child, expressed affection, and commented upon scenes of domestic harmony.[9] Yet while such poems of mother's love and domesticity occur relatively infrequently in classical Tamil poetry, they are the sine qua non of pillaittamil poetry.

Several influential feminist critics in the West have argued that literature dealing with motherhood and the domestic sphere has been, until recently, neglected or denigrated by scholars because the dominant power structure dismisses it as part of women's sphere. According to their critique, because the prevalent literary tradition assumes that "great" literature deals with war, politics, and other aspects of public life, it marginalizes such literature of the domestic. As Virginia Woolf asserted when describing this attitude: "This is an important book, the critic assumes, because it deals with war. This is an insignificant book because it deals with the feelings of women in a drawing room."[10] Closer to our own time, Tillie Olsen has analyzed this devaluation of the women's sphere in Western literature and its relegation to the category of less important literature: “Power is seldom recognized as the power it is at all, if the subject matter is considered woman’s: it is minor. . . .”[11] Male pillaittamil poets and connoisseurs, in contrast, neither neglect nor denigrate domestic themes. Instead, they embrace the theme of domesticity as a setting and source of imagery for expressing love toward the divine.[12]

The motif of the extraordinary child gives the genre its distinctive subject matter and ethos. To prevent misunderstanding, it is necessary to take into account that not every part of every verse in every pillaittamil deals exclusively with domestic themes. For example, many verses written in the genre depict heroic deeds performed by the deity after he or she grows to adulthood. In other pillaittamil verses, poets focus on creating carefully crafted artwork with puns, plays on words, formal literary ornamentation, or alliteration as their main focus. Nonetheless, in every verse the themes of childhood and domesticity play some role, even if it is limited to the last few lines of the verse. Furthermore, pillaittamils contain more verses in which the themes of domesticity and childhood predominate than any other genre of Tamil poetry.

The following pillaittamil verse to the Hindu God Murukaṉ provides an example of the emphasis on childhood and depiction of domesticity so significant to the genre; poets and artists usually portray Murukaṉ, one of Śiva’s sons, as young and vigorous. This particular verse comes from a section of the pillaittamil in which the speaker beckons the baby. In it the mother expresses her love for Murukaṉ in many ways. She seeks to protect her divine baby from malevolent forces by drawing a *tilak,* an auspicious mark, on his forehead. She offers to adorn him with radiant jewels, nurse him with her breastmilk, bathe him, and shower him with kisses. With each promise, she encourages him to come to her. This god is accessible; indeed, the baby needs the mother’s loving care. Her offers emphasize the baby’s smallness and vulnerability—he takes tiny steps, she must keep him clean, he depends upon her for nourishment. All her requests present the deity as the endearingly winsome object of the speaker’s affection. In such a situation, one finds the deity eminently approachable.

And yet the last six lines of this verse subtly alter the dynamics between mother and infant. The speaker praises Murukaṉ's sharp spear, reminding the listener of his powerful deeds of demon-killing that preserve the world. The speaker also lauds the deity's seaside shrine, Tiruccentur, emphasizing that his divine presence there has enriched the surrounding land, on which rise many-storied houses whose prosperous owners display radiant jewels. The poet even reminds us that this young baby nursing at its mother's breast is, as an adult, the husband of beautiful Vaḷḷi, whose own breasts have already begun to grow round and full. That the maternal narrator calls the baby to come and nurse at her maternal breasts by invoking the erotic breasts of Vaḷḷi indicates the poet's conflation of present and future time.

Tiruccentūr Piḷḷaittamiḻ 54

Come so I can fasten your waiststring, adorned with rare jewels.
Come so I can slip a ring 'round your finger.
Come so I can draw a tilak *on your brow.*
Come and play in the lane.

Come so I can lift you to my lap and hug you.
Come so I can bathe you in fresh rosewater.
Come suckle ambrosia from my full breasts.
Come and receive kisses.

Come let me wash the dirt from your body.
Come and speak a few words.
Come let me see your tiny steps.

Dwelling in Tiruccentur,
where towering houses abound with lustrous gems,
Murukaṉ with the sharp spear, come.

Vaḷḷi's budding breasts, fragrant with sandalpaste,
are like tender coconuts.
Husband of that woman, come.[13]

In this verse the poet juxtaposes the scenes of God as infant with a refrain about God as adult. In a sense, the verse transcends specific times, by simultaneously addressing the deity directly as a child yet with reference to adult deeds performed. By conjoining the two, the poet reminds us that Lord Murukan̲ is both child and grown man, charmingly helpless and miraculously powerful, an experiencer of female attention both as son and husband. The domestic scene in the main part of the verse enables us to envision Murukan̲ as near and dear; the refrain emphasizes his extraordinary potency and power.

Depiction of domesticity and divine power interrelate in a quite different fashion in a selection from another pillaittamil. In the verse Mīn̲āṭci creates her home and performs housework there. The verse's first section depicts Goddess Mīn̲āṭci, mother of Murukan̲ and wife of Lord Śiva, at work constructing her house: the walls, central supports, roof, and lights. The walls support the Cakravāla Range of mountains, which, according to Hindu mythology, surround the cosmos. The central pillar is Mount Meru, the *axis mundi* that joins heaven and earth. The vast sky, illuminated by the sun and the moon, forms the roof. Thus, when this little girl builds her playhouse, she simultaneously performs a cosmogonic act.

Goddess Mīn̲āṭci washes and stacks up the kitchen vessels, but those vessels are also all the worlds, rinsed by her in the waters of the deluge at the end of the eon. Dishwashing must be done again and again, because each day cooking pots and vessels get dirty; the poet identifies the soiling of kitchenware with Śiva's repeated destruction of the universe. Despite her husband's mad acts of violence, she constantly cleanses and recreates the world with her dishwashing. In the refrain, the poet abruptly redirects our attention, lauding this goddess as a tiny infant who amuses herself by swaying back and forth as she gradually learns how to move her tiny body. When this child plays, the universe is her playhouse.

Maturaimīn̲āṭciyammai Piḷḷaittamiḻ 15

You prop up the eight mountains
to support the high encircling Cakravala Range.
You plant Mount Meru in the middle as a pillar.
You cover the top of the sky,
then you hang the sun and moon as lamps.

In the dashing waters
you wash the old cooking vessels—
all the worlds—
and stack them up.
Then you cook sweet ambrosia
from fresh food.

Mother, you've done this many times.

While you do this
the great madman Śiva with the umattai *flower*
wanders through the courtyard of space
destroying your work again and again,
and then comes before you,
dancing.

You never get angry.
Every day,
you just pick up the vessels.

Tender young girl
who plays house with the ancient universe,
sway to and fro.

Only daughter of the southern king
and the king of the Himalayas,
sway to and fro.[14]

This pillaittamil verse turns images of domesticity into language about the salvific and universe-renewing acts of the divine. In this verse, the poet has elevated "women's work" to a cosmic metaphor, while affectionately praising an extraordinary divine child.

The Paruvam Structure

In order to savor the poetry of the highly conventionalized pillaittamil genre, one must understand its governing assumptions and overall framework. Each verse of a poem occurs in one of ten carefully sequenced *paruvams,* or sections; familiarity with this ten-part structure enables the connoisseur to appreciate the subtleties of each poet's treatment of a paruvam. Like the skeleton of a body, the paruvam structure supports and connects the poetry of the pillaittamil. The ten paruvams of a pillaittamil function in ways that might be seen as analogous to the classical Indian system of musical ragas. The well-trained listener knows the mood associated with each raga and the notes of its required scale. Although the performer begins with an elaboration of the scale of the raga and takes it as the musical foundation of the composition, true artistry reveals itself in the performer's ability to improvise within the raga. This structured creativity brings delight to musically sophisticated listeners. Each of the paruvams, like each of the ragas, provides a structure within which invention flourishes.

The Tamil term *paruvam* has two main sets of meanings, one relating to the notion of maturation and the other denoting a section of a larger entity. A specific example of the maturation meaning occurs when the term is used to indicate a period during which some activity takes place. The section meaning occurs when the term refers to a chapter, canto, book, or other subdivision of a piece of literature. Stages in life are called paruvams; sections of epics are called paruvams. As a technical term in pillaittamil poetry, the term has both meanings, because it denotes a stage of development in the life of a child, as depicted in a specific section of the poem.[15]

A paruvam takes as its subject matter a specific childhood activity: for example, a child giving the mother a kiss, a little girl bathing in the river, or a little boy beating a toy drum. Each paruvam possesses a name, usually based on a key word in a paruvam's assigned activity. For example, the paruvam where the mother asks the child for a kiss literally bears the name "kiss" *(muttam)*, the paruvam where the girl bathes in the river is named "playing in the water" *(nīrāṭal)*, and the paruvam where the boy beats a drum is called "little drum" *(ciṟu-paṟai)*. The final phrase of each verse in a given paruvam, which I have called a "refrain," functions to specify the paruvam. The refrain is a short consistent phrase with which all the verses in that paruvam close, such as "clap your hands" or "beat your little drum."

Each standard pillaittamil contains ten paruvams; each paruvam, except the first, usually contains ten verses.[16] Note that the paruvam anchors the verse, but need not limit it. That is, the verse must relate in some way to the paruvam's prescribed activity and must end with the prescribed refrain; if it does so, the verse may then make reference to any period in the life of the deity. Consider, for example, the verse in which the mother promises to adorn and nurse the baby, translated above. It comes from a pillaittamil composed of 103 verses in praise of the Lord Murukan̲. This verse belongs to the paruvam in which each verse depicts the mother beckoning to the baby. The refrain identifies it as part of the "come" paruvam, but the poet remains free simultaneously to refer to the wife of the grown deity without controverting the prescriptions of the poetry.

Numerically, most pillaittamils include between 101 and 103 verses. If each paruvam contained ten verses, one might expect all poems to possess one hundred verses. In Indian tradition, however, certain numbers are considered more auspicious or favorable *(mangalam)* than others. Just as when one bestows a monetary gift it is auspicious to give 101 rupees, rather than 100, a pillaittamil will usually contain slightly more than a flat 100 verses. These additional verses occur in the pillaittamil in at least two ways. Poetic prescriptions say that the first paruvam may contain up to eleven verses, and many poems do. Alternatively, a number of poets precede the first paruvam with one or more pre-poem invocations to, for example, Gaṇeśa, the deity worshipped at the beginning of artistic endeavors.[17] Although some poets have written smaller-scale pillaittamils that contain five, seven, or nine verses in each paruvam, the vast majority of pillaittamils contain ten verses in all paruvams except the first. The number of verses in a particular pillaittamil can be less than ten, but nearly every pillaittamil has neither less nor more than ten paruvams.

As Table 1 shows, the paruvam structure provides the organization and sequencing of a pillaittamil. Consider, for example, the second verse translated above, taken from a 102-verse pillaittamil addressed to Goddess Mīn̲āṭci, here envisioned as "the dishwasher" and cosmic purifier. The verse comes from the paruvam in which the mother encourages the baby to move gently back and forth. That paruvam is the second on the paruvam list found in the left-hand column of the table. Said to be named after the undulating movements of a young reddish plant, the paruvam calls on the infant to sway gently (middle column), a request made explicit in the refrain (right-hand column).

The ten paruvams turn out to be a surprisingly heterogeneous

TABLE 1. THE PARUVAMS OF A PILLAITTAMIL

NAME OF PARUVAM	TOPIC	REFRAIN
1. *kāppu* protection	invoking a series of deities to protect the child	Protect [this child]
2. *ceṅkīrai* tender young greens	encouraging the baby to move its body gently	Sway to and fro
3. *tāla* tongue	lullaby/encouraging the child to move its tongue	Talelo [like la la la]
4. *cappāṇi* handclapping	asking the child to clap its hands	Clap your hands
5. *muttam* kiss	asking the child for a kiss	Give me a kiss
6. *vārāṉai/varukai* coming	asking the child to come	Come
7. *ampuli* moon	asking the moon to be a playmate for the child	Moon, come and play
Male Alternatives		
ciṟṟil little house(s)	girls entreating the boy not to knock down their little house(s)	Don't destroy our little house(s)
ciṟupaṟai little drum	encouraging the boy to beat on his little drum	Beat your little drum
ciṟutēr little chariot	encouraging the boy to play with his little chariot	Drive your little chariot
Female Alternatives		gently
ammāṉai [game like jacks]	encouraging the girl to play *ammāṉai*	Play jacks
nīrāṭal bathing	encouraging the girl to bathe in the water	Bathe in the water
ūcal swinging	encouraging the girl to swing on a swing	Swing on the swing

group. Because the term "paruvam" carries with it the sense of growth, one might expect the paruvams to form a sequence of infant and child development, with the activity in each paruvam becoming more difficult, requiring increasingly mature mental and physical skills. Some developmental thrust occurs in the sequence of the paruvams, but that development is also cross-cut by literary and religious elements which have also shaped the paruvam structure.

The first paruvam, for example, provides a ritual entrance into the pillaittamil. In this "protection" *(kāppu)* paruvam, the poet requests divine assistance to guard the child from danger. Each verse in the paruvam appeals to a different deity to watch over the tiny infant. Within the internal logic of the pillaittamil, the protection paruvam enables the mother to enlist a set of powerful divine guardians—each with his or her special powers—for her infant. From the perspective of the pillaittamil poet as well, these multiple entreaties for protection prove crucial; they begin the poem auspiciously and allow the poet to praise (and himself receive merit from) deities in addition to the one to whom he addresses his pillaittamil.

Tamil literary tradition interprets the second and third paruvams variously. A favorite explanation of the second paruvam's name, *ceṅkīrai,* breaks it into *cem,* "red," and *kīrai,* "vegetable greens." Imagine vegetable greens whose stalks, when young, have a slightly reddish tinge (like beet or rhubarb stalks) and which, when small and tender, sway gently in the breeze. Most *ceṅkīrai* verses depict some kind of gentle undulating movement on the part of the baby.[18] Paruvam three, *tāla* (tongue), always includes the refrain *tālēlō,* an onomatopoetic lullaby equivalent to the English "la la la." Some scholars argue that this paruvam encourages the child to move its tongue and prattle, an explanation that accounts for the word "tongue" in the paruvam name.[19]

Next follow paruvams that need little exegesis. In the fourth paruvam, *cappāṇi,* the mother asks the child to clap his or her hands. The fifth paruvam asks for a kiss *(muttam).* The sixth paruvam called *vārāṉai,* or the variant title *varukai,* both of which mean "coming," depicts the mother calling the child to come hither.

In pillaittamil tradition, the seventh paruvam stands out as the most challenging, with particularly wide scope for poetic creativity. In this "moon" *(ampuli)* paruvam, the mother addresses the lunar sphere shining in the sky, asking it to come play with her baby. In order to entice the moon to come and provide companionship for the child, poets employ a number of rhetorical strategies, including threats, arguments about rank and status, and even bribes (chapter 2 of this book examines this fascinating paruvam in detail).

The first seven paruvams remain constant in all pillaittamils, but the last three paruvams differ in notable ways. Most important, the paruvam system branches into two types, depending upon the sex of the child.[20] This bifurcation can be seen in the middle of Table 1, which provides two alternatives for paruvams eight, nine, and ten. These last three paruvams can also vary in order. Table 1, therefore, does not give numbers for the last three paruvams.

Of the three paruvams in the male branch, two paruvams are rather straightforward. In the *ciṟupaṟai* (little drum) paruvam, the speaker encourages the boy to beat on his drum. In a similar paruvam, *ciṟutēr* (little chariot), the speaker tells the boy to drive his toy chariot. The most unusual paruvam for males bears the name *ciṟṟil,* or "little house(s)." Unlike all the other paruvams in the pillaittamil genre, the poet adopts not the maternal voice but that of a little girl or group of little girls playing in the sand by the seashore. The girls entreat the little boy not to destroy their tiny houses, which they have built with such care.

For paruvams in the female branch, three paruvams are found most often, although some variation occurs. The first female paruvam, *ammāṉai,* bears the name of a girl's game similar to jacks, in which players throw balls or round seeds into the air. A second paruvam for females, *nīrāṭal,* depicts bathing, splashing, diving, playing, wading, cavorting, and otherwise enjoying a dip in the waters of a river, pond, or reservoir. A third paruvam for girls, *ūcal,* calls the girl to play on a swing. A few other paruvams occasionally appear.[21]

Poets must work within the confines of this ten-paruvam system in order to produce a poem clearly recognizable as a pillaittamil. Connoisseurs evaluate the skill of the poet according to how successfully he balances invention and convention, maneuvering within the paruvam to create fresh and artful approaches to the subject matter for each paruvam. The pillaittamil verses translated in this book reveal the range of opportunity for religious and poetic creativity present within the paruvam framework.

Criteria for Selection of Poetry

AT THE OUTSET, the reader must be forewarned that this book is not a comprehensive study of all pillaittamils ever written. Some older pillaittamils no longer exist, while others remain only in fragmentary form. Some pillaittamils were published not by commercial presses for general purchase but by religious institutions for free distribution to guests at ritual occasions and to monastic libraries, so they were not collected in any systematic way. A number of pillaittamil publications have succumbed to mice or mildew. Several pillaittamils, once considered lost, are only now in the process of being reprinted as a result of the revival of interest in Tamil Islamic literature. There are also some pillaittamils that are not particularly distinguished or original, as is the case in any literary genre. Finally, the analyses here cannot be exhaustive because poets continue to develop the genre and compose new pillaittamils, for example, to recently popularized gods and goddesses.

Due to all these factors, as well as the practical one of limited space, this volume is intended to whet rather than to sate one's appetite to read more pillaittamils. As far as I know, no other anthology of pillaittamils exists in English; when other scholars join me in translating more pillaittamils into English, no one will be more pleased than I. In the meantime, however, I offer the volume's bibliography for further reading. It can guide Tamil readers who want to continue their exploration of the genre beyond the poems chosen for translation in this book.

Every anthology develops from a set of choices and limitations. I have chosen to focus primarily upon pillaittamils from ongoing religious communities, where poets and devotees continue to support and respect the writing and publication of pillaittamils as poetic expressions of their ultimate concerns. There is no doubt that these poems have currency in Tamil society: members of each community transmit them institutionally through republication, writing commentaries, quotations and citations, and, in some cases, through public recitation or musical rendition. Thus, the texts represented in this volume emphasize those pillaittamils that are well known and respected within particular religious communities.[22]

Each of the first five pillaittamils featured in this volume stands as a preeminent example, in some senses representative of a particular religious community. For example, my choice of Hindu pillaittamils developed in response to conversations with Tamil literary connoisseurs. To discover which texts they considered to be the finest pillaittamils, I consulted Hindu academics and also queried literati of a more traditional scholastic bent, including those attached to monastic institutions or temples. On everyone's "short list" were the two pillaittamils featured in chapter 3 and chapter 4 of this book, representing some of the most artful poetry that Hindu writers have offered in the genre. Similarly, the text I chose from the Muslim pillaittamil corpus had been recommended by a group of Tamil Muslim intellectuals and adopted as required reading on a university syllabus as a representative text from Tamil Islamic literature generally.

My sampler draws attention to how the genre adapted to new subject matter, indicating key points in the history of the genre as it expanded its range of religious, social, or political affiliations. Two Hindu pillaittamils to deities appear, one addressed to a god worshipped at a seaside shrine and another to a goddess in a major Tamil city. Included as well is a Hindu one addressed to a saint and written by a revered holy man closely associated with a monastic establishment at the height of its political, economic, and social power. Muslim and Christian examples of the genre appear in chronological order. I also show how the genre now has been used to praise the heroes and heroines of Tamil cultural movements of the latter twentieth century.

The poetry in the anthology has been selected to reveal the flexibility of the genre, a feature that enabled it to retain its importance to individual poets and cultural institutions over time and across social boundaries. Consider, for example, the statement of the Christian mechanical engineer who wrote the pillaittamil featured in chapter 7. Rather than rejecting the genre because it did not speak to his concerns, he rejected the notion that engineering and writing Christian pillaittamils were mutually exclusive. Because he wanted a pillaittamil that reflected both parts of his world, he composed one about Jesus, but also about electrons, computers, and hydroelectric power. He and many other pillaittamil poets throughout history have perceived the genre as a form that they could adapt and make their own.

Equal in importance to including pillaittamils of historical and religious significance was the importance of including poetry that displays a mastery of the formal qualities valued in Tamil poetry. Discussion of these formal qualities appears in Tamil prescriptive texts, commentaries on particular poems, poetic practice, and legends about divine recognition of excellent pillaittamils, so there was a great deal of critical textual evidence to guide me in my selections. The anthology features some of the most artful and carefully crafted of pillaittamil verses. I paid particular attention, as well, to verses that had a clear overall design, parallel verbal structures, a controlling metaphor, a narrative line, or a central poetic conceit. In addition, the reader has many chances to sample verses that demonstrate the shaping influence of the paruvam structure in a particularly compelling, cogent, or delicate way.

I have also included a couple of verses whose artistry lies in elaborately ornamented juxtaposition of mellifluous Tamil sounds. It is nearly impossible to convey in translation the nuances of such poetry because its art lies in resourceful use of the special linguistic capacities of Tamil semantics, syntax, and phonology. To represent this strand of pillaittamil poetry, therefore, I analyze one such verse in great detail in chapter 4 through transliteration of the original Tamil and analysis of phonetic strategies in composition. Pillaittamil lovers relish this verse because, among other reasons, it uses aural effects distinctive to the Tamil language. In an indirect way, however, the detailed analysis required to present the sophistication of this verse to non-Tamil readers reveals an implicit criterion for selection of poetry for translation. Included are few verses that could not be translated into English without losing their distinctive form and nuances of meaning. In such cases, only the original Tamil can convey fully and directly the poetic skills of the author.

Far easier to render effectively through translation is pillaittamil poetry that achieves its effect through wit and humor, so this kind of poetry is well represented in my anthology of translations. Especially clever are the moon verses in which the speaker uses threats, flattery, cajoling, insults, lunar lore, astronomical information, mythology, and references to recent space travel to persuade the moon to come to earth and act as a playmate for the extraordinary child. Equally charming and often amusing are the verses in which little girls beseech the little boy not to destroy their sandcastles. This richly erotic poetry, masked as childish play, incorporates much of the sensuality and suggestiveness of classical Tamil love poetry and does so with tongue-in-cheek wit that often pokes fun at the seriousness of devotional genres of petitionary prayer.

To give some sense of the pillaittamil's peripheries, chapter 8 explores the limits beyond which a poem seems to lose its "pillaittamilness" by analyzing two political poems. Both technically belong within the boundaries of a pillaittamil in that each addresses a baby and contains verses in all ten paruvams. Yet the first of these pillaittamils seems lifeless and, for the most part, lacks skill or freshness. Lest one think that its banality derives solely from its political polemic, consider the second pillaittamil. Addressed to E. V. Ramasami, political critic and militant atheist, it makes clever use of the protection paruvam, includes several cleverly crafted moon verses, probes the meaning and effect of some of Ramasami's dearly held beliefs about the nature of reality, and playfully mocks certain familiar pillaittamil refrains. This second poem pushes at the pillaittamil's boundaries while maintaining the creative spirit of the genre.

The poems upon which I chose to focus in each chapter were also texts for which I could uncover information about cultural context, especially the circumstances of composition, performance, intended audience, and reception. The amount and quality of information available varied from poem to poem. Sifting through temple legends and artwork, publication records, and monastic memoirs enabled me to reconstruct aspects of the cultural context of pillaittamils composed in previous centuries. Interviews with living poets provided me with information about why and how they choose to write pillaittamils.

This sampler of pillaittamil poetry explores not only the art of the poetry, but also how artfully pillaittamils perform cultural work. The brief introduction before the set of translations in each chapter of Part Two highlights and analyzes notable aspects of the poetry's cultural context. Part Two thus foregrounds both formal and contextual perspectives on pillaittamils, exploring different aspects in each chapter.

Following a Translation

TRANSLATORS ENGAGE IN a process of negotiating between and across cultures; such negotiations take especially complex forms when one translates from a genre as shaped by such poetic conventions as are pillaittamils. Never entirely successful in their negotiations, translators have only the option of deciding which of the many facets of translation they will highlight in their work. The translations in this volume focus not on replicating surface effects such as meter, alliteration, or puns. Instead, using the resources of the English language, they aim to reproduce the overall shape and effect of the original verse, within the context of the pillaittamil's paruvam structure.

To illustrate some of the challenges of translating even fairly straightforward pillaittamil poetry into English, I set out below three stages of a translation, moving from the most literal to the one that most effectively reproduces the poetic effects of the original in English. The first translation functions as a diagram of poetic units, revealing some of the richness of individual imagery. The second translation supplies contextual information that the poetry's intended audience would have taken for granted and reveals the links between different parts of the verse. The final version fits individual units of meaning into the overall shape and momentum of the verse, allowing various interpretations to emerge.

I have chosen as my example *Tiruccentūr Piḷḷaittamiḻ* (hereafter *TCPT*) 15 from the "sway to and fro" paruvam, which eulogizes Lord Murukaṉ's prowess on the battlefield. The verse depicts how the lord unsheathes his spear and goes to war, filling the battlefield with dead bodies and voracious ghouls who feast upon them.[23] Seeing this, the divine infant simply smiles. Most of the verse, in sum, recounts actions that take place on the battlefield.

One challenge for the translator, therefore, lies in conveying the relationships between the many actions (verbal forms) in this piece of poetry. Grammatically *TCPT* 15 comprises a single sentence. Version 1 of the translation indicates all the key verbal forms by capitalizing them. Tamil verbs occur in two forms: finite (completed action) and nonfinite (adverbial participle). *TCPT* 15 is composed of a series of adverbial participles, with its only finite verb in the refrain. This verbal series indicates not separate actions but actions in relation to the final action. Thus, even the rudimentary translation of Version 1 suggests that Murukaṉ's adult conquest of enemies and subsequent events on the battlefield are seen in relation to the final action, a request for the baby to gently sway to and fro.

In Tamil, modifiers precede the main noun; in contrast, ordinary English syntax presents the noun first and follows with the modifying clause. I use the symbol < to indicate this left-branching phenomenon. For example, consider the phrase "beautiful golden crowns snatch who < ghouls / ball PLAYING." (The English would be "ghouls who snatch beautiful golden crowns play ball.") The literal translation shows how Tamil intensifies the expectations in this line. Encountering "beautiful golden crowns," the Tamil reader would expect praise of great acts of heroism performed by majestic monarchs. These expectations are thwarted upon reaching the noun "ghouls," forcing the reader to radically readjust expectations. When ghouls play ball with the crowns of monarchs, it can only be the context of defeat on the battlefield, since the opportunity to feed on the dead attracts ghouls to the site.

Version 1: Word-for-Word Translation

1. *excellence* SHOWING

2. *hot sun the color of [is] < top of short blade*
    excels which < spear from sheath [you] having unsheathed
    cruel mouths opening of < tiny eyes huge she-ghouls DANCING

3. *horrid headless bodies uncontrollably* MOVING

4. *old buffalo high neck on < Dark-colored Yama*
    both hands waving PLEADING

5. *body [on] eyes with < Lord* LAUDING

6. *big big top place < space without*
    vultures MOVING

7. *beautiful golden crowns snatch who < ghouls* PLAYING BALL

8. *Vindhya-Mountains-and-Desert of < Mistress*
    with three-prong-ilai-headed trident
    fresh rich blood of < flood in mud PLAYING

9. CONQUERING

10. *small smile* PLAYING *< Young One,*
11. *to and fro* SWAYING-GRACE

12. *red color tuft white cock banner with < you*
13. *to and fro* SWAYING-GRACE.

The body of the verse in the second version of the translation tells us of Murukaṉ's entry into battle and the carnage that follows. The first two verbal units depict him readying his weapon as divine and human spectators sing his praises. Murukaṉ unsheathes his powerful spear, capped by a gleaming lethal point—an image of potency and the power to prevail. The verbal units that follow show the consequences of his victory, as ghouls and vultures arrive to gorge on the corpses. Against the backdrop of convulsively writhing human torsos come the female ghouls who act as ladies-in-waiting to Goddess Kālī, who loves to wade in the blood of war. Her attendants, described using a Tamil literary device in which opposite adjectives are paired, are said to have huge, cruel mouths for chomping on human flesh and tiny eyes that lack compassion. Yama, the deity responsible for bringing the dead to hell, desperately begs Murukaṉ to end the killing; he can no longer accommodate any more people in his overcrowded realm. The sky, a place envisioned as spacious and nearly infinite in size, becomes choked with carrion-eating vultures. Even Indra, King of the Gods (identified by his epithet "One with eyes on his body"[24]), bows at Murukaṉ's feet. Serving as a benchmark, Indra shows that Murukaṉ has reached a state so powerful that even the divine monarch does obeisance to him.

The verse ends with Murukaṉ viewing the scene, a smile playing on the lips of the youthful warrior. The term for "youth" or "youthful one" is Kumaraṉ, a popular epithet for Murukaṉ, also known as "Young God." Immediately afterward, comes the refrain asking the little one to "sway to and fro." The refrain connects the childhood motif to the adult depicted in the body of the verse.[25] That function proves crucial here, because except for the mention of the warrior's youth, the rest of the verse contains no mention of themes related to childhood. The refrain effects a link between the bloodthirsty adult warrior and the little child toward whom the speaker feels affection and love. The relationship between actions on the battlefield and the child's smiling movement suggests his latent victorious power and its potential for expression.

Version 2: Contextual Information Added

1. [Onlookers] call attention to the excellence [of Murukaṉ as warrior]

2. [You, Murukaṉ] unsheathed from its sheath
the spear which possesses an excellent short blade
whose top is the color of the hot sun
[because you did that,]
huge she-ghouls with tiny eyes [serving Goddess Kālī]
open their cruel mouths

3. Gory headless bodies dance convulsively
4. Dark Yama [God of Death] [riding] on the high neck of his ancient buffalo
waves both his hands pleading [that Murukaṉ not kill anyone else
because hell is already over-crowded]
5. The God with eyes all over his body [Indra, King of the Gods] lauds you
[even though he is the king and you are just a little baby]
6. The zenith of the very high sky has no place left
[because it overflows with] vultures circling [over corpses]
7. Ghouls snatch lovely gold crowns [from the heads of kings who died in war]
and play ball with them
8. The Mistress of the Vindhya Mountains and the desert [Goddess Kālī]
plays with her triple ilai *[pear-shaped] pronged trident*
in the muck flooded with fresh rich blood
9. [All this is occurring because] you conquered [your enemy in battle]
10. O Youth [upon whose lips], a small smile plays
11. Graciously sway to and fro
12. You whose war banner [bears the emblem] of the red-tufted white cock
13. Graciously sway to and fro.

The third translation attempts to replicate the shape, momentum, and poetic effects of the verse as a whole and make the verse comprehensible to the modern reader of English.

Version 3: Unstilted English

Onlookers praise you.

Because you have unsheathed your spear
with its short sharp blade and surface gleaming like hot sun,
huge female ghouls with tiny eyes
open their cruel mouths and dance.

Gruesome headless bodies
convulsively dance.

Dark Yama, mounted on the neck of his ancient buffalo,
throws up his hands and pleads.

Even the lord with eyes all over his body
lauds you.

The lofty zenith of the universe
is choked with circling vultures.

Ghouls snatch splendid gold crowns
and play ball with them.

The Mistress of the desert and the Vindhya Mountains
bathes her trident with three pear-shaped prongs
in muck with a flood of thick fresh blood.

Young one who has conquered,
a faint smile plays on your lips.
Graciously sway to and fro.

You whose banner bears the red-tufted white cock,
graciously sway to and fro.

The final version portrays the verse's grammatical cohesion in visual form. The momentum of the verse can be understood as deriving from a series of verbal sequences, one after another, that eventually dash against the refrain. Each verbal unit receives its own space (a line or lines), while a blank line marks where one unit ends and the next begins. Because the verbal marker comes last in each unit in Tamil, I have tried to make the verb occur in the second half of the verbal unit if possible. The translation's vertical form helps to represent the elongated syntax and diction of the Tamil. Its list-like quality helps to indicate multiple events occurring simultaneously or sequentially. The abrupt change of tone and pace at the English refrain replicates the grammatical and semantic changes in the original Tamil.

The refrain links all that has been depicted in the body of the poem with the image of God as a tiny baby. The speaker encourages the baby to try to move gently to and fro. She asks that warrior, whose prowess the poet emphasizes by mentioning his banner that sports the spunky red-tufted cock, to undertake the simple task of swaying back and forth. Both the adult warrior and the child are very much present in the poem, as if temporal distinctions have become irrelevant or as if the warrior is perpetually present in the child. The refrain, thus, calls attention to the juxtaposition of the victorious warrior with a child just beginning to gain control over his muscles.

How should we read that smile? The ending allows us to interpret the verse in several (nonexclusive) ways. According to convention, a warrior should not be arrogant about his victories. So Murukaṉ can be seen as allowing himself only a small smile when he contemplates his success in battle. Or, the moment of the smile can be viewed as a foreshadow of his coming greatness—a kind of mental rehearsal for the demon-killing to come in the future. Alternatively, if temporal order has been transcended, we can see the omniscient child reflecting upon his great victories, which have always existed because they are eternal. From yet another perspective, the faintly amused smile may indicate how God laughs at the pretensions of all those who foolishly try to defeat his power.

At a deeper level, the juxtaposition suggests that the dramatic events of everyday existence are nothing but divine play. Just as the ghouls play ball with the splendid crowns of once-famed warriors, God plays with his human supplicants. The idea that the world is the result of divine sport is a long-established one in Hindu philosophy. The gruesomeness of battle, which this verse deliberately heightens and exaggerates, stands as evidence of the futility of all earthly endeavors. Seeing all these events, the innocent child-god simply smiles, at the fleeting quality of victory, and sways back and forth. The tiny smile that plays on his lips emphasizes the irony of it all. In a sense, the verse allows the reader to see the deity unleashing his powers to defeat the demons, but the refrain withdraws these powers. They return inside the body of this small gentle baby, amusing himself as he sways back and forth.

Building upon the discussion of domestic themes, the paruvam framework, and the translation issues provided in this chapter, the remainder of the book provides a poetry sampler, intended to display systematically the diverse forms of poetic invention fostered within the pillaittamil. Throughout the translations in this volume, I select a verse whose construction or interpretation is particularly complex, terse, unusual, or significant in its community and analyze it in the introductory essay to the chapter to highlight the multiple facets of a verse and the diverse meanings occurring within a single pillaittamil.

With the background information provided about the paruvam sequence that chapter 1 provides, the reader can now move on to chapter 2, which displays range not across paruvams but within one. This second chapter focuses entirely on a single paruvam, by consensus the most challenging one in the pillaittamil. By looking at how several poets have created verses asking the moon to be the child's playmate, this chapter reveals the array of creativity that can occur within a single, conventionally circumscribed, poetic situation.

CHAPTER TWO

ASKING FOR THE MOON, TAMING THE TIGER

THE MOON *(ampuli)* paruvam provides an excellent example of the aesthetic of virtuosity that plays a large role in pillaittamil composition. In this paruvam the poet must address his poetry directly to the moon, using various forms of cajolery or intimidation to convince the moon to act as playmate for the extraordinary child.[1] According to Tamil literary tradition, moon verses pose the greatest challenge to the poet who seeks to write a pillaittamil. As the saying goes, "Among the paruvams, *ampuli* is the tiger."[2] That is, among the ten paruvams, poets find the moon paruvam the hardest to master. A tradition has developed that poets usually compose moon verses by adopting one of four established rhetorical strategies *(upāyams):* (1) similarity *(cāmam),* demonstrating their compatibility as playmates; (2) difference *(pētam),* emphasizing the child's superiority; (3) the offer of a gift *(tā<u>n</u>am),* promising the moon a reward; or (4) punishment *(taṇṭam),* threatening the moon with unattractive consequences, if he refuses to act as playmate.

An aspiring poet shows his mettle by writing a moon verse according to traditional paruvam conventions, yet showing inventiveness within those restraints. A small twist, a clever variation, skillful incorporation of material from myth, a different perspective, a striking juxtaposition, a cosmic threat—all of these appear in moon verses. They bring pleasure, surprise, relish, and amusement to the listener or reader through a fresh approach. The aesthetic here, thus, involves virtuosity within the constraints of the formal structure.

Unlike all the other paruvams in the pillaittamil, here the poet addresses not the baby but the moon, in an attempt to persuade the moon to come and play with the child. Because the poet uses only one main rhetorical strategy in each verse, moon poetry tends to possess a large degree of internal coherence. The premise of the moon as companion encourages the poet's playfulness, so the audience expects the verses to be cogent and amusing. In addition, the poet needs to master and draw upon the corpus of moonlore available to him in order to compose clever and evocative verses.

Poets of different religious and political affiliations have used imagination and resourcefulness to write in the moon paruvam. Within its four traditional strategies, they explore the challenge of expressing their ultimate religious concerns and sentiments. Their treatment of this paruvam demonstrates the extent to which they, despite their individual affiliations with particular ideologies, see themselves as part of a shared poetic tradition. To show the pleasures of reading moon verses and to demonstrate the way poets from different ideological backgrounds work within shared literary frameworks, this chapter presents verses that ask the moon to come play with Hindu deities and a saint, a great monarch, the Prophet Muhammad, Baby Jesus, and an atheist hero.

Moonlore and Poetics

In Indian tradition, the need for calendrical and astrological calculations fostered careful observation of the moon's cycles and characteristics. Astrologers' knowledge of the monthly cycle of waxing and waning informs many discussions of the auspicious and inauspicious days in a month. Literary texts assume familiarity with lunar shapes such as the full orb or a sliver-like crescent moon. The periodic eclipse of the moon, although a relatively uncommon occurrence, is noted, as are the irregular markings of the moon's surface.

Within Tamil poetic tradition, imagery about recurrent lunar patterns flourishes.[3] Poets regularly use the moon's full spherical form as an image for a radiant and shapely face, coining the familiar adjectival phrase "moon-faced," applicable to a lovely woman or a handsome man. In crescent form, the moon conventionally resembles the pleasing curve of a comely maiden's brow or the magnificent arc of a royal elephant's tusk. The waxing and waning of the moon often serves as an image of the moon's lack of constancy, especially when contrasted with some unchanging entity. In some texts the dispelling of darkness by the full moonrise stands, in figurative terms, for the destruction of ignorance by wisdom. Many poets portray the relentless heat of the sun as searing the earth, withering the crops, and causing despair in times of drought; in contrast, the cool light of the moon soothes the spirit, refreshes the body, and is thought to make the crops flourish.

The irregularities of the moon have also fostered speculation. The patterned markings on the moon's surface have been viewed as forming the shape of a hare. What Americans perceive as the "man in the moon" is perceived as the "hare [or rabbit] in the moon" in India. Another tradition holds that the moon is filled with the divine elixir of immortality, whose taste is marvelously sweet. Poets often portray the cakravāka bird, which perches silhouetted in a high treetop against the background of a full moon, as fond of this ambrosia. The bird is thought to peck at the moon to drink some of its ambrosia, causing the pockmarks on its surface.

Astronomical observations of the moon led to cultural speculation, elaboration, embellishment, and narrative. For example, since pillaittamil poets portray the moon as a male, some poems depict him as a husband of multiple wives, namely, the stars, believed to hover around him, ready to do his bidding. The moon's periodic disappearance has been explained as the result of a series of events. According to a well-known myth, a demon stole some of the elixir of immortality while the gods were busy with other matters, but when the moon saw the demon's theft, he reported it to Viṣṇu, who sliced the demon's body in two. Since the demon drank the elixir of immortality, he could not die, so he continued to live, but in two separate parts, named Rāhu and Ketu. These two pursue the moon to get revenge and periodically catch their prey. Rāhu contains the throat, but the stomach is lodged in Ketu, so when Rāhu swallows the moon, instead of going into the stomach, the moon exits from the bottom of Rāhu's body. An eclipse, then, begins when the moon enters Rāhu and ends when the moon emerges from the upper part of the demon's body.

In addition, narratives about the moon occur within the literature of a specific religious tradition. For example, in popular Islamic tradition the Prophet Muhammad is said to have split the moon in the presence of King Habib.[4] Hindu poems in this chapter feature a number of references to the story of the churning of the ocean, an act that produced both the elixir of immortality and the moon itself. The churning not only gave the gods the gift of immortality but established the moon in the sky.[5] Śaivite tradition also figuratively describes Śiva as the whole world, with the moon and sun as his two eyes.

In Indian poetic tradition, a set of lullabies and other children's songs has always posited a special relationship between the moon and a little baby. For example, a charming incident in the Hindi devotional poetry of Sūrdās tells of how Baby Kṛṣṇa's foster mother tries to stop his fussing: she draws his attention to the full moon in the sky, which Kṛṣṇa then demands as a toy. His mother fills a big silver bowl with water, hoping that when the baby peers in and sees his own face next to the moon, he will be satisfied. As she encourages him to look in the bowl, she sings a nursery rhyme:

Uncle Moon so far away,
Uncle Moon so far away,
Uncle Moon so far away,
Uncle Moon so far away,
Whose brilliance sways in these small waves—
He swallows the whole celestial bowl
And sprinkles just a cupful here.
But make that cupful go away:
The moon will pout and rage!

Unfortunately when Kṛṣṇa sticks his finger into the bowl of water, the ripples cause the image of the moon to dissipate (making the moon "pout and rage"), so Kṛṣṇa begins to cry.[6]

Lullabies also feature the theme of the moon as playmate. For example, the motif of a parent showing the child the moon in play occurs in a shadow puppet enactment of the story of Rāma performed in the Nagerkoil area of Tamilnadu. As Rāvaṇa bathes the body of his grown son slain in battle, he poignantly laments: "At night I used to hold you in my lap and feed you soft rice until the moon rose; then I pointed to it and sang, 'Come down, little moon, come down and play with my little boy.' And you, when you saw that rabbit in the moon, you jumped up and down, trying to catch it!"[7] The idea of the moon's descent appears in a familiar song sung by mothers in Tamilnadu as they encourage the baby to eat its dinner:

Moon, moon, come running!
Don't stop, come running!
Climbing on top of the mountain, come!
Bring jasmine flowers when you come!
Lay them at the center of the house![8]

The moon verses in a pillaittamil thus share with a set of children's songs the idea of the moon as playmate.

In addition to the link between children and the moon, many Tamil poets have been fascinated with the moon. While ascetics might gaze directly at the sun all day as a form of mortifying the flesh, poets write about how they find the cool beauty of the moon particularly appropriate for inspiring their composition of love poetry. In fact, in honor of the first moon landing by an American astronaut in 1969, a group of Tamil poets held a nighttime poetry recitation in the moonlight; each poet recited a verse celebrating the moon.[9]

Thus, we can see that at both the popular and the literary level, yearning for the moon has, on numerous occasions, become the subject for poetic adornment and elaboration. The repositories of celestial information and the cultural traditions of moonlore provide a skillful pillaittamil poet with numerous resources for composition. A survey of how poets draw upon those resources demonstrates the scope for creativity within the moon paruvam.

Similarity

THE SIMILARITY STRATEGY builds upon the notion of compatibility. The poet attempts to convince the moon that he and the child share so many characteristics or accomplishments that they would make excellent playmates. The evidence upon which poets draw, in order to make their case, ranges from heroic deeds to personal assets. In addition, some of the most sophisticated similarity verses develop around a series of puns, enabling the poet to show off semantic virtuosity, while simultaneously using the same word to say appropriate things about both the child and the moon.[10]

The verse below (from *Muttukkumāracāmi Piḷḷaittamiḻ,* composed by Kumarakuruparar and addressed to Murukaṉ, the son of Śiva) represents a virtuoso example of such punning. The verse falls into two sections; after the first part, which can be read as applying to both the moon and Murukaṉ, comes the explication, in which the poet concludes that the two would make good companions. My translation of the first part presents two different ways of construing its meaning—one about the moon and one about Murukaṉ. In the first section, each of the stanzas of the verse contains a verb with a semantic range broad enough to apply both to the moon and to Murukaṉ. Each stanza also contains a "swing phrase," upon which the dual interpretation rests. In the first stanza, for example, the swing phrase is *muḻu mati,* which can mean either "full moon," referring to a lunar phase, or "complete wisdom," referring to an attribute of Lord Murukaṉ. Some stanzas require a bit more decoding. For instance, stanza three has as its swing phrase *karattāmarai. Tāmarai* means lotus and *kara* can mean either "hand" or a form of the verb "to conceal." In the case of the moon, this stanza alludes to the belief that the lotus closes its petals at night to conceal and protect its honey, while the water lily opens up to bask in the moonlight. In the case of Murukaṉ, when he closes his lotus-like hands in a gesture of greeting upon seeing his beloved hillwoman, Vaḷḷi, her mouth opens into a smile as beautiful as a blooming water lily.

The verse combines familiar lore about the moon with allusions to myths particular to a specific religious tradition. The tradition that moonlight makes the lotus close and the water lily open, for example, is one available to any Tamil poet. Conversely, the myth about Murukaṉ's love for Vaḷḷi, the hillwoman, appears in the Hindu corpus of stories about the consorts of Murukaṉ, a pool of poetic imagery from which a Hindu poet draws to fashion imagery that his Hindu audience will understand.

Muttukkumāracāmi Piḷḷaittamiḻ 62

[Reading 1: About the moon]

Because, filled with ambrosia,
you come as the full moon god
in a form praised throughout the
worlds

Because you appear
in the huge, surging ocean of bliss
into which the sky river crashes

Because when the secretive lotus
closes,
the water lily opens
like the mouth of an uninhibited
hillwoman

Because you pour
benevolent gracious coolness
so that crops thrive
as life in all the worlds

Because you are one of the celestial
eyes
of Śiva, whose matted hair
holds the crescent moon and the
Ganges

[Reading 2: About Murukaṉ]

Because, filled with ambrosia,
he comes as the god of complete
wisdom
in a form praised throughout the worlds

Because he appeared
from the huge, surging ocean of bliss
into which the sky river crashes

Because he joins his lotus-hands in
greeting,
the mouth of the uninhibited
hillwoman
will open like a water lily

Because he pours
beneficent cool grace
so that lives—the crops
in all the worlds—thrive

Because he is the spark
from the eye of Śiva, whose matted
hair
holds the crescent moon and the
Ganges

This noble one resembles you, Moon.
There's no other companion like him, you see.

With the one who created the world of the gods
and all the other worlds as well,
Moon, come to play.

With Skanda who came
to make gorgeous Kantapuri prosper,
Moon, come to play.[11]

The second example of a similarity moon verse comes not from a religious text but from a pillaittamil praising the Tamil cultural hero, E. V. Ramasami. As a potent social and political force in the public sphere of Madras from the 1920s to the 1960s, E. V. Ramasami espoused atheism as a form of liberation from the "mystification" of religious ideologies and rejected caste distinctions. The poet, Mu. Singaravelu, strings his verse together around the imagery of light and enlightenment. Since both Tamil and English contain semantic overlaps between light and enlightenment, a single translation can convey both meanings that the poem provides. The verse displays the same overall structure as the previous verse, with the first two-thirds simultaneously applicable to both E. V. Ramasami and the moon:

Periyār Piḷḷaittamiḻ 62

You shower resplendent ambrosia
and new light spreads through the world.

When you spread fresh light everywhere
new waves surge up in the rolling blue sea.

The thick darkness yearns for a place to rest,
fleeing in all directions.

Kind people find their hearts joyously refreshed
because of your glowing light.

You bear the large unchanging blemish
and pour cooling grace on everyone.

Because you [moon] shower cool moonlight,
you shine forth as this father [E. V. Ramasami] shines.

So, with the radiant luminary whose rays spread in all directions
Moon, come to play.

With the one who makes the world of the gods
and all the other worlds tremble,
Moon, come to play.[12]

This verse plays on literal and figurative meanings of light. The moon's radiant light dispels the darkness and influences the tides in the ocean. The atheist orator spreads the light of knowledge, originating waves of thought that swell forward, rocking society. Just as the moon cools the heart with shimmering light yet avoids debilitating heat, Ramasami cools people's hearts by instructing them in humanistic values, delivering them from the searing and destructive heat of caste ideology and humiliation.

The verse also plays upon the moon's spots, using them as a way to reflect on the socially constructed nature of concepts such as beauty and blemish. According to literary tradition, the image of the hare on the face of the moon can be viewed as a flaw in its otherwise pearly texture and effulgence. Ramasami too bears what, from the upper-caste gaze, appears to be a blemish: Brahmins view him as marked and flawed by his non-Brahmin (low-caste) status, ranking him inferior to upper castes. Rather than shame, however, E. V. Ramasami feels pride in serving as spokesman for other Shudras, rejecting the hegemonic power of a judgment created by Brahmins to keep low-caste people oppressed. Both he and the moon, though perceived as blemished, spread the light of well-being among people, so they would be compatible.

A close look at one section of the refrain in the two similarity verses reveals that Singaravelu plays a subtle joke by using a slightly altered phrase employed centuries earlier by Kumarakuruparar in the verse translated above. In Kumarakuruparar's refrain section, he asked the moon to come play with "the one who created the world of the gods and all the other worlds as well." The verse gives the moon the message that this deity is so powerful that he created the entire universe—the world of the gods and all other worlds. Singaravelu, inspired by that refrain in the famous earlier moon poem, also refers in his refrain to the world of the gods and all the other worlds in the universe. From the atheist's point of view, such worlds are fabrications, created for ideological reasons by Brahmins to keep lower castes from questioning their low status. E. V. Ramasami's unmasking of their imaginary status makes the whole epiphenomenal religious superstructure tremble in fear of losing its power to delude low-caste people.

These cleverly structured verses create imaginative praise of an extraordinary child through a description of lunar characteristics. In a similarity verse, the link between moon and child may be semantic or contextual. In the first translation of a similarity verse, playing with multiple meanings of the same term enabled the writer to create two self-contained but entirely different readings of the same Tamil words. In the second example, the same phrases were applicable to the moon in a literal sense and to the child in a figurative sense. Pillaittamil lovers savor the verbal facility and cleverness necessary to create a moon verse based on similarity.

Difference

WHILE SIMILARITY VERSES often stretch the limits of language and poetic ingenuity because the moon differs so greatly from most religious figures praised in pillaittamils, difference verses provide poets with broad scope for inspired—and often humorous—play. Essentially, a poet employing the difference strategy argues that the extraordinary child surpasses the moon in so many ways that the moon should consider himself privileged to act as the child's playmate. Sometimes the poet emphasizes the baby's superiority, other times the moon's inferiority.

The moon verse below by Oṭṭakkūttar, which comes from the oldest extant pillaittamil, focuses almost entirely on the greatness of the extraordinary child, saying little about the moon. Taken from the fragmentary *Kulōttuṅkaṉ Piḷḷaittamiḻ*, dated ca. the twelfth century, it praises the great Chola monarch, envisioning him as both victorious warrior and embodiment of Lord Viṣṇu on earth.[13]

Kulōttuṅkaṉ Piḷḷaittamiḻ 76

Behold, all the eight directions are temples
for his eight elephants streaming with rut.

Behold, the eight caves serve as his huge prisonhouses
where he throws kings who refuse him tribute.

Behold, the seven overflowing oceans are ponds with fragrant unguents
where he sports with his consorts, Śrīdevī and Bhūdevī.

Behold, the seven fertile groves and the seven worlds are flower gardens
where he enjoys going in procession.

Behold, the seven mountains, where pearls are always found,
serve as stalls for his elephants.

Great Mount Meru is the martial throne
where he has carved his tiger emblem.

His royal parasol is the top of the universe.
Therefore, Moon, come to play.

With the incomparable one,
possessor of victory,
and lord of the lineage of Manu,
Moon, come to play.[14]

This verse praises the Chola king as a world conqueror whose kingdom extends throughout the cosmos. The body of the verse elaborates upon the symbolic meaning of the extraordinary monarch's attributes. As a victorious hero, he has defeated many neighboring kings on the battlefield; those who refuse to submit to his sovereignty by paying him tribute spend the remainder of their days trapped in his prisons. Knowledge of his valor extends to the ends of the earth, since he has carved the tiger emblem of his renowned lineage on Mount Meru, where the gods dwell. In celebration of his victory, his royal procession passes through all the seven worlds.

In keeping with a long tradition that the king acts as an embodiment of Viṣṇu, the Preserver, the poet suggests that this monarch preserves the welfare of his kingdom. His just and effective rule brings prosperity to his lands, where pearls can be found in abundance, and his eight high-spirited and potent temple elephants protect all the directions. As the human embodiment of Lord Viṣṇu, he sports with Viṣṇu's two wives, Śrīdevī and Bhūdevī. Just as the ideal king creates fertility by insuring the cultivation of the earth,[15] Chola Kulōttuṅkaṉ unites with Śrīdevī, the goddess of prosperity, and Bhūdevī, the earth in the form of a goddess. Flanking him on either side, these goddesses bestow wealth, happiness, and fertility to the kingdom's citizens.

In Tamil literary tradition, the king's parasol symbolizes the protection that the king provides to his citizens. The more his parasol of kingship protects them from harm, the more just and effective a king he is. The hyperbole at the end of this verse suggests that Kulōttuṅkan's parasol spreads so wide and rises so high that it acts as an umbrella for the entire universe. In comparison, the moon can only be viewed as an utterly inferior being—only one of the many entities that benefit from the shade of the king's parasol. The verse may say little about the moon, but the message comes through clearly: the moon should consider it his privilege to play with such an extraordinary child.

To get a sense of the range of creativity within the difference strategy, compare the use of cosmic imagery in the verse just translated with the use of iconographic imagery in the verse below. In Civañāṉa Cuvāmikaḷ's poem *Kuḷattūr Amutāmpikai Piḷḷaittamiḻ,* he praises Goddess Amutāmpikai, a consort of Śiva, who is worshipped in a shrine in Kuḷattūr near Madras. The long matted hair of her husband Śiva provides a dwelling place for many items and creatures. For example, according to myth, the Ganges River graciously agreed to descend to earth, but fear arose that the force of her fall would cause terrible damage to the land. Śiva came to the rescue, breaking the river's descent by allowing it to land in his thick locks first and then flow down to earth. For this reason, poets and icon-makers usually portray Śiva with the Ganges River in his hair. As a Śaivite goddess, the Ganges is often considered to be one of Śiva's female consorts, or even one of his wives. Similar stories exist to explain the presence of others found in Śiva's hair, many of whom appear on the list that begins the verse.

The moon appears on this list too, but, as the poet is quick to point out, the lunar orb is only one of many with a small claim to Śiva's hair. In contrast, Goddess Amutāmpikai possesses a vastly different relationship to Śiva. When she joins with Śiva to take on an iconographic form called Ardhanārīśvara, the resulting deity appears as half god and half goddess—split right down the middle, with a female breast on one side and a male chest on the other. In this form the goddess shares fully 50 percent of Śiva's body. Clearly she surpasses the lowly moon, who can claim only a tiny bit of the great god's body.

Kuḷattūr Amutāmpikai Piḷḷaittamiḻ 67

All of these—
the Ganges River
snakes
the tumpai flower
a thickly woven garland of pure, golden cassia flowers
a skull
the feather of a crane
fragrant ūmattam flowers, from which fragrant honey drips,
Agni, the fire god,
the erukku plant
cool aṟuku grass
the celestial mantāram flowers, showered from above by the gods,
and flowers picked and strewn by the sages—
they stay
in the Lord's forest of matted hair.

So you have nothing but a tiny claim
on his hair, do you?

But the goddess lives,
taking as her own exactly one half
of all the flawless thirty-two parts
of Śiva's body.

So, she is greater than you.
Of that there is no doubt.
With her, Moon, come to play.

With Amutavaḷḷi from Kuḷattūr,
whose beauty ever increases,
Moon, come to play.[16]

In the next verse, from Kumarakuruparar's pillaittamil to the Goddess Mīṉāṭci in Madurai, the poet devotes most of his attention to the moon, while implying that the goddess greatly surpasses him in many ways. The poet builds his verse around astronomical and religious insults to the moon.

Maturaimīṉāṭciyammai Piḷḷaittamiḻ 64

They say you are the by-product
spit out after the gods and their families
churned, poured, drank,
and enjoyed the celestial ambrosia.

They say you are the leftovers
vomited by the black planet,
which radiates fiery poison.

They say you are a consumptive,
full of blotches
and covered with shrinking skin.

They say people should not look at you
on a certain day each month.

The sea-girt earth utterly despises you.
No refuge except this one, you see,
removes the terrible impurity of those like you,
who try to flee with orbiting stars.

With the young elephant cow
who bathes in the Vaigai River
which floods the Kaṟpaka Forest
with its high surging waters,
Moon, come to play.

With the fair creeper,
consort of the god with the pure golden bow,
Moon, come to play.[17]

Kumarakuruparar mocks the moon for its disappearance during an eclipse, its waning and waxing, and its mottled surface. Other poets have alluded to these familiar features of the moon, but this verse's humor comes from the imaginatively pejorative ways in which the poet interprets the moon's behavior. For example, since the moon's size decreases, the poet accuses it of wasting away, afflicted with consumption.

The insults the poet hurls at the moon imply that the moon has become thoroughly polluted and desperately needs the purification that only a visit to the temple of Goddess Mīṉāṭci can give him. The moon even originated in an insignificant way: as a mere by-product of the central project of securing celestial elixir when the gods churned the ocean. Then, during an eclipse, Rāhu swallowed the moon, which later emerged from the bottom of Rāhu's body undigested. Food tasted and tainted by another's saliva is impure, so the poet derides the posteclipse moon as polluted. Furthermore, since the moon's skin contains blotches and shrinks, he must be treated as defiling, like lepers and consumptives. Finally, during the fourth lunar crescent, people must avoid looking at the unlucky moon, whose sight on that day is considered inauspicious.

For all these reasons, no hope of salvation exists for the moon unless he visits the temple where the goddess dwells. Ever since Indra purified himself of the sin of brahminicide by bathing there, the auspicious site has been renowned as a place of purification. As proof of the power of the goddess, the poet calls attention to the abundant waters of the Vaigai River in Madurai. In his refrain, the poet eulogizes Mīṉāṭci's effect on her city by commenting that the Vaigai River in Madurai rises as high as the heavens, filling the Kaṟpaka Forest there with its life-giving waters. This piece of hyperbole suggests that Goddess Mīṉāṭci can purify and bring auspiciousness to both the terrestrial and the celestial world. Thus, a visit to her provides the only hope for the degraded moon.

All three examples using the difference strategy argue that the extraordinary child far surpasses the moon in eminence and power. In the first two verses the poet achieves his goal by emphasizing the greatness of the baby, while the last verse makes the same point by emphasizing the flaws of the moon. In all three, the difference strategy implies that the moon should feel himself fortunate indeed that such a marvelous baby would deign to accept the moon as a companion.

Giving

The strategy of giving (or bribery, as some call it) promises that the child will save the moon from some peril or give him something he dearly wants, or both. This strategy enables the poet to praise the hero or heroine of the poem by making reference to great deeds accomplished in his or her adult life, while simultaneously attributing certain anxieties to the moon. In the following verse, Seyyitu A<u>n</u>apiyyā portrays the Prophet Muhammad according to Tamil moon-lore, as well as according to legendary accounts preserved in Muslim popular tradition.

Napikaḷ Nāyakam Piḷḷaittamil̲ 69

Behold, he is the king who will end the suffering
that the cakravāka bird causes you.

Behold, he is the shimmering-tailed peacock
who will remove the trembling
that long-bodied Rāhu causes.

He will stand before you in Mecca,
city of justice that appeared as a ruler
for the sea-girt world.

For the sake of King Habib,
the sovereign of kings,
on the new moon day
he will command you to come
on the right path without delay.

Before he does that,
come with your waxing beauty,
and worship his lotus feet with love.

With the precious Prophet,
son of Aminar,
Moon, come to play.

With the greatest of prophets
from the Quraish lineage,
praised by the whole world,
Moon, come to play.[18]

This verse reveals what the poet imagines to be the moon's fears. According to Tamil literary tradition, the cakravāka bird tortures the moon by pecking at his surface in order to drink ambrosia. A<u>n</u>apiyyā promises that the Prophet will end the moon's pain, presumably by destroying or frightening away the cakravāka bird, if the moon comes to play with the baby. The poet also alludes to the moon's anxiety that the snake Rāhu might swallow him again. Likening the Prophet to a peacock, the snake's natural predator, the poet suggests that Muhammad's gift of protection will rescue the moon from the threat of ingestion.

The rest of the verse confirms the greatness of Muhammad by drawing attention to his marvelous effect on the moon. According to Islamic legends about the life of the Prophet, he causes the moon to come before him (and splits it) to prove the power of Islam to King Habib. The poet insinuates that the Prophet can command the moon and will do so, when so requested by King Habib. Therefore, the poet urges the moon to throw himself at the mercy of the powerful Prophet for protection from the cakravāka bird and the relentless pursuit of Rāhu.

Although a poet can draw upon a great deal of legend and lore, as the previous verse shows, moon verses can also incorporate topical material in a witty way and still remain comfortably within the conventions of the paruvam. In *Śrī Vaiṣṇavi Piḷḷaittamiḻ*, poet Sadhu Ram advises the moon of the potential danger posed by scientific projects aimed at space exploration. Written soon after the first human steps taken on the moon, the verse tells of the willingness of the extraordinary divine girl to protect the moon, even if Westerners try to colonize it, thereby destroying its formerly untouched splendor.

Śrī Vaiṣṇavi Piḷḷaittamiḻ 63

Using the scientific perspective
that they have developed,
Westerners won't leave you alone.

They make attempt after attempt,
trying to establish
some kind of house on you.
If it becomes practical
for the people of the earth
to emigrate there,
then where is there room
for your ancient glory?

And afterwards, even the celestials
won't esteem you, Stupid Moon!
Who began calling you "intelligent?"

Consider this:
If you come here quickly
and fall at her feet in worship
the threat to your greatness will end
and you can be saved.

Moon, right now come and play.
With Vaiṣṇavi who lives in Ambapuri,
Moon, right now come and play.[19]

If the gift verse can be seen as a form of persuasion in which the opponent receives an offer of a present, the punishment strategy suggests that when the moon refuses to cooperate, harsher measures are also available.

Punishment

THE TERM *taṇṭam* derives from a Sanskrit word, *daṇḍa,* meaning staff, and eventually comes to connote punishment and retaliation.[20] A common type of punishment verse threatens that whatever measures are necessary, in order to get a proper playmate for the child, will be taken. The following verse, (from Pakaḻikkūttar's *Tiruccentūr Piḷḷaittamiḻ* to Murukaṉ), contains a carefully detailed threat beneath its seemingly polite invitation to the moon. The speaker might be described, in today's terms, as making an offer that is too good—and too dangerous—to refuse.

Tiruccentūr Piḷḷaittamiḻ 68

The ancient Mandara Mountains still exist
so we can churn sweet ambrosia as in the old days,
can't we?

The wide ocean—that deep moat—it didn't turn to mud
and dry up into a bed of sand,
did it?

Did Indra and his gods in the sky die?
Did a huge darkness settle in?
Did the seven outer worlds become empty?

The huge snake Vasūki,
his long teeth flowing with poison,
he didn't split into pieces,
did he?

Incomparable Vali still has a tail,
doesn't he?

Foolish moon,
what isn't possible if this boy wants it?

With the lord of the gods,
the one from Tiruccentur,
who wields the sharp spear,
Moon, come and play.

With Murukan̲ who rides his peacock,
making the steep mountains tremble,
Moon, come to play.[21]

Pakal̲ikkūttar assumes that the listener knows precisely how the moon originated. Using Mount Mandara upside down as the churn and two snakes as churning ropes, the gods churned the sea to get the celestial nectar. As a by-product of the churning, they also produced the moon. The speaker inquires—in a way that insinuates the answer is already known—whether all of the principal items and actors in the famous churning project are still available. Then the poet conveys how much little Murukan̲ wants the moon to be his playmate, noting that the deity always gets what he wants. Implied is that if this moon refuses, Murukan̲ can surely cause another moon to be churned out who will be more cooperative.

If most punishment verses suggest that the extraordinary child can get a playmate through the use of force, the Christian punishment verse below, written by Aruḷ Cellatturai, locates the source of punishment elsewhere. The moon must fear not the extraordinary child, portrayed as kind and loving, but the resolve of modern Tamil poets, who will cease praising the moon in poetry unless he agrees to act as a playmate for Jesus.

Iyēcupirāṉ Piḷḷaittamiḻ 70

Poets with Pure Tamil as their life-breath
have praised you in many ways
in the verses they composed.

So, with pride,
you wander in the cloud-filled sky.

Young Tamil poets drink in from all sides
the beauty of the Baby who comes here
tottering with charming steps,
holding the hand of the woman
linked to precious Tamil of the Sangam.

If you don't hurry
to join him and play, right now,
poets will exclude you
from all their writings.

That's a loss you'd never accept.
Don't hesitate.

With the one who knows eternity
and who is the raft
that takes us to the other shore
to the feet of God,
Moon, come to play.

With the son of God
seated at the right side of precious God,
Moon, come to play.[22]

Most Tamil poets share a love for the Tamil language and a pride in its long literary tradition. In this verse, Cellatturai melds that pride in Tamil with love for Jesus in an appropriate visual image: he portrays the little baby tottering along uncertainly while clasping the hand of Tamil Tay—Tamil poetry conceived as a mother. This image suggests that Tamil poetry nurtures the figure of the Blessed Child in Tamilnadu. Poets too will do their part in caring for the fate of Baby Jesus, but will ignore the moon if he refuses to come play with the child.

The threat of punishment strategy enables pillaittamil poets to draw upon many literary strands within Tamil literature. The tone of confrontation and resolve in the two examples here typifies poetry in which poets employ the punishment strategy. The martial ethos of a number of punishment verses indicates the extent to which a genre supposedly devoted to celebration of the happy child encompasses a range of themes, all the way from commentary on poetic practice (poets' praise of the moon) to thinly veiled threats of coercion (the threat to rechurn the ocean).

War Strategies Transformed

LONG BEFORE PILLAITTAMILS, treatises on statecraft mentioned four basic strategies employed by a successful king. One of the most influential of these treatises, attributed to a king's counselor named Kautilya, the *Arthaśāstra,* lays out four strategies for extending a kingdom beyond its current boundaries: conciliation, bribery, dissension, and punishment. Conciliation involves friendly persuasion, especially convincing officers of the enemy king that their interests would be better served were they to aid their king's opponent. If conciliation does not succeed, Kautilya advises bribery to win over seditious men in the enemy king's army. Should both strategies fail, he recommends cultivating dissension (the "divide and conquer" strategy) among the enemy king's supporters, especially imprisoned princes, neighboring kings, or independent chieftains. Only as a last resort should a king practice force, the final method.[23]

Kautilya's discussion reveals a heretofore unexamined similarity between the strategies and the four strategies traditionally utilized in the moon paruvam of a pillaittamil. One need not argue that a specific passage from the *Arthaśāstra* exerted direct influence on the development of the moon verses, a perhaps undocumentable claim. It is more likely that over time the four strategies, as an individual unit of analysis, were incorporated into the body of knowledge to be mastered by those educated for religious and political leadership.[24] By the time that the pillaittamil developed, the four strategies probably formed part of the intellectual resources from which sophisticated poets could draw for their own purposes, just as they drew upon moonlore, mythic traditions, and iconographical conventions.[25] Whatever the historical connection between the two, close scrutiny suggests that the pillaittamil's moon strategies bear a striking resemblance to the techniques originally conceived in a martial situation.

The pillaittamil does, however, reconfigure the four strategies both in relation to their original sequence and their semantics.[26] According to the *Arthaśāstra*, one should proceed sequentially, trying earlier strategies before finally turning to war. In contrast, rather than a four-part sequence, the pillaittamil strategies form two contrasting pairs: similarity/difference and generosity/punishment. More important, within the pillaittamil tradition the four strategies are not seen as sequential but as equally viable alternatives. A poet can utilize any of these strategies, or not, without assembling their verses in a set order. In addition, the first two strategies have shifted their semantic range. In the *Arthaśāstra*, one undertakes friendly persuasion *(sāma)*, followed by the cultivation of dissension *(bheda)*, but in the moon paruvam the first two strategies entail identification of similarities *(cāmam)* and differences *(pētam)* between the moon and the extraordinary child being praised.

Despite these shifts, the four strategies seem to have carried their martial subtext with them into the pillaittamil. Scholar Aradhana Parmar aptly summarizes the overall thrust of the four strategies in the original context of statecraft when he says, "The whole purpose of Kautilya's foreign policy is to increase one's power mainly at the cost of the natural enemy. This increase in power is intended to be the first step towards the realisation of the ambition to conquer the world."[27] The martial tone—the drive to get what one wants, the urgency or veiled threat, the emphasis on proclaiming the immense power of the child and denigrating the worth of the opponent—shapes moon poetry in explicit and implicit ways. This poetry works with antagonism. Nowhere else in a pillaittamil does one find the kind of crude threats, insults, and expressions of contempt that occur in the moon paruvam. Just as a king ritually taunts his enemy and threatens to bring about his downfall, the speaker of the moon verse insults the moon (in highly stylized poetic ways) and threatens the moon with all kinds of dire consequences if he refuses to come play with the baby. Kautilya's strategies are about power—the power to overwhelm the enemy. Pillaittamil moon verses concern the power to overwhelm the moon through persuasion, convincing him to come play with an extraordinary child.[28]

Moon poetry explicitly deals with play: the poet requests that the moon come to play with the extraordinary child. But the poet, too, has scope for play within this paruvam, because of the range of strategies as well as the opportunities for wit, humor, and punning. The poetry in the paruvam ranges from statecraft to iconographic conventions, moon phases to cosmology, myth to morality, lunar landings to metaphors of enlightenment. Pillaittamil tradition has identified this paruvam as the tiger of paruvams; these translations show why the paruvam functions as a benchmark of virtuosity.

Every time readers move through a single pillaittamil, they can experience the standard pillaittamil sequence of paruvams. This chapter, however, provides an experience not found in any single pillaittamil text. Here the reader can move from text to text, seeing how different poets play with the seventh paruvam. The translations in this chapter provide examples of how the pillaittamil assumes and participates in an aesthetic of virtuosity. The analyses in this chapter demonstrate the extent to which conventions and expectations exist for moon poetry. In spite of those poetic restraints, or perhaps precisely because of those poetic restraints, connoisseurs of the genre celebrate poetry that maneuvers within those conventions to produce something inventive and fresh.

The chapter deliberately juxtaposes moon verses written by poets with differing religious (and, in one case, nonreligious) affiliations. The Hindu pillaittamil tradition was well established prior to Muslim and Christian adoption of the genre, but when Muslims and Christians adopted it, they did so as a Tamil enterprise, not a Hindu one. They employed the pillaittamil genre as a set of poetic options whose conventions provide a general literary framework for particular religious expression. These poets draw upon the conventions of a genre that was not originally theirs to make a space for themselves within the history of the genre. Thus, although all poets who write in the moon paruvam request the moon as a playmate, Hindu poets draw on a body of Śaivite mythology, Muslim poets draw upon legends from the life of the Prophet, Christians draw upon accounts of the salvific powers of Jesus, and atheists celebrate their leader's defeat of demonic superstitions. Mastering the pillaittamil conventions, they become established poets in the genre and expand its scope by bringing in new ways of taming the tiger.

PART TWO

PILLAITTAMILS FOR READING

2. *Pulling a Little Chariot.* Wall painting in the shrine at the Dharmapuram Matha (photograph by Michael H. Fisher).

CHAPTER THREE

THE FLORESCENCE

THE PILLAITTAMIL GENRE began to flourish with the composition of Pakaḻikkūttar's *Tiruccentūr Piḷḷaittamiḻ* (henceforth *TCPT*). While several extant earlier texts contain some or almost all of the features characteristic of the pillaittamil genre, *TCPT* is the first fully articulated devotional pillaittamil and stands at the beginning of a long line of successors.[1] Later poets and connoisseurs praised *TCPT* and measured their own work against it. Pakaḻikkūttar set out certain poetic strategies for particular paruvams. Later poets built upon, elaborated, ignored, embellished, subtly transformed, and pushed these strategies to their limits. Essentially, Pakaḻikkūttar's text established the pillaittamil as a productive genre. It is appropriate, then, that the translations from *TCPT* (which appear after this introduction to the poem) provide the reader with sample verses from all ten paruvams. In addition, for selected paruvams, several verses are provided. Thus, the reader can appreciate the scope of the paruvams in one of the earliest and still influential pillaittamils.

Author and Text

PAKAḺIKKŪTTAR GREW UP in a village in the Ramnad area. Most scholars date his birth sometime after the mid-fourteenth century and his death sometime in the first quarter of the fifteenth century.[2] *Pakaḻi* means arrow, so some legends take this as evidence that the author came from a community of arrow-making blacksmiths, while others explain the name differently.[3]

According to tradition, Pakaḻikkūttar, originally a Vaiṣṇava devotee, suffered terrible stomach pains for a long time. One day an ancestor who had been a devotee of Murukaṉ (son of Śiva) appeared to him in a dream and asked him to sing a pillaittamil. The poet then saw that sacred ash and a leaf had been bestowed upon him. He awoke to find a palm leaf beside him upon which to compose poetry. After prayer to Lord Murukaṉ cured his illness, he composed his pillaittamil to the deity as manifested at the Tiruccentur shrine.[4] A center of pilgrimage in the Tirunelveli District, Tiruccentur lies by the seashore near the Mannar Straits, between India and Sri Lanka. Evidence suggests that the shrine to Murukaṉ there is quite old (some claim as early as second century), and ninth-century inscriptions attest to the site's importance from that period.[5] A place of great natural beauty, Tiruccentur provided Pakaḻikkūttar with a whole set of seaside imagery (waves, sands, shore, pearls, conches), which he incorporated into his poem as part of his praise for Murukaṉ's shrine.

Research into the dissemination of *TCPT* demonstrates its enduring popularity. Manuscript versions are many, and its reprint history is impressively continuous from the time that we began to have systematic records about its printing history in Tamilnadu. Publication data indicate that in the first three-quarters of this century, it was a favorite text to publish and distribute freely as an act of religious merit on special occasions in the Śaivite monasteries of the Thanjavur area. More recently the Saiva Siddhanta Publishing Works Society (henceforth SISS) has reprinted the poem a number of times.[6]

Legend and customary usage also attest to the esteem in which this pillaittamil was held. According to legend, Lord Murukaṉ found the poem that Pakaḻikkūttar sang to him so beautiful that the deity gave the poet a golden necklace. There is a widespread Tamil saying that means "The pillaittamil of Pakaḻikkūttar is great Tamil [poetry]."[7] When connoisseurs wanted to praise a later pillaittamil poet, they would often refer to him as similar to Pakaḻikkūttar (see chapter 6, where a nineteenth-century poet is given that honor), indicating that *TCPT* constituted a benchmark for later pillaittamil writers. Pakaḻikkūttar's text became, in effect, the pattern for later generations of pillaittamils that flourished over the centuries.

Since almost all pillaittamils possess at least one hundred verses, it would be impossible to translate an entire pillaittamil in this volume and still have room to show the myriad ways that various poets from different ideological communities have composed within the genre. Still, by selective sequential sampling, the reader can experience the process of moving through the paruvams of a pillaittamil. This chapter's translations are arranged to make that possible by providing at least one example from each paruvam. The verses translated occur in paruvam order: protection, sway to and fro, lullaby, handclapping, kiss, come, moon, little drum, little house, and little chariot.

Another pleasure for a pillaittamil reader involves lingering within a particular paruvam, relishing the various ways a poet depicts the same activity throughout each paruvam. For the protection paruvam, two verses in this chapter suggest the diverse concerns of the poet when he invokes the aid of gods and goddesses to protect the divine infant. The translations also include two verses from the kiss paruvam to demonstrate how the use of a pun can generate elaborate variations on a theme. Finally, the reader will find four examples of the little house paruvam, each employing a different form of persuasion. The connoisseur's knowledge of the paruvam structure creates an appreciation for the poetic subtleties achieved by pillaittamil poets both across and within paruvams.

Protection as Prescribed

SOUTH INDIAN ARTISTS performing classical dance concerts or musical recitals often precede the performance with a prefatory poem, song, or prayer. Performers refer to this piece as *mangalam*, "auspicious." Some prefatory pieces invoke the deity's presence, some praise the deity, some ask for divine help so that all obstacles to the successful completion of the performance can be overcome, and many combine these. According to tradition, such ritualized beginnings bring blessings, both because they consecrate the artist's work and because they provide members of the audience with the opportunity to hear auspicious words of prayer. One could describe the pillaittamil's protection paruvam as a highly embellished equivalent of the *mangalam*.

Like the prefatory piece that begins a performance, the protection paruvam initiates the listener or reader into the pillaittamil poem. Each of the verses in the paruvam asks a particular deity or set of deities to protect the child whom the poet lauds in the poem. The paruvam can be conceptualized as a process of ritualized entrance. It brings the audience into the world of a mother concerned about her tiny baby's welfare. One can also see it as an initiation into the religious world of the poet, because the protection paruvam identifies, verse by verse, the deities whom the poet and the audience considered to be capable of powerful acts of protection.

The protection paruvam invokes an umbrella-like coverage to shield the child from dangers that rain down upon the vulnerable. Since each verse in the paruvam invokes the aid of a different deity (and the last verse often invokes all the remaining gods), the range of protection requested is vast. The protection paruvam also invokes multiple auspicious results, because within it the poet brings together many references to the salvific acts of protection that gods and goddesses have performed in the past. Such references bear witness to and provide evidence of the power of these protectors. If one earns merit from a single song of praise, one earns even more merit with multiple ones. If a child benefits from one deity as protector, that child benefits even more from a host of deities.

Formally, the protection paruvam constitutes a set of niches, into which the poet places requests to particular deities. *Pāṭṭiyal*s, traditional texts on poetics that provide specific directions for the writing of pillaittamils (and other genres), give detailed instruction about how a poet should fill the niches in the protection paruvam.[8] The first extant, and most influential, *pāṭṭiyal* text, *Pa<u>nn</u>iru Pāṭṭiyal,* includes a list of deities who may fill protection niches. The instructions draw particular attention to the first niche of the paruvam:

> The god taken up first in the invocation is [Viṣṇu] who wears in his crown the sacred basil, whose flowers are fragrant. He is appropriate to be mentioned first since [he is] the Lord of Protection, since he unites with the Lady of the Lotus [Lakṣmī], and since he is the Lord with the crown, armlet, thick garland of flowers, earrings, sacred thread, jewelry with excellent gems, and sapphires.[9]

This admonition seems particularly intriguing since the vast majority of pillaittamils, including *TCPT,* are Śaivite, yet Viṣṇu must occupy the first niche; the arbiters of literary form caution that the paruvam should function to ensure protection, and Viṣṇu preserves the universe.

Pakaḻikkūttar fills *TCPT*'s first protection niche as follows:

TCPT 2 (protection 1): Addressed to Viṣṇu on behalf of Murukaṉ

Indra, with mountainous shoulders
fragrant with fresh sandalpaste
where Śacī perches, praises him.

Śiva, from the zenith of the sky,
worships him.

He is the learned guru
who taught Tamil to great Agastya,
King of the Potiyal Mountains.

Protect Murukaṉ of Centur,
who lives west of the roaring ocean.

You created Brahmā,
enthroned on the sweet red lotus
with a rich golden stamen.

To join Brahmā, you created
the primordial generative Prakṛti.

Considering how to make all things prosper,
you put a measure of yourself
in all created beings.

Only you hold the conch and wheel
for protection, Viṣṇu.

Protection verses include two components of praise, one to the baby and one to the protector. The poet demonstrates the preciousness of the child to the deity by proving the child's praiseworthiness. Pakaḻikkūttar emphasizes the child's greatness by focusing on the awe Murukaṉ inspires in other eminent gods and gurus. For example, Pakaḻikkūttar tells us that along with his consort Śacī, the sovereign of the gods, Indra, eulogizes Murukaṉ. So too does Lord Śiva. Even Agastya, the great grammarian, considers Murukaṉ his literary preceptor. Such a baby clearly deserves protection.

Praise of Viṣṇu's protection is considered especially efficacious, since he preserves the universe; the poet fills the opening niche of his protection paruvam just as the *pāṭṭiyal* texts indicate. Pakaḻikkūttar praises Viṣṇu both to express appreciation for his glorious acts of protection and to convince him to perform the same kinds of deeds to protect the little baby. The poet emphasizes Viṣṇu's responsibility to maintain his creatures by noting that Viṣṇu himself created Brahmā, the creator god, and Prakṛti, from whom all matter came. Viṣṇu even invested each creature with a tiny bit of his own divine nature. Therefore, the poet reasons, Viṣṇu should protect this baby with his own special weapons, the conch and the discus, which prove effective against danger.

The *pāṭṭiyal* texts tell us that a verse to Lord Śiva can occur in the protection paruvam only after the first verse had been designated for Viṣṇu. Not only that, but the protection verse to Śiva must avoid all reference to Śiva's destructive aspects:

> The established tradition when they speak [of Śiva] is to mention the Ganges River, the moon, the ko<u>nr</u>ai garland, along with the auspicious axe and the daughter of the mountain [Pārvatī] in order that the name, iconographic symbols, and other things become apparent. They should not mention killing and cruelty when they say, "May the god with the spreading matted hair [Śiva], along with the seven mothers, protect with grace."[10]

The arbiters warn that the poet must uphold the goal of protection by avoiding reference to Śiva's destruction of the world at the end of time. Rather, poets should fill their verses with auspicious attributes of Śiva, such as the beauty of his consorts and his protection of the earth from the impact of the Ganges River's descent from the sky. In accordance with prescriptions, *TCPT*'s second protection verse (see translation following this introduction) opens by praising how Śiva gave the crescent moon and the Ganges River refuge in his matted hair. Again in accordance with prescriptions, within the first few lines Pakaḻikkūttar invokes Pārvatī (there called Umā), the consort who acts as a mediator between petitioners and Śiva. The line noting that Śiva protects his devotees when they worship him with words acts as a reminder that this verse praises Śiva with words in order to win protection for Baby Muruka<u>n</u>.

The fundamental rhetorical pattern of a protection verse remains essentially the same throughout the protection paruvam. One section of the verse praises the deity invoked for protection; the other section praises the divine infant for whom protection is requested. The phrase in which the poet asks the deity to protect the baby connects the two parts of the verse. The poet can express praise for either deity by enumerating salvific deeds, such as the defeat of demons; the poet can draw attention to the iconography of the deity, especially the powerful weapons he or she holds, such as the spear or trident; the poet can also laud the consort of the god or goddess as an indication of the added power, auspiciousness, or compassion that the consort contributes to his or her partner.

Possibilities of a Pun

ALTHOUGH PRESCRIPTIVE TEXTS for pillaittamils say a great deal about candidates for niches in the protection paruvam, other than naming the remaining paruvams, *pāṭṭiyal* texts give little information about them. Within the lineage of pillaittamil writers themselves, however, certain poetic conventions developed in less formal ways. One such convention developed around the name for the paruvam that requests that the baby give the speaker a kiss, *muttam*. Since *muttam* can mean either "kiss" or "pearl," there is ample opportunity for word play that Pakaḻikkūttar exploits. Another poetic convention in *muttam* verses is the conceit that pearls appear in many places—not just in oysters. A particularly auspicious source of pearls remains the right-whirling conch; since most conches swirl to the left, right-twisting conches are rare and precious. Tradition says pearls also appear in tusks of rutting elephants, the ripe head of a paddy stalk, bamboo, plants, and rainclouds.[11] A clever poet can make this list of places to harvest pearls into a charming verse.

Two of Pakaḻikkūttar's *muttam* verses play with the notion of multiple sources of pearls. *TCPT* 41's refrain (translated after this introduction) reminds us that Murukaṉ's shrine at Tiruccentur stands by the seashore. Because Murukaṉ fills the shrine with his auspicious presence, fertility and richness surround it. The ocean waves lapping at the shore are not, however, the only source of pearls. The rest of the verse explores the nature of these and other pearls, all of which are found lacking in comparison with the wonderful pearl of a kiss that Baby Murukaṉ gives.

Pakaḻikkūttar combines the motif of the many kinds of pearls/kisses with another sophisticated literary technique in *TCPT* 51. As in *TCPT* 41, the vertical structure of the verse comprises a list of pearls, which the women in this verse disparage, preferring Murukaṉ's pearl of a kiss instead:

TCPT 51 (kiss 11)

We never like the strings of small raindrop pearls
from the clouds
which made their home in the sky
put to shame by our hair—
where dotted bees flit
drinking honey and resting.

We decided we never want the white pearls
found in the ancient pond
into which the fish dove
put to shame by our eyes—
which extend to the bright fish-shaped jewels
worn in our ears.

We aren't pleased by the pearls
from Kāma's right-whirling conches
which cannot even be compared to our necks—
like the trunk of the soft areca tree
with fronds of flowers and green leaves.

Nor will we touch the bright pearls
from the bamboo
put to shame by our lustrous shoulders.

Instead, with your coral lips,
grant us a pearl of a kiss.

Rider from Tiruccentur
mounted on the feathered peacock,
with your coral lips,
grant us a kiss.

Not only do the women disparage the pearls, but they do so by judging them according to a particular set of aesthetic criteria. In classical Tamil love poetry, the poet uses a set of conventionalized similes to describe a woman's physical features. Poets repeatedly compare the dark glossy hair of a beautiful woman to the luminous, blue-black, monsoon skies. They formulaically praise shapely eyes by likening them to the gracefully curved body of a carp. A lovely neck is said to resemble an areca trunk. Comely shoulders have the roundness of a bamboo plant. Pakal̲ikkūttar inherited all of these familiar comparisons as part of his poetic heritage and put them into play in this verse. In this case the women's beauty surpasses even that of the lovely skies, fish, trunk, and plant. So the pearls from those inferior places are discredited by the women, who prefer, instead, a kiss from Murukan̲.

Pakal̲ikkūttar takes the kiss/pearl pun and subtly creates an erotic resonance to be savored by the literary connoisseur. Although both of the kiss verses reject all other kinds of pearls as inferior to Murukan̲'s kiss, the second one does so in a richer and more allusive way. By simultaneously combining the *muttam* pun and the poetic conceit of female beauty, Pakal̲ikkūttar manages to create a clever, sensual, poetically sophisticated verse—all around the motif of a baby's kiss.

Strategies to Save Little Houses

Pakal̲ikkūttar shows consummate literary skill in his treatment of the little house paruvam, which is unique among pillaittamil paruvams. First, in the other nine paruvams of the pillaittamil, the poet generally takes on a maternal persona. By contrast, in the little house paruvam the poet assumes the voice of little girls playing at the seaside. Second, all the other paruvams except moon verses revolve around praise for the baby. In contrast, the overall rhetorical strategies in the little house paruvam express mock criticism or reproach of the child and attempt to dissuade him from particular actions. The girls fear that the boy will knock over their playhouses; they try to prove to him that such an action would be wrong or inappropriate. Third, the setting and tone of this paruvam differ from all other paruvams.

The narrative situation of the little house verse has roots in ancient Tamil love poetry (dated ca. first to third centuries C.E.), which has continued to influence Tamil literary tradition in numerous ways through the centuries. One link between little playhouses and classical Tamil poetry is a shared landscape, that of the seashore *(marutam)*. Traditionally, Tamil poets portray the heroine's anxious feelings about her separation from the hero against the backdrop of the ocean landscape.[12] In the little house paruvam of the pillaittamil, however, we usually find not a single heroine but several young girls. Furthermore, their anxiety derives not from separation from the hero, but from fear that he will knock down their little houses. A second link to ancient love poetry is the dramatic situation: a boy threatens a playhouse built in the sand by the shore. A famous ancient poem depicts a young heroine amusing herself at the seaside by making a little sandcastle. The hero teases her, threatening to knock it down in order to get her attention.[13] The pillaittamil tradition has taken this vignette, stylized it, and transformed it into an unusual paruvam.

Although pillaittamils do not explicitly identify the age of the youths in this vignette, a number of *pāṭṭiyal* writers identify the boy as just reaching manhood and the girls as just developing their womanly figures.[14] It comes then as no surprise to those familiar with ancient Tamil poetry that in many Hindu little house verses, the girls describe themselves to the boy in ways that emphasize their physical beauty—their slim waists and voluptuous breasts. In a parallel way, they describe the deity in terms of his physical strength and prowess, qualities characteristic of the hero thought to be attractive to women. Thus, for a well-read audience, little house verses contain an explicit eroticism that would have been heightened by the seashore setting.

Other literary strategies overlay this erotic subtext. In this paruvam, the poet must use his ingenuity to provide the little girls with a plausible strategy for persuading the boy to desist from destroying the little houses. Pakaḻikkūttar depicts the girls employing tongue-in-cheek teasing and cajoling, as well as beseeching their tormentor for mercy. The reader can savor a number of excellent examples of the creative possibilities within this paruvam. Consider for example, *TCPT* 87, a set of attempts to dissuade young Murukaṉ from his threatened act of destruction.

TCPT 87 (little house 4)

You are truly great,
performing all three functions.

You created the entire wide world
around which Aruṇa drives his seven horses
in a chariot with fluttering banners.

You preserve the world you created.
You destroy it.

Your intention is to seize
entire cities of your enemies, isn't it?

Is it really prowess
to destroy the homes
we made as playhouses?

We are just little girls
with anxious eyes,
waists burdened
with the support of our heavy breasts,
and flower-like hands reddened
from sifting sand.

With your holy lotus feet,
sought by Indra and the other gods,
don't destroy the little houses of us little ones.

Rich one of Tiruccentur,
where the waves cast up pearls,
don't destroy our little houses.

In this little house verse, the girls begin by flattering Murukaṉ with the compliment that he performs all three cosmic processes: creation, preservation, and destruction (even though each one is usually assigned to the three great gods Brahmā, Viṣṇu, and Śiva respectively). The girls emphasize the greatness of his deeds to contrast them with the lowly act of destroying a playhouse. They urge him instead to perform his assigned duty of destroying demons who threaten the order of the universe. Surely, the destruction of a little girl's playhouse shrinks to insignificance before the other tasks that he must complete. In fact, by knocking down their little houses, he acts as a bully rather than displaying prowess.

Switching tactics, the girls now highlight their frailty. To win Murukaṉ's sympathy, they complain that building in the sand has exhausted them, and stress their fear of his impending attack. The poet provides descriptive details—waists so slender that they are barely strong enough to support their breasts, hands grown red and sore from sifting sand—that reaffirm their need for protection, rather than destruction. The refrain implies that the powerless girls are inappropriate foes for Murukaṉ, since even the powerful warrior and chief of the gods, Indra, comes to bow at his feet in obeisance. Surely Murukaṉ, worshipped by the gods, should pick an enemy with strength equal to his own and should show compassion toward the girls who have placed their trust in him.

The little girls use a different ploy to manipulate Murukaṉ in *TCPT* 93 (see translation below). There the girls carefully shift the blame for a potentially destructive act away from Murukaṉ himself, arguing that his nursemaids are to be blamed for his behavior, not him. As early as classical Tamil poetry, the figure of the nursemaid plays a role. She lives with a family, taking care of the little baby. Later on it becomes a convention that special children have more than one nursemaid. As evidence of Murukaṉ's greatness, he has a whole set of such servants, whom the little girls blame for allowing him to approach their sandcastles. The verse then moves into a devotional mode. The little girls remind Murukaṉ that he is the deity to whom they turn for protection: If he attacks them, their world will be shattered. Abandoned by their chosen deity, they have nowhere to turn. They appeal to him as children from families who have been devoted to him for generations, beseeching him for protection. The verse thus culminates with a cry for aid from a powerful god.

Yet another little house verse uses the occasion when the girls have been "playing house" as the backdrop for their plea for protection. *TCPT* 84 (translated below) gains much of its charm from its playful perspective on the fabrication of domestic activities. After building their house, the girls stock it with the equipment and ingredients for cooking. Conches function as pots, honey as cooking liquid, pearls as grains of rice, and flower petals as vegetables and spices. The girls are imitating housework. Their poignant plea, "See how eagerly we cook our precious rice," is almost a parody of the young Indian wife's desire to please her in-laws and husband with her culinary devotion.

In this kind of verse the pleas of the girls have the pattern of supplications to a deity. The girls are terrified that Murukaṉ might destroy their carefully created homes. The refrain serves to remind the hearer of Murukaṉ's tremendous power. His feet are redolent from the head of Indra because that great and powerful king of the gods has bowed in submission, the poet reminds his reader. The verse suggests that without the divine compassion of Murukaṉ, the domestic existence of everyday life will be endangered.

Range Within a "Child" Genre

ALTHOUGH THE PILLAITTAMIL genre focuses on the extraordinary child, within the genre's boundaries lie poetry whose subject matter includes everything from battle accounts to bedtime narratives, from stories of Murukaṉ's uncle (Kṛṣṇa) cavorting with the milkmaids to a survey of the different kinds of auspicious drums played in heaven. One could argue that in some pillaittamils, the connection to childhood can become quite tenuous. It would be more accurate to say, however, that while the rest of the verse is not necessarily limited to material dealing with childhood, the refrain keeps the poetry anchored to that theme. In fact, a powerful aspect of pillaittamil poetry is the surprising way that poets dart back and forth between childhood and adulthood. Depictions of varied activities may fill *TCPT*, but the refrain always brings the reader back to the extraordinary child.

Consider, for example, *TCPT* 12, which testifies to Murukaṉ's war prowess by depicting the fear he inspires throughout the cosmos. The verse begins with the arrival of Murukaṉ, riding on his fierce peacock. Murukaṉ's coming disturbs the cosmic elements: the northern mountains collapse, the seas dry up, and the mountain range that circumscribes the cosmos trembles. The sun and moon disappear from sight when Murukaṉ gallops so swiftly that the huge clouds of dust he produces obscure the heavens. Indra, the king of the gods, promptly surrenders, offering to pay whatever tribute Murukaṉ might demand. Even Śeṣa, the serpent upon whom Lord Viṣṇu rests, fears his predator, the peacock, and writhes in terror. The refrain, however, brings the reader's attention back to the fact that the deity addressed is a mere infant. A mother gently requests that the powerful warrior, who inspires such fear as an adult, sway to and fro, like a tender young plant swaying in a breeze. The link with the theme of childhood reasserts itself in the refrain, making the reader juxtapose all the martial deeds just described with the image of a small child.

Just as some verses deal primarily with the hero's adult deeds but reintroduce the child theme at the end, other verses deal with the baby throughout the body of the verse, but the refrain jolts the reader into realizing that this tiny, seemingly helpless, baby performs acts of miraculous power. For example, *TCPT* 28, a verse about a mother seeking to lull Baby Murukaṉ to sleep, is more than just a verse about a baby. In contrast to the verse analyzed above, the refrain emphasizes Murukaṉ's adult activities, even though the entire rest of the verse is about him as an infant. In an attempt to get Murukaṉ to settle down, his mother recites a head-to-foot litany of the glittering ornaments that the infant wears, starting at the top with his earrings and working all the way down to his anklets.[15] Trying another tack, she asks him to consider his poor devotees, who exhaust themselves by trying to keep up with him. Next, she expresses her worry that if he does not stop running around, perhaps the evil eye (a malevolent force aroused by envy of the beauty and vulnerability of young children) will cause misfortune. That tack does not work, either, so she attempts to make the idea of sleep attractive by describing the rich gems that adorn his cradle. Confessing her frustration and love, she asks the little baby to just lie down and suck his finger, hoping that he will fall asleep eventually.

In the refrain, however, the poet reminds the reader of the power of this great God, depicted earlier in the verse as a helpless baby. Murukaṉ is so powerful that his presence in the Tiruccentur shrine brings prosperity to those who live around it. Brahmā, the creator of the world, and Pārvatī, the great goddess, both worship him. The majority of the verse concerns the baby, but the refrain reminds us of Murukaṉ as a powerful adult.

As readers move through the translations in this volume, they will see how much Pakalikkūttar did to sketch approaches to composition within each paruvam. For example, Pakalikkūttar's treatment of the little house paruvam provides the template for some of the most sophisticated poetry found within the pillaittamil genre. In the following chapters we will see how other poets maneuver within, elaborate upon, or depart from some of the patterns established by Pakalikkūttar. Over the centuries, within the conventions of the genre, poets develop new and sophisticated perspectives on some of the basic poetic strategies prevalent in particular paruvams. Kumarakuruparar, who wrote the pillaittamil analyzed in the next chapter, was particularly masterful at using the pillaittamil's paruvam structure resourcefully and integrating into the text the mythic and sonorous elaboration so admired by pillaittamil connoisseurs.

TCPT 3 (protection 2): Invoking Śiva on behalf of Murukaṉ

In his jungle of red matted hair
the crescent moon, the Ganges, and snake wander.

The Pure One hugs Umā, whose breasts press close to him.

He protects devotees who worship him with words.

He swallowed the terrible fiery poison
that emerged from the fish-filled surging ocean.

Once, that true dancer performed the pavuri,
while his golden gem-filled anklets resounded.

His mounted arrow, strong as a reinforced bow,
forced the back of the northern mountains to bend and crawl.

His smile blooms with a laugh, like a flawless full white moon,
to destroy the jungle of darkness with ever-brighter light.

He took on an accessible form.
He nourished precious Sanskrit and Tamil.
He is the Lord in Madurai and in the Silver Hall.

We praise his fragrant feet
so he will protect Murukaṉ,
who keeps the Kuṟava Lady ever in his thoughts.

Murukaṉ longs for her full breasts
peaked as the Himalaya mountains,
fragrant with kumkum *and sandalpaste,*
in which sweet, striped, humming bees flit.

While the beating brass drum and mṛdangam *shake,*
the Strong One fights on the battlefield,
where so many aged ghouls dance
that no room remains for the enemy demons' army.

This younger brother is more mature in compassion
than the elephant-faced god, flowing with rut.

This prattling son rejoices
when he can sleep in the bed of Pārvatī's flower-hands.

This husband throws himself into tender union
with the Tree God's daughter, fragrant with thick blossoms.

Protect Murukaṉ whom famed Sarasvatī worships,
Lord Skanda who bestows sweet poetry!

Umā: Śiva's consort.

poison: When the gods churned the ocean to get heavenly ambrosia, a terrible poison emerged, but Śiva protected everyone by swallowing it.

pavuri: The specifics of this particular dance are unclear.

Silver Hall: The shrine in Chidambaram, where Śiva is worshipped in the form of a dancer.

Kuṟava Lady: Murukaṉ's consort Vaḷḷi, a woman from the hills.

kumkum: Saffron powder worn on the forehead by women, usually as a sign of auspiciousness, and applied to other parts of the body as an unguent.

mṛdangam: A cylindrical two-headed drum played with both hands.

the Strong One: Murukaṉ.

elephant-faced god: Gaṇeśa.

Tree God's daughter: In Indra's heaven stands his famed Kaṟpaka Tree. This epithet refers to his daughter.

Skanda: Another name for Murukaṉ.

TCPT 12 (sway to and fro)

The long, spotted, and striped snake Śeṣa,
with poisonous teeth like thorns
has many heads and they all writhe.

The northern mountains collapse.

The seven deep seas,
whose waterfronts abound with leaping fish,
dry up.

Sūra<u>n</u>, with twisted fangs, feels fear.

The moon and the sun completely disappear
behind the red dust.

The zenith of the universe,
where patient gods dwell,
is pierced.

Demons are afraid.

The shining Cakravāla Mountains tremble.

Frightened Indra, armed with his thunderbolt,
measures out the tribute
which you demand.

Warrior mounted on your peacock,
sway to and fro.

God with the sharp spear,
who is pleased with Alaivay,
where waves wash ashore,
sway to and fro.

Śeṣa: The cosmic serpent upon whom Viṣṇu sleeps.

Sūra<u>n</u>: Another name for Padmāsūra<u>n</u>, a demon whom Muruka<u>n</u> defeats in battle.

Cakravāla Mountains: A circular mountain range that surrounds the cosmos.

Alaivay: Another name for Tiruccentur.

TCPT 28 (lullaby 8)

Who hasn't seen the beauty of
your studded and dangling earrings,
your twelve arms, heavy with garlands,
your six faces, radiant in unchanging kingly splendor,
your waistband, your anklet, your jeweled belt like lightning,
your tinkling bells and other gems?

Look at those who fall at your feet:
dust has fallen on their soft fragrant hair,
their limbs have grown weak,
and their bellies are sunken.

Nothing good will happen if you crawl around.
The evil eye may fall on you, bringing misfortune.
Come to sleep on the grand bed
inlaid with gold and mountain gems.

Child who is my life,
you give me a gorgeous smile
but you won't go to sleep.

Won't you just lie there and suck
the ambrosia of your finger?
Won't you prattle sweetly?

Skanda, who enriches the prosperous city
of southern Centur, where the waves dash,
Little one begotten by Śiva,
tala, talelo.

Son of the supreme goddess,
boy worshipped by Brahmā and Pārvatī,
tala, talelo.

---

studded and dangling earrings, anklets, waistband, etc.: It is customary for a young child to wear a waistband and some jewelry, but this child's adornments are particularly ornate because he is a deity.

TCPT 35 (clap 5)

The seven great cloud-covered worlds
are meditation diagrams
which you delineate.

Even the wishing tree
is only a garden grown
for weaving lovely flower garlands
to place on your shoulders.

Excellent Indra and his gods
are those who never forget your holy name.

The peaked golden mountain
is the jewelbox where you keep
your collection of sacred ornaments.

The waves of the ocean
are water that washes the flesh
from your famed spear.

The seven groves and all their islands
are the track where your handsome-feathered peacock
practices running.

Handsome-chested One bedecked with garlands,
since all this is so,
armed with the sharp spear in Tiruccentur,
clap your hands.

With the sharp spear in Tiruccentur,
where conches drift onto the shore and cast pearls,
clap your hands.

---

meditation diagram: A mandala or image of the cosmos used to enhance concentration.

Wishing tree: A celestial miraculous tree that yields whatever one desires.

The Golden Mountain: Mt. Meru, the mountain that forms the axis of the cosmos.

The seven groves: The seven continents, in Hindu cosmology.

TCPT 41 (kiss 1)

Tossed about by roaring waves,
right-whirling conches drift up on white sand,
suffer harsh labor pains,
and give birth to pearls.

They have a price.

Huge rutting elephants
who stagger in their frenzy
bear crescent-moonlike tusks
that produce pearls.

They have a price.

The green paddy plant,
its thick head stooping with sheaves of grain,
produces cool pearls.

They have a price.

Clouds bestow pearls.
A price can be named for them.

But the pearls from your fruit-like mouth
are priceless.
Murukan̲, give me one of those kisses.

Primordial one of Tiruccentur,
where the sea showers pearls,
give me a kiss.

TCPT 56 (come 5)

Even when you feel hunger
as tiny as a sesame seed,
you get sad and move to and fro.
Your little tummy contracts,
you are about to cry,
your lovely coral lips pout,
and then you shed tears.

You jump up, you quiver,
you move to your cradle's side,
and kick your legs.

You suck your thumb
and droplets flow
from the corner of your mouth.

You crawl slowly,
dangling the fish-shaped earrings
that brush across your shoulders.

You smile a little,
you sit on my lap.
Then you sob, whimper,
and gaze at my face.

Prattling little one,
happily nursing nectar
from beloved Umā's breast,
fragrant with sandalpaste,
come.

Husband of Vaḷḷi,
the woman with budding breasts
like tender coconuts,
come.

Vaḷḷi: A young girl from the mountain tribe, one of the two wives of Murukan̲.

TCPT 67 (moon 5)

Among the forest of spreading hoods
belonging to strong thorny-toothed cobras
whose mouths flow with poison,
one cobra with a soft spotted body
and a huge gaping mouth
burned with ravenous hunger.

That cobra drank the west wind,
swallowed the wind rising in the east,
scooped up and gulped down the north wind
and the southern breeze.

Then it ate the plump sun.

Now, no target is left
except your place, and you're not
strong enough to stand up to the cobra.

So, join Murukaṉ.
You can stay here and play.

If you come,
a peacock endowed with strength
will come to your aid.
So, Moon, come and play.

With the Young One who rides the peacock,
under which writhes the head of a snake,
Moon, come and play.

---

under which writhes the head of a snake: Murukaṉ rides on a peacock, the natural predator of snakes. Since the moon fears the cobra will destroy him, he can take refuge with Murukaṉ, whose peacock feeds on snakes.

TCPT 77 (little drum 4)

In every street and road belonging to Indra,
who sits in a grove under the shady Pārijāta Tree,
the clear auspicious sounds of wedding drums
resound.

Everywhere in the city of Kubera,
whose garland has flowering buds and spreading petals,
the booms of beating drums
resound.

Kāma's clear surging ocean of musical instruments
resounds.

The Tiṇṭimam drums, played by musicians
who eagerly perform auspicious songs of blessing,
resound.

So, people think it must be a special festival
and in every town, instruments play
and the exalted four Vedas, chanted by the lords of the gods,
resound.

Beat your little drum, too.
Destroyer of the lineage of powerful demons,
who battled you in war,
beat your little drum.

---

wedding drum: The celestial inhabitants of Indra's realm have the privilege of enjoying sensual pleasures, including sexual union. The euphemistic phrase "wedding drum" indicates a "wedding" or coupling that occurs when an inhabitant enjoys a tryst with a celestial nymph.

Kubera: The god of wealth.

Pārijāta Tree: One of the five evergreen trees growing in heaven.

Kāma: The god of love.

TCPT 84 (little house 1)

We little girls
make the outer walls of our little houses
with pearls from golden conches
which surround the fragrant golden water.

We make our cooking pots
from right-whirling conches.

We fill pots with rich honey
that seeped from red lotus buds
growing in newly planted fields.

We cook our rice
made of pearls from bamboo.

We make our curry
from freshly picked bunches of flowers
grown in a grove as fragrant as rosewater.

See how eagerly we cook our precious rice.

With your fair young feet,
redolent from the head of Indra,
don't destroy our little houses.

Rich one of Tiruccentur,
where waves cast up pearls,
don't destroy our little houses.

TCPT 85 (little house 2)

It's not destruction of the playhouses
made by lovely girls
that worries us.

It's that the pearls
might irritate and bruise
your beautifully soft, anklet-clad, sacred feet.

And when the God of light
who wears the pure white crescent moon,
picks you up,
hugs you to his face,
and seats you on his broad shoulders,
won't dust settle there?

And if that innocent lady
who does not grow old—
even though
she has given birth to all the worlds—
seats you on her lap,
nurses you,
and lifts you to her face,
won't the fine red dust on your feet,
clad in warrior's anklets,
settle on her?

Don't destroy the little houses
of us little ones.

Rich one of Tiruccentur,
where the waves cast up pearls,
don't destroy our little houses.

God of light: Śiva, Murukan̲'s father.

that innocent lady who does not grow old: Pārvatī, Murukan̲'s mother.

TCPT 93 (little house 10)

Shouldn't we hate your nursemaids, not you?

They bathed you on the steps
leading down to the Tamraparni River,
renowned for its unfailing riches.
They put jewels of all kinds on you.
They picked you up and suckled you,
hugging you close.

And then,
they let you out into the street.

You are not the kind to knock down
with a kick of your feet
the little houses
which we made with our own hands,
eagerly sifting sand and gathering pebbles.

If our protector begins to destroy things,
to whom will we go with our worries from now on?

Great One, we have been your slaves for generations.
Don't destroy our little houses.

King of Tiruccentur,
where the waves cast up pearls,
don't destroy our little houses.

---

slaves: Here used to mean "devotees," those so devoted to Murukaṉ that they consider him their master and themselves his servants or slaves.

TCPT 95 (little chariot 2)

He entered the house of milkmaids
against whose pungent blouses,
full young breasts press.
Quietly he ate the white curds
set aside.

Then he pushed over the pot,
scooped up the white butter,
rolled it into a ball and ate,
his eyes closed in pleasure,
and wiped his luscious red mouth.

On that day Kṛṣṇa played,
rolling his large cart with his ankleted feet.

Nephew of that unique Dark One,
roll your cart to drive away the enemy,
old karma
that disheartens your devoted servants.

Roll your wheel of command
through all the worlds in this universe
and the universe above.

So you can roll over the mountain
of enemy demons' heads,
roll your little chariot.

Majestic young one with the rooster banner,
roll your little chariot.

---

that unique Dark One: Kṛṣṇa, in his form as mischievous butter thief and lover.

the old karma that disheartens your devotees: Devotees feel helpless because of the consequences of their past actions, but Murukaṉ can destroy that evil karma because of his prowess in all kinds of battle.

CHAPTER FOUR

A TEMPLE AND A PILLAITTAMIL

IN THE SEVENTEENTH century Kumarakuruparar composed *Maturai Mīṉāṭciyammai Piḷḷaittamiḻ* (henceforth *MMPT*) and presented it to Tirumalai Nāyakkar, ruler and patron responsible for a major set of renovations on the Mīṉāṭci Cuntarēśvaraṉ Temple in the city of Madurai. Pillaittamil connoisseurs cherish *MMPT* for its mellifluous verse and the subtle imagery with which the poet describes the life of Goddess Mīṉāṭci and her marriage to Lord Śiva. The poem also has come to be intimately bound up with the devotional practice of the temple, in both artwork and music. Considered to be one of the finest pillaittamils ever written, *MMPT* has been shaped by—and has itself shaped—the temple culture for whose glorification it was written.

Legends of Lauding the Goddess at Madurai

EXTANT TRADITIONS ABOUT Kumarakuruparar present him as a talented, prolific, and wide-ranging poet.[1] Although his date of birth is unknown, he was born of Śaiva Vellāla parents in Srivaikuntham (in the Tirunelveli area) and is said to have traveled to North India in 1655 and died ca. 1688.[2] He was, according to tradition, mute until the age of six, when the grace of Lord Murukaṉ at Tiruccentur (see chapter 3) restored his speech. In gratitude, he composed a poem to the deity, thereby commencing his literary career. As a youth he was initiated into monastic life by the fourth abbot of the Dharmapuram Matha. After studying Sanskrit, Tamil, philosophy, poetry, and asceticism there, he wrote many devotional texts, among which *MMPT* stands preeminent.

The Mīṉāṭci Cuntarēśvaraṉ Temple in Madurai has a long history of patronage by influential devotees. The Pandiyans, who ruled the southern part of Tamilnadu during the eleventh and twelfth centuries, worshipped principally at the temple, which stood at the center of their capital city. Temple chronicles narrate the fourteenth-century destruction of Madurai by Muslim invaders. With the end of the Madurai sultanate and the rise of the Vijayanagar Empire, new patrons for Hindu temples became active. The lineage of Vijayanagar governors who ruled over Madurai were Nāyakkars, Telugu-speaking warriors who patronized local temples as an expression of their new sovereignty. Tirumalai Nāyakkar, the last Nāyakkar ruler who supported religious architecture in the area, was known as an ardent devotee of Goddess Mīṉāṭci. Traditional histories of the temple say that Tirumalai Nāyakkar shifted his capital from Tirunelveli to Madurai at the request of the goddess herself; he funded the large-scale renovation and rebuilding that the temple underwent (1623–1659).[3] He also ordered calendrical changes in the annual temple festival to facilitate opportunities for acts of devotion to the goddess by the devotees who venerated her when she went out in procession.[4]

In pillaittamil history, however, Tirumalai Nāyakkar's most crucial act of patronage was his link to Kumarakuruparar's *MMPT*. According to tradition, in the course of making pilgrimage to various Śaivite temples, Kumarakuruparar visited Madurai and composed a pillaittamil to Goddess Mīṉāṭci. Legend tells us that the goddess appeared to Tirumalai Nāyakkar in a dream, directing him to arrange for a recital of Kumarakuruparar's poem before a learned assembly.[5] After inviting the poet to recite, the king made elaborate arrangements for the event.

On an auspicious day, Kumarakuruparar began reciting his poem in the large hall of the temple. According to a well-known legend, while the poet was explaining to his audience the requirements of the fifth paruvam ("come"), the goddess took on the outward form of a temple priest's young daughter and went to sit on the ruler's lap, happily enjoying the poet's recitation. As Kumarakuruparar was explaining verse 61 of his pillaittamil, the goddess expressed her appreciation by garlanding the poet with a string of pearls, and then she disappeared.[6] Her divine approbation of the pillaittamil, and that particular verse, has been echoed by many other connoisseurs of pillaittamil poetry, so they demand our close attention.

Savoring a Single Verse

THE PILLAITTAMIL METRICAL structure provides a poet with numerous opportunities for developing elegant imagery and pleasing alliteration. The earliest corpus of Tamil literature primarily used the *aciriyam* (or *akaval*) meter; each verse had a limit on its number of lines, and each line was composed of four metrical feet. Later medieval genres, including the pillaittamil, adopted the extended *aciriyam (aciriya viruttam),* which increased the length of a line, thereby making the poetry's structure more expansive and flexible.[7] This elongation of meter generated "expansive diction, elevated semantic choices, and long metrical structures" in the hands of skillful poets.[8]

Tamil literary connoisseurs have identified Kumarakuruparar as just such a skillful poet, singling out *MMPT* as exemplary in its mellifluousness, created by the arrangement of patterns of sound considered pleasing to the ear. They have also admired its deft, subtle, and suggestive incorporation of mythological incidents. In addition, they recognize Kumarakuruparar as masterful in his use of familiar poetic conceits and ornaments in ways that give them a fresh twist. Traditional connoisseurs of poetry use terms such as *mellicai* (soft sounds) and *o̱luku vaṇṇam* (flowing rhythm) to describe the kinds of poetic musicality prevalent in the poem.[9] As defined by Tamil metrical and poetic standards of his time, Kumarakuruparar excelled in poetic craftsmanship.

Certain verses in the poem have earned the status of classic examples of poetic beauty. Among these classic verses, none is more beloved than the one known familiarly among connoisseurs by the first two words of the verse in Tamil, *"toṭukkum kaṭavuḷ":*

MMPT 61 (come 9)

Fruit of the string of ancient songs
composed about the divine!

Fragrant taste flowing from sweet Tamil
with its full, honeyed, poetic themes!

Lamp lighting up the temple of the mind
of each devotee who roots out egotism!

Soft young elephant playing among the rising peaks
of the Himalaya Mountains!

Painting come to life, envisioned and contemplated
in the holy mind of He who transcends
this world girt by tossing oceans!

Young vañci creeper
in whose forest of tresses bees drink!

Come, great life whom Malayattuvacan̲ begot!
Come, come.

Echoing Mīn̲āṭci's assessment of this verse at the poem's debut, one modern scholar and connoisseur has written in praise, "How can we measure and describe the unfathomable beauty, excellent taste, and depth of meaning in the song (61) which moved the Goddess to listen to it in a human form?"[10] Initially, the outside observer might be puzzled by the praise heaped upon this verse, if considering only the criteria of rhetorical unity or narrative drama. For the verse's attraction arises from a complex set of techniques that include, among others, deft stringing together of alliterative patterns across the stanzas of the verse, the use of certain resonant consonants, vocative imagery, and the expression of devotional sentiment.[11]

Tamil connoisseurs have praised verse 61 for Kumarakuruparar's ability to "string" together parts of the verse according to certain established patterns. As one poetician observes, such stringing *(toṭai)* beautifies a poem in the way that a string of flowers adorns the wearer.[12] Among the various kinds of stringing, Kumarakuruparar makes major use of *etukai* and *mōn̲ai*, both indicated on Table 2.

TABLE 2: STRINGING AND VOCATIVES (*MMPT* 61)

toṭukkum kaṭavuṭ pal̲ampāṭal

toṭaiyin̲ payan̲ē nar̲ai pal̲utta

tur̲aittīntamil̲in̲ ol̲uku nar̲uñ

cuvaiyē akantaik kil̲aṅkaiyakal̲n

teṭukkum tol̲umparuḷakkōyir̲

kēr̲r̲um viḷakkē vaḷarcimaya

imayap poruppil viḷaiyāṭum

iḷamen̲ piṭiyē er̲itaraṅkam

uṭukkum puvan̲an̲ kaṭantu nin̲r̲a

oruvan̲ tiruvuḷḷattilal̲a

kol̲uka el̲utip pārttirukkum

uyirō viyamē matukaramvāy

maṭukkum kul̲ar̲kāṭēntum iḷa

vañcik koṭiyē varukavē

malayat tuvacan̲ per̲r̲aperu

vāl̲vē varuka varukavē

etukai

mōn̲ai

vocatives

Verse 61 contains *etukai* at the beginning of each of the four stanzas. *Etukai* governs the class of sounds in the first syllable, and the alliteration and form of the remainder of the word. Etukai occurs at the beginning of each stanza. Note the recurrent syllables *ṭukkum*, which, according to prescriptions for *etukai* and the vowels preceding the *etukai* phrase *(ṭukkum)*, must be non-long vowels (*o, e, u, a* rather than *ō, ē, ū, ā*). Another form of stringing, *mōṉai*, involves repetition of initial sounds occurs across metrical feet. Kumarakuruparar's verse displays the *mōṉai* pattern in the third, sixth, fourteenth, and last lines of the verse.

Admirers also call attention to the beauty of the verse because of Kumarakuruparar's choice of consonants. The reader unfamiliar with the Tamil alphabet and its analysis by Tamil grammarians can consult the table below, which summarizes the ways in which consonants are categorized:

HARD	SOFT	MIDDLE
k	ṅ	
c	ñ	y
ṭ	ṇ	
ṟ	ṉ	r ḻ
t	n	l ḷ
p	m	v

According to Tamil poetics, the most artful poetic phrases contain as few doubled hard consonants and as many soft and middle consonants as possible. In *MMPT* 61—except as part of the *etukai*—there are very few doubled (adjacent) hard consonants. In contrast, the poem abounds with soft and middle consonants. Among middle consonants, the Tamil letter *ḻ* remains a favorite of Tamil connoisseurs. *Ḻ*, a unique letter and sound, appears only in the Tamil alphabet. Produced in the middle of the throat with the tongue pulled back, its sound possesses an unusual resonance. Both its special status and its sonic reverberation distinguish it from all other sounds. Table 3 indicates the presence of the letter *l,* as well as soft and middle consonants. Note that every single line of the verse contains multiple examples of sounds considered pleasing by Tamil connoisseurs of poetry. The large number of nasals *(m* and *n)* tells us how pleasingly resonant the verse will sound when recited.

TABLE 3: MELLIFLUOUS SOUNDS (*MMPT* 61)

toṭukkum kaṭavuṭ pal̲ampāṭal
toṭaiyin payan̲ē nar̲ai pal̲utta
tur̲aittīntamil̲in ol̲uku nar̲uñ
cuvaiyē akantaik kil̲aṅkaiyakal̲n
teṭukkum tol̲umparuḷakkōyir̲
kēr̲r̲um viḷakkē vaḷarcimaya
imayap poruppil viḷaiyāṭum
iḷamen̲ piṭiyē er̲itaraṅkam
uṭukkum puvan̲aṅ kaṭantu nin̲r̲a
oruvan̲ tiruvuḷḷattilal̲a
kol̲uka el̲utip parttirukkum
uyirō viyamē matukaramvāy
maṭukkum kul̲ar̲kāṭēntum iḷa
vañcik koṭiyē varukavē
malayat tuvacan̲ per̲r̲aperu
vāl̲vē varuka varukavē

soft consonants
middle consonants
l̲

Tamil poetic analysis credits a certain kind of sound with the ability to deepen the devotional fervor of a verse: the vocative phrase, marked by the phoneme *ē* at its end. One way poets express devotional sentiment is to address an epithet or laudatory phrase directly to an intended audience, here Goddess Mīṉāṭci. The vocative's long *ē* sound enables the reciter to hold onto the auspicious phrase a little bit longer than usual and savor the opportunity to praise one's chosen deity. Vocatives always occur in pillaittamil refrains, but in some poetry (including verse 61), they appear throughout the verse. The poet uses the vocative again and again to put himself into a direct, personal relationship with Goddess Mīṉāṭci. In fact, as Table 2 shows, this entire verse consists of vocative phrases of praise.[13]

The imagery in these vocative phrases abounds with admiration and affection. Kumarakuruparar addresses Goddess Mīṉāṭci as the fruit or consequence of ancient songs, because when devotees sing these divine songs, they can envision her. Kumarakuruparar invokes not just sight but fragrance and taste as well in his adoring praises. The goddess becomes one to be savored when beautiful Tamil praises are uttered. The devotee need not even travel to a temple for worship because the goddess can dwell in the mind of a devotee; if egotism has been dug out, like a tuber, the goddess enters the mind to bestow the light of knowledge, says the poet.

In this verse, Kumarakuruparar's use of many relatively short vocative phrases enables him to envision Goddess Mīṉāṭci in multiple forms: as a little girl or graceful as a baby cow elephant, cavorting on the peaks of the Himalayas; as a sinuously shaped woman with fragrant flower-filled tresses, and as the goddess who bestows her presence and divine knowledge on her devotees. Kumarakuruparar also suggests the complexity of her parental relationships. As a form of the Goddess Pārvatī, she is daughter of the Himalaya mountains, where she played as a young girl. Yet the next line in the verse reminds us that in this birth she was begotten by Malayattuvacaṉ, the Pandiyan king. In the refrain, the poet emphasizes that both her divine father and her human one gratefully celebrate her vitality. Goddess Mīṉāṭci herself singled this verse out as one of her favorites, according to legend, and the verse's construction demonstrates the care and craftsmanship that went into it.

Mythology, Fertility, and Sensuality

OTHER VERSES IN *MMPT* display poetic patterns of larger scale, especially those built around a well-known myth or a single controlling image. In particular, Kumarakuruparar excelled in integrating the requirements of a specific paruvam with nuanced references to particular myths, especially *Tiruviḷaiyāṭal Purāṇam,* a collection of myths recounting the sports *(līlās)* of Lord Śiva. This collection depicts various salvific acts Śiva performed to help his devotees, but Kumarakuruparar draws on its stories primarily in relation to the circumstances under which Goddess Mīṉāṭci was trained as a warrior, fought in battle, and came to fight with and then marry Lord Śiva. A look at two verses from *MMPT* demonstrates how Kumarakuruparar alludes to mythic incidents well known in *Tiruviḷaiyāṭal Purāṇam* as the basis for verses that elaborate on the emotional depth of Goddess Mīṉāṭci's love for Śiva.

One verse (89) uses the paruvam describing bathing in the river as an occasion to consider the greatness of a deed performed by Lord Śiva, as recounted in the *Tiruviḷaiyāṭal Purāṇam.* Bathing verses evoke well-being and security. They describe newly risen (fresh, *putu*) waters, that provide just enough water to prevent both drought and floods. The water fills streambeds in a way that makes it perfect for bathing. As verse 89 begins, Mīṉāṭci enters just such a cool, flowing river. Bathing (neither swimming nor washing) can include submerging oneself in the water, diving beneath its surface, splashing water at a friend, rinsing off one's clothing, or simply wading in shallow water to enjoy the caress of the fresh breezes coming from the river.

Mīṉāṭci's companion, Goddess Lakṣmī, invokes a beloved story by reminding her that long ago on this very spot, Lord Śiva carried earth to build a dike along the riverbank to prevent a flood. This brief allusion would bring to the mind of the Hindu reader the entire story of Śiva's gracious deed. During a catastrophic flood, the king ordered all his subjects to bring earth to help construct levees. One old woman, too poor to hire someone to do the required work and too weak to perform it herself, rejoiced when a young man came to carry out her allotted share of work: He turned out to be Śiva himself, who undertook the lowly task out of compassion.[14] When the young Mīṉāṭci contemplates the kindness of this deed, her heart melts and she weeps. Lakṣmī slyly stops this stream of tears by suggesting her divine tears might cause another flood, requiring Śiva to carry earth yet again.

Kumarakuruparar increases the sense that acts of gods mix with the play of a little child through hyperbole of a type greatly admired in highly ornamented Tamil poetry in the refrain of verse 89. Because the waters of the Vaigai River in Madurai rise high, they provide fertile waters for the lands surrounding it, which grow thick with groves filled with trees, where all nature flourishes. There the bees produce so much honey that it is said to flow like waterfalls. This sweet cascade attracts the auspicious white elephant Airāvatam, mount of Indra, the Lord of the Gods. He and his wife play in the honeyed waterfall, just as young Mīṉāṭci plays in the refreshing waters. This impossible image suggests unearthly abundance on earth. The hyperbole undermines the boundaries between celestial and terrestrial, merging the abundance of the heavenly world with the fertility of the earthly world. The verse manages to combine the basic mood of the bathing paruvam with praise of Śiva's compassion. Kumarakuruparar uses the paruvam, in an ingenious way, to suggest the tremendous love that the Goddess Mīṉāṭci feels for Lord Śiva, swelling into open emotion as she reflects upon his salvific deed, just as the waters of the river swell.

Kumarakuruparar excels at combining a refined and understated eroticism with mythological richness as, for example, verse 34 demonstrates. According to the myth of Mīṉāṭci's birth, her father, who had asked for a son, receives instead an infant daughter with three breasts. Her father determined to raise her as a male warrior and had her trained in the arts of war. Then, after conquering all the directions, she went into battle. Instead of winning the war, she gained Lord Śiva as her husband. At that moment, her third breast disappeared. Verse 34 depicts the moment when she sees Lord Śiva (the God with golden Mount Meru as his bow), her husband-to-be, and as a result her third breast disappears. The thrill of war changes to the excitement of love. Her eyes pour ambrosia, rather than bloodthirstiness.

MMPT 34 (clap 2)

In battle your tiny waist swayed
in your golden chariot with its lotus finial
when you faced the God
with golden Mount Meru as his bow.

One of your three breasts, little girl,
disappeared as you thought of heart's union
with your worldly wise husband.

You bowed your head in obeisance
and gazing at your nipples,
the corners of your eyes streamed ambrosia.

You sighed,
and tiny beads of sweat filled your brow.
Your bashfulness was genuine.
You stood there astonished,
like a painting come to life.

The end of one finger
embraced the tip of the bow,
planted in the ground,
and your other hand crawled
up and down the bowstring,
stroking it.

Clap with those fair hands.

Creeper, who was born with Tamil
and grew up in ancient Madurai,
clap your hands.

This imagery prefigures their eventual sexual union. At the same time, it conforms to the paruvam, which calls for attention to actions connected with the heroine's hands. The verse's focus on the hands holding the bow enables the poet to lead directly into the refrain, "Clap with those fair hands."

The Poem and Temple Arts

KUMARAKURUPARAR RELIED UPON the corpus of myth connected with the Mīṉāṭci Cuntarēśvaraṉ Temple to inspire his composition. In turn, after he composed his poem, temple artists used some of Kumarakuruparar's poetic imagery to inspire several paintings and a set of sculptures. Patrons and craftsmen have identified, selected, and emphasized certain aspects of *MMPT* as a way of visually accompanying devotional practice in the temple.

Artwork inspired by *MMPT* before the entrance to the inner shrine or sanctum *(garbha gṛha)* where the Goddess Mīṉāṭci's icon is worshipped frames the worshipper's experience of devotion. Before entering the shrine, the temple visitor encounters on the wall a brightly colored painting (periodically repainted) depicting the legend of Kumarakuruparar's first recital *(araṅkeṟṟam)* of *MMPT.* Portrayed according to the traditional account, the painting shows two scenes of the recital. One side depicts a charming little girl sitting on the ruler's lap, listening to the poetry. The other side shows the same girl placing a necklace of pearls around Kumarakuruparar's neck in praise of his composition. Goddess Mīṉāṭci had quite appropriately taken the form of a little child to listen to a pillaittamil addressed to her in the form of a child.

Immediately above the painting, one finds a panel framed in red, on which has been written Kumarakuruparar's mellifluous verse 61, just analyzed. At the bottom of the panel stands a caption for the painting below: "Goddess Mīṉāṭci graciously gives a pearl necklace to Kumarakuruparar, who had sung a pillaittamil." Thus the artwork on the wall takes the famous verse 61 to represent the entire *MMPT* poem. Clearly, the verse was regarded as the most precious gem in the poem; Goddess Mīṉāṭci rewards the poet for his labors with another gem, a set of precious pearls.

After passing these paintings, devotees enter the shrine room, where they again encounter visual images related to *MMPT.* A devotee usually begins worship by circumambulating a shrine room in the auspicious direction. In the process of doing so in the Mīṉāṭci Cuntarēśvaraṉ Temple, the worshipper passes before a set of sculpted panels, in standard paruvam order, that illustrate selected verses from

MMPT. Each panel contains a relief depicting some scene, moment, or piece of imagery from a verse written by Kumarakuruparar. Beneath each sculpture the worshipper finds the paruvam labeled, accompanied by a short summary of the relief. The panels make it possible for worshippers to experience key moments in Kumarakuruparar's text while they perform their ritual circumambulation of the goddess.

To represent the poetry of Kumarakuruparar in sculpture, however, requires selectivity and ingenuity. Consider, for example, Kumarakuruparar's protection verse (translated below) to Sarasvatī, patron goddess of learning and fine arts. Kumarakuruparar has structured the verse in two parts. The first part, praising Goddess Sarasvatī, envisions her in her most characteristic iconographic pose, seated on a lotus. As she sits surrounded by bees, whom poets conventionally portray as buzzing around women with beautiful eyes, the bees' sweet hum cajoles the petals of the divine lotus into opening, thus allowing a full view of the goddess. Enthroned there, Sarasvatī sifts through a Tamil text that sets out prescriptions for settings of love poetry, savoring the pure, rich Tamil verses contained as exemplars in the guide to poetics which she reads. The poet compares Sarasvatī to a goose because, according to convention, a goose can discern and drink only pure rich milk, even when it is mixed with water. The goose motif also links her with the baby whose protection is requested. In Indian literary tradition, poets compliment a woman who walks with grace by comparing her gait to that of a goose. Yet Mīṉāṭci *gave* the goose its gait, just as she gave the doe its tender glance and the parrot its charming prattle. Therefore Sarasvatī, the learned muse and patron of Tamil, will surely appreciate the uniqueness of Baby Mīṉāṭci (referred to in the verse as "the Paṇḍiyan lady") and protect the little goddess who bestows upon creatures their qualities that all poets celebrate.

The sculptural depiction, in contrast, focuses attention on the verbal icon in the poetry, the image of the goddess on the lotus. In the context of ritual practice, devotees revere this familiar iconographic image because they value her fostering of music, poetry, and education. In representing a verse from the protection paruvam, the artist focuses on a single image, rather than trying to reduplicate the poetic complexity of the poem. The sculptural representation is iconically driven, rather than directly related to the full range of imagery in the poem.

Besides selectivity, the sculptor also uses conflation to represent verses from the protection paruvam. In sculptural panels based on other paruvams, a panel's content is generally based upon a single verse so only a few of the ten verses are represented. Representation of the protection paruvam differs because the sculptor wants to represent as many of the deities invoked as possible. Since only a few panels are allotted to each paruvam, the artist cannot include a separate panel for each of the deities invoked in the eleven protection verses by Kumarakuruparar. Instead, the panel conflates different niches. *MMPT*'s verse 8 to Lakṣmī (goddess of prosperity and wife of Viṣṇu), verse 9 to Sarasvatī (goddess of arts and wife of Brahmā), and verse 10 to Durgā (the fierce goddess and wife of Śiva) all come together in a single scene. The goddess of prosperity, in the posture of blessing, and the goddess of the arts, playing a veena, appear on the left of the panel. On the right side sits the fierce goddess, mounted on her lion. In the middle lies Baby Mīṉāṭci in her cradle. The sculptural equivalent of a "joint photo" results. Just as the pillaittamil takes advantage of each niche in order to enlist maximum protection for the baby, the sculptor makes the most of the limited space allotted to provide the maximum opportunity for worshippers to gain blessings by seeing many deities.

This tendency to conflate reaches its culmination in the final sculpture for this paruvam. Representing the last two verses in the protection paruvam there, the sculptor depicts the seven mothers (verse 10), as well as the thirty-three gods (verse 11). These thirty-three deities are considered capable of protection, but not sufficiently significant (or individualized) for each to have a single niche.[15] The thirty-three are Vedic deities, classified into groups (the Aśvin twins, the eight Vāsus, the eleven Rūdras, and the twelve Suns). By the time *MMPT* was written, these ancient deities were vestiges, rather than full deities toward whom worshippers held strong devotional feelings.

Two unusual features in Kumarakuruparar's protection verse to the thirty-three gods reflect their minor status in the divine hierarchy: (1) it is a very long verse and (2) there is no description of the deeds of the thirty-three gods at all. They appear only in the very last lines of the verse. Kumarakuruparar mentions neither their individual names nor even the names of their category of deity (e.g., twins, suns). Instead, in shorthand form, he remarks only that the two, eight, eleven, and twelve protect Mīṉāṭci. The rest of the verse demonstrates the greatness of Goddess Mīṉāṭci: she sends the great Chera and Chola monarchs into retreat, innumerable earthly kings do obeisance to her and pay whatever tribute she demands, the rivers of her southern lands outsplash the great northern Ganges River, cosmic Mount Meru does obeisance to the mountain range in Mīṉāṭci's kingdom, and so forth.

Marginalization of the thirty-three gods is even more extreme in the temple sculpture. In this panel the seven dancing mothers, surrounding baby Mīṉāṭci lying in her crib, fill three-quarters of the space in the sculpture. In the remaining one-quarter on the right side of the sculpture, the thirty-three gods rise like a huge tower to the very top of the sculpture, their faces shrinking in size as one moves to the top edge of the artwork. The sculptor maximizes his chance to give the devotee a vision of many powerful deities; still these thirty-three lack individual characteristics and barely figure in the main focus of the panel.

Several panels employ a bitemporal mode of representation in order to capture visually the complexity of Kumarakuruparar's verse. The famous bathing verse (analyzed earlier) in which the goddess weeps, thinking of her husband's compassion, for example, finds a prime place in the sculpture. On the left of the panel Goddess Lakṣmī recounts how Śiva carried earth, in the center Mīṉāṭci plays in the water, and on the right we see Lord Śiva with a heavy basket of earth on his head, an incident from a previous mythic age. If the poetry plays with the intermingling of past and present, the sculptural panel represents two different times in a single scene to suggest the lingering presence of the memory of the Lord's compassion.

Bitemporal sculpture also enables a simultaneous depiction of both literal and figurative imagery. For example, an especially beloved verse from the jacks paruvam (verse 82, translated below) receives a rendering that shows both an action and a poetic image to which that action is compared. In this verse, the poet urges the little girl to throw her jacks up into the air. Since her celestial jacks are emeralds, sapphires, and pearls, Kumarakuruparar compares them to birds—

the green parrot, the dark cuckoo, and the white swan who are Mīṉāṭci's pets. He likens the jacks to messenger birds flying to the celestial world to tell Lord Śiva of Mīṉāṭci's love for him.[16] The sculpture depicts both the literal and figurative events: on the left side of the panel Mīṉāṭci throws up the jacks; above her head fly three birds heading straight toward Lord Śiva.

Music, as well as visual art, draws from *MMPT* to contribute to

3. *Jacks Turn into Messenger Birds.* Sketch of a sculptural relief in the Mīṉāṭci Temple by Brian Meggitt (original in the collection of the author).

the devotional life of the temple. The complex daily round of liturgy in the temple includes selections from many scale types *(paṇs)* in Tamil music and from various textual sources, performed at different times of day.[17] Vocal recitation usually takes place daily, but selections differ from day to day.

For an ordinary evening concert that I observed in 1987, the immediate audience varied from three people at the beginning to a high of thirty. Because of the amplification system, the notes of the invocation to Vināyakar resonated down the wide temple corridors. Devotees joined the audience in a leisurely manner. Since the performance took place in a major passage of the temple, worshippers came by constantly on the way to the shrine; many stood and listened for a while before continuing their devotions.

This performance occurred on the floor across from the entrance to the shrine, near enough to the electrical room so that the microphone could be plugged in. The singer *(ōtuvār),* Caṅkita Puṣṇam Poṉ Muttiyar, had been trained in recitation in Annamalai before coming to the Mīṉāṭci Temple. He was accompanied by two instrumentalists. The musical program contained four basic parts. The musicians started with a traditional invocation to Vināyakar that usually begins religious concerts. Next they played some pieces from *Tēvāram,* the collection of songs by three Śaivite poet-saints that laud the Mīṉāṭci Temple. Third came three verses from *MMPT,* including the beloved verse 61. Also chosen were a *muttam* kiss/pearl verse and a lullaby verse. Finally, there was a closing piece.[18]

Visitors to a Hindu temple often keep in their home some reminder of a favorite sacred site. Some bring home from a temple visual images, such as stone, metal, or plastic icons of the deity or colored posters and pamphlets. Due to the ease with which audio cassettes can now be reproduced relatively inexpensively, devotees can also bring into their homes performances of selections from *MMPT.* Consider one such musical keepsake, a tape recording featuring singer S. Janaki accompanied by R. Ramanujan. Recorded on the label of AVM Music Service, the tape presents a taste of *MMPT* that reveals certain musical and poetic presuppositions. Most immediately noticeable is the choice of musical style; rather than classical Karnatic music, as one might expect, Ms. Janaki sings in a catchy upbeat style usually called *filmi* (film music style). Despite the cinematic ambiance suggested by the music, however, the choice of selections indicates an attempt to represent the pillaittamil according to the distinctive features of the genre. Most of the verses rendered in song emphasize Goddess Mīṉāṭci as a child.

Furthermore, the recording presents ten verses, replicating in spirit the ten-paruvam structure of the pillaittamil. Only one example from each paruvam appears on the tape, so the selection of which niche to present from the protection paruvam clearly took some thought. Traditionally a Hindu pillaittamil begins with a verse to Viṣṇu, but if only one protection verse is to be sung, the intended audience for this tape would probably prefer a prayer to a Śaivite deity. Those who decided the content of the tape have solved the problem by not including a selection from the protection paruvam at all. Instead, they take the verse to Vināyakar that precedes the entire pillaittamil, thus insuring that they have propitiated the deity responsible for auspicious beginnings. In a sense, this choice accords with the theory of the protection paruvam, even if it means that no actual protection verse from the paruvam appears in the recording. Ms. Janaki sings a verse from each of the other ten paruvams and, as one might well expect, her selection from the fifth paruvam turns out to be the beloved verse 61, into which she puts a heartfelt emotional resonance.

MMPT remains, thus, not only a poem that pillaittamil connoisseurs savor but part of a living tradition of worship. The veneration shown to the celebrated verse 61 represents the admiration for *MMPT* in Tamil literary tradition. Kumarakuruparar worked skillfully within the conventions of particular paruvams to create imagery that was evocative, appropriate, and fresh, yet still grounded in Hindu mythic tradition. He had to do so while simultaneously choosing words whose sounds enabled him to accomplish the feats of aesthetic virtuosity that provide the verse with its mellifluous qualities. Kumarakuruparar's poetry also shapes the ritual experiences of pilgrims to the Mīṉāṭci Temple in Madurai. Because painters, sculptors, and musicians have created representations of *MMPT*'s poetry in the midst of the temple, thousands of pilgrims who come to worship also have the opportunity to savor the poem. *MMPT*'s poetry dramatizes and celebrates the power of a sacred site. Hearing the poem or viewing scenes based upon it enables the devotee to savor the power of that sacred place.

MMPT 10 (protection 9)

Addressed to Goddess Sarasvatī on behalf of Mīṉāṭci (the unique Pandiyan lady)

Goddess Sarasvatī sits sifting in her house,
a lotus in bloom.
Its golden stamens gush honey,
while bees joyously make sweet music.
In response the long lotus petals,
shaped like silver serving trays,
open.

She drinks in the lucid ambrosia of the divine text
which identifies the five landscapes of love
found in the clear ocean of Tamil.

The unique Pandiyan lady,
even at a very early age,
gives generous gifts:
  sweetly flowing tender prattle to the young green parrot
  youthful beauty to the merry peacock
  a glance to the doe
  a graceful gait to the fledgling royal goose,
    with a comb like a blooming red kiñcuka flower,
  and innocence to the girls who play with her.

We bow at the excellent feet
of the peerless white goose, saying,
"Please protect her."

---

the divine text: A grammatical/poetic digest, setting out the prescriptions for classical Tamil love poetry, which poets set in five different landscapes, each associated with a different phase of love.[19]

MMPT 12 (protection 11)

Addressed to the thirty-three gods on behalf of Mīṉāṭci

The Chera turns his back in battle, retreats,
and runs with the Chola into the forest.

Countless monarchs stand dejected
in the courtyard, saying,
"Here is our tribute. You measure it."

Word spreads in the eight directions that
these kings of the earth,
those guardians of the directions,
and the gods,
wait in attendance.

The Sun God swelters in his own heat,
brooding jealously over the lineage
of the white ambrosial moon.

The excellent rivers—
Kumari, Kavery, Vaigai, and Tamraparni—
flow more bountifully than the splashing Ganges.

Mount Meru, the dwelling place of the gods,
praises and worships the many-peaked Potiyal mountain.

The Siddhars sing of her:
"Mother of two sons and all the gods,
yet still a virgin."

Heavenly women who rejoice in the kuṟavai
join hands and dance with lovely earthly women.

The royal goose sent by Brahmā joins in friendship
with the geese of the seven oceans.

Dark Viṣṇu's Garuḍa and young Murukaṉ's peacock
play together in the same nest.

On the harsh battlefield
the celestial elephant that Indra drives
falls into a pit, like earthly elephants.

The two goddesses on their lotuses
approach the eternal golden pond
and share a lotus there.

Those Pandiyans who adhere to Manu's laws,
as did the king of the Himalayas,
prosper, receiving our King Śiva
as their good son-in-law.

People ask, in confusion:
"Who are the celestial people?
Who are the earthly people?
Which is the golden world?"

All this happens because
our three-breasted mother appears
to make lovely Southern Madurai flourish.

Those who protect together
the beauty of our mother
are the thirty-three gods:
the two, the eight, the eleven, and the twelve.

---

brooding jealously over the lineage: The sun feels jealous that the great Pandiyans claim descent from the moon, rather than the sun.

kuṟavai: A dance performed by women, especially in cowherd communities.

geese of the seven oceans: According to myth, the Pandiyan king's mother wanted to bathe in the seven oceans but was too elderly to travel, so Śiva brought all seven oceans to Madurai.

Garuḍa and the peacock: These two divine vehicles are usually rivals.

Indra's elephant: This celestial elephant, belonging to the king of the Vedic gods, is usually portrayed as invincible, but he is trapped just like ordinary elephants during battle with Goddess Mīṉāṭci.

the two goddesses on their lotuses: The two goddesses, sometimes rivals, share the same lotus in the golden tank at Mīṉāṭci's temple due to her greatness.

People ask, in confusion: They wonder how such heavenly splendor can appear on earth.

MMPT 14 (sway to and fro 3)

Standing there, your inner joy bursts forth
and even before your holy father asks you to come,
and beckons you once,
you rush over on all fours
and feed him the sweet ambrosia
of your childish prattle,
so refreshing that it quenches his burning hunger.

You lie in fragrant saffron and sandalpaste
spread on his broad chest,
and clasp his broad hands that extend to his radiant feet.

You climb on his broad shoulders,
around which garlands of fresh flowers,
entwined with sonorous Tamil, bloom.
Then you sit on the nape of his neck.

Green peacock, stand there and dance,
as your lovely mouth gleams with clear moonlight
and rich green light glimmers around your body
like emeralds.

Sway to and fro, incomparable daughter
of the king of the beautiful golden mountains
and of the Pandiyan king.
Sway to and fro.

---

father calls you: This is one of the few pillaittamil verses where the poet concentrates on the father-daughter relationship.

Hands . . . feet: According to conventions about male beauty in Tamil poetry, a handsome man will have wide hands and long, long arms.

green peacock: The poet uses this epithet because in iconography the Goddess Mīṉāṭci is usually portrayed as green.

flowers composed of sonorous Tamil: The Pandiyan king was a patron of Tamil poetry, so the musicality of Tamil verse is described as a garland of fresh flowers that adorns him.

MMPT 18 (sway to and fro 6)

The moonlight of your smile,
pouring from your face,
dances.

The jewels in your hair
dance.

The gem on your brow,
your vine-like curved eyebrows,
and the murippu jewel
dance.

Your warring fish-shaped eyes and their rivals,
the two fish earrings,
dance.

When you move your feet,
your ankle bells tinkle
and dance.

Your thin sinuous waist,
weary from the weight of your clothes,
dances.

All moving and unmoving things
and the vast universe,
contained in the shining embryo
that makes your heavy stomach
hang over your navel,
dance.

Sway to and fro, goddess who wears a crown
so that the earth can flourish.
Sway to and fro.

---

fish-shaped eyes: Women's eyes that are round at the nose and thin near the ear are said by poets to resemble a fish. Here Kumarakuruparar sees Mīṉāṭci's eyes as competing with her fish-shaped earrings.

shining embryo: Mother Mīṉāṭci bears the entire universe in her womb.

MMPT 33 (clap 1)

In the middle of the deep darkness,
when everyone else sleeps,
Brahmā, the god with eight eyes,
leaves his round-stemmed lotus seat.

Viṣṇu, living in his supreme dwelling,
leaves his spotted snakebed.

Earth and universe tumble down,
the eight mountains collapse into the seven oceans,
the oldest mountain in the universe,
which served as Śiva's bow,
and the Cakravāla Mountains
whirl round.

Meanwhile, in unison, Viṣṇu and Brahmā,
play the breast-shaped cymbals
in a rhythm appropriate
for the pure dance of the god
who wears ūmattam flowers filled with honey,
and dances in a circle.

To mark the time,
clap your hands, too.

Creeper born along with Tamil
who grew up in ancient Madurai,
clap your hands.

---

eight eyes: Brahmā has four heads and rests on a lotus.

spotted snakebed: Viṣṇu sleeps on the cosmic serpent.

Earth and universe tumble: Śiva is in the process of destroying the world.

the god who wears ūmattam flowers: Śiva.

creeper who was born along with Tamil: "Creeper," is a term for a beautiful woman in Tamil poetry, referring to how she sinuously wraps herself around her lover. "Born with Tamil" refers to her birth in ancient Madurai during the time of the Tamil poetic academies.

MMPT 37 (clap 5)

From the corners of your black ocean-like eyes,
whose shapeliness surpasses your fish-shaped earrings,
you pour ambrosia,
casting clear waves of compassion.

You lay the divine child,
who set fire to the white waves,
on your small, fair, round, swaying ankles.

You bathe him,
kiss the top of his head,
apply fragrant oils to his hair
and put on holy ash.

You put milk from your full breasts
into a conch-shaped cup
and then feed him by coaxing open his lips.

You sprinkle his body with fresh talcum
put him to sleep on your young golden thighs
and lay him in a small cradle,
adorned with huge gems.

Goddess, clap those lotus hands
that rock the cradle,
while you sing lullabies.

Creeper, who was born with Tamil
and grew up in ancient Madurai,
clap your hands.

---

the divine child: Murukan̲, who set the ocean aflame during the battle in which he defeated the demon Sūrapadma. Here Baby Mīn̲āṭci is depicted in her maternal role, caring for her young infant.

holy ash: Worn by a devotee of Śiva as a sectarian marking on the forehead after being offered to a holy icon and then returned as a blessed substance.

MMPT 40 (clap 8)

The flying arrows, Śiva's henchmen, the Kālīs,
Bhairava who fought in battle like a lion among dogs,
and others
all scattered.

Lord Nandi stopped standing still
and ran away.
When you saw his handsome chest
followed by his handsome back,
your young laughter poured moonlight.

You've forgotten how you once played
in the front yard of tall Mount Kailasa.

Now you wage war,
you bend the strong bow,
you arch the strong bows of your eyebrows,
and you shoot lotus arrows.

Mīṉāṭci, goddess who conquered the god
with the mountain as his bow,
clap your hands.

Goddess who nurtures Daughter Earth
beneath the shade of your royal umbrella,
clap your hands.

Śiva's henchmen, the Kālīs, Bhairava: In battle, Goddess Mīṉāṭci defeated Śiva's *gaṇas,* a gang of truculent attendants, and the Kālīs, goddesses full of destructive power. She even defeated Śiva himself in his fierce and horrific form as Bhairava.

his handsome chest . . . his back: Śiva's bull vehicle was so frightened of Goddess Mīṉāṭci that the handsome animal turned and fled, to Mīṉāṭci's amusement.

how you once played: In her birth as Pārvatī, she was the daughter of the Himalaya Mountains and played as a child on its high peaks.

MMPT 47 (kiss 5)

In the ghat of Kanya Kumari,
where waves war with beach and mountain,
there are pearls.

In the port of Korkai,
pearl fishermen dive
for heaps of pearls.

In the Tamraparni River,
with its large cool bathing ghats,
like clear moonlight
pearls appear.

On the broad slopes
of the refreshing Potiyal Mountains,
waterfalls shower cool pearls.

Put those pearls away
in a corner of your little house
where you play with young girlfriends,
wearying your waist,
thin as a withering vine.

Pearl with long tresses
fragrant with perfumed vapors
and sweet-smelling oils,
with your mouth luscious as fruit,
give me a kiss.

Goddess whose three breasts
are a feast for the three eyes
of the luminous one,
give me a kiss.

---

ghat: Steps down to a riverbank or ocean.

the luminous one: Śiva, who has a third eye in the middle of his forehead.

MMPT 65 (moon 4)

The goddess overlooked that you ran away
after robbing the holy beauty
flowing from her bright face
when you rose as the full moon
in your new white garb
and poured streaming ambrosia

and that you stole the beauty
of her radiant forehead,
when you shed moonlight
as the crescent moon

and that you sit there
while fished-eyed women
offer cow dung and worship you.

and that you live on her husband's crown
along with her co-wife.

So she called you for play.
Isn't it, therefore, just
to speak of the great compassion
of this woman?

With the princess who gave kings their crowns,
so they could place the entire earth
on their shoulders and comfort their subjects
moon, come to play.

With the vine of rubies
who unites with the god
carrying the pure golden bow
moon, come to play.

---

offer cow dung: Reference to a lunar rite performed by women.

co-wife: The Ganges River shares Śiva's matted hair.

vine of rubies: The fair-skinned Mī<u>n</u>āṭci.

MMPT 82 (jacks 10)

Your jacks—
lustrous emeralds,
perfect sapphires,
and a set of white pearls—
spill brilliant light.

Woman whose flower garlands drip with honey,
take, in turn, one of each gem
and throw it sky-high.

When they reach the Lord
with the eye in his forehead
they will look as though,
you sent messengers:
the green parrot you carried on your hand
the pleasing dark cuckoo you raised
and the young white swan
to report of your ever-increasing love.

Lady of Madurai,
where the king of the geese
embraces and sleeps with his mate
in the richly watered fields,
play jacks.

Lovely auspicious one,
whose beauty only continues to grow,
play jacks.

Lord with the eye in his forehead: Śiva.

king of the geese: The king of geese can sport in the fields of Madurai with his mate, as if they were in a pond, because water is so abundant (hyperbole to indicate the fertility of land in Mīṉāṭci's city).

MMPT 89 (bathe in the water 7)

In front of the bathing ghat
where the cool waters descend,
the woman on the blooming white lotus said
"This is the place where our Lord carried earth."

The thought moved you.
Your heart melted,
your eyes reddened,
and you stood shedding a flood
of joyous tears.

So she said,
"Wouldn't it be too much
to make him do the job again
by causing another flood?"

Bathe in the newly risen water of Madurai,
whose groves have honey flowing like cascades,
where Airāvatam, whose curved tusks are dipped
in the pollen of honey-filled flowers
from the fragrant kaṟpaka tree,
sports in the honey together with his long-haired mate.

Golden doll of the Lord
of the Poruṉai River,
bathe in the newly risen water.

---

woman on the blooming white lotus: Lakṣmī.

Airāvatam . . . sports in the honey: Honey is so abundant in Mīṉāṭci's city that Indra's celestial elephant comes to sport in the honey, as if it were a flowing river.

mate with tresses: Often when poets describe the hero and heroine playing in the water, they comment on her beautiful tresses. This convention seems to have been extended to the elephant's mate, despite the fact that she does not have tresses.[20]

MMPT 91 (bathe in the water 9)

Your fragrant garland,
which the Vine of Words and the Vine of the Lotus
plucked and wove for you,
your red tilak,
which the Beautiful Woman put on,
and the kumkum,
painted in rainbow shape
on your large breasts—

the high waters plunder them all
revealing your natural beauty
and making a feast
for the eyes of the Lord,
while you play.

Golden Vine, your eyebrows
are so even and well-curved
that they are worshipped even by Indra's bow
and the bow held by the warrior with the fish banner,
along with his vine-like wife.

Young Vine from the Himalayas,
bathe in the newly risen Vaigai waters.

Goddess of the Tamraparni ghat
and the Kumari ghat,
bathe in the newly risen waters.

Vine of Words: Sarasvatī, goddess of learning and the arts.

Vine of the Lotus: Lakṣmī, who sits enthroned on the lotus.

Beautiful Woman: Indrāṇī, wife of Indra.

Golden Vine, Young Vine: Goddess Mīṉāṭci.

Warrior with the fish banner: Kāma, God of Love.[21]

CHAPTER FIVE

THE HINDU MONASTIC MILIEU

NO SINGLE ENGLISH term or phrase can adequately describe the role that T. C. Mīṉāṭcicuntaram Piḷḷai (henceforth Pillai) played in nineteenth-century Tamil literary culture. He began as a child prodigy gifted at composing verse, matured into an astonishingly prolific poet-scholar, and won reverence in his old age as a literary mentor. He was a champion in rhetorical and grammatical debate, poet laureate at Tiruvavatuturai Monastery, and—not least—a pillaittamil writer. Because his most gifted disciple wrote a lengthy biography of his spiritual preceptor, a detailed account of Pillai's life exists.[1] A look at Pillai's education and his place in the monastic milieu, as well as the circumstances under which he composed his poetry, provides us with a revealing view of the creation of nineteenth-century pillaittamils.

Of the many pillaittamils Pillai composed, one stands preeminent: *Cēkkiḻār Piḷḷaittamiḻ* (henceforth *CPT*), addressed to a beloved Śaivite saint. This text is representative of a whole stream of pillaittamils written to saints, gurus, abbots of monasteries, and other religious specialists whom devotees worship as extraordinary and, in some cases, divine beings. In this pillaittamil, Pillai emphasized the superiority of Śaivism, as well as the greatness of the Veḷḷāḷa (dominant non-Brahmin landholding) lineage, to which both Cēkkiḻār and Pillai belonged.

Literary Training

PILLAI GREW UP surrounded by love for Śaivite devotional texts. Born in 1815, he lived in the Tirucchirappalli region, where his devout Veḷḷāḷa father taught secular and religious writings, including poetry composition. At an early age he attended his father's school and studied, among other skills, writing on palmleaves, the fundamentals of grammar, recitation of poetry, and exegesis of texts. The father recognized his son's unusual skill in poetry and trained him well. The boy spent his spare time writing imitations of famous compositions by earlier poets. His talents brought him invitations to the homes of influential citizens, who requested that he recite poetry and expound upon its meaning. When he was introduced to leading scholars of his time, they encouraged him to develop his artistic potential. Even at a young age, he composed extemporaneous verse with ease, a talent for which he became famous as he grew older. After his father's death when Pillai was fifteen, the townspeople continued to support his studies.

Pillai worked actively to locate and master a large number of religious and grammatical texts. Whenever he heard of a place where someone possessed a noteworthy palmleaf manuscript, he would travel there to study it and then copy it for his own library. When he exhausted the resources in his own area, he moved to the city of Tirucchirappalli, a center of religious learning. Teachers specialized in a particular text (for example, *Kamparāmāyaṇa*), accepting students to study that text with them; after Pillai mastered a particular text, he moved on to the next teacher. He sought out intellectual mentors and through his persistence, talent, and enthusiasm persuaded them to teach him—no matter how reclusive they were.[2]

Pillai's literary and religious life were closely bound together. A pious man, he lived according to the promise made to his father that he would never miss a day's recitation of verses from *Tēvāram* and *Tiruvācakam*.[3] After he became established as a teacher, he regularly traveled on pilgrimage to religious temples, accompanied by his pupils. Temple officials considered themselves honored by his visit and requested that he compose poems celebrating their shrine. Pillai created verses that celebrated the major legends about the temple, using elaborate imagery and learned conceits that were metrically correct and filled with auspicious and sonorous words.

Poet Laureate

PILLAI SOUGHT ANSWERS to questions that he had about the meaning of certain lines of poetry by consulting learned men; this enterprise led him to visit the *matha* (monastery) at Tiruvavatuturai, one of the largest and most influential Śaivite *matha*s in South India, known as a center of philosophical and literary virtuosity.[4] Under the abbot's leadership, some monks performed austerities, philosophical study, and worship, while others managed the vast lands of the monastery. Pillai's biographer aptly describes the sights of the monastery that made the greatest impression on the first-time visitor: monks in their radiant ochre robes, influential men who came from afar to pay homage to the monks, famous scholars and musicians for whom the monastery acted as patron, and attendants who punctiliously carried out the prescriptions of daily worship (I:33–34/11).

When Pillai arrived, he was granted an audience with the abbot, to whom he did obeisance by reciting verses and offering fruit, according to the established custom. After the abbot tested his knowledge by asking him to recite several verses, he explicated certain poems about which Pillai had queries. Pillai found the whole visit exhilarating and returned for consultation often, occasionally enrolling in the classes in Saiva Siddhanta philosophy held at the *matha*. Over the years, he composed numerous literary works, which were published through the generosity of wealthy patrons, and his fame spread. Even so, he continued to maintain close ties with this monastery.

In the early 1860s the abbot of this monastery created the position of Tamil poet laureate and appointed Pillai to it as part of the abbot's program to patronize Tamil (in addition to Sanskrit) learning. To initiate his new bond with the monastery, Pillai was invited to an elaborate ceremony during which he was invested with the title "Mahā Vidvāṉ" (One of Great Knowledge) and presented with shawls and other appropriate gifts. Members of the monastic establishment showed their respect by giving him the seat of honor in the area where the laymen (nonmonks) ate. He received his own residence and two attendants to care for his everyday needs, freeing him to concentrate on his work (I:202/51). The monastery became his home base, even though he continued to journey to holy places, act as visiting scholar-in-residence at numerous important centers of learning throughout Tamil country, and travel to consult palmleaf manuscripts.

At the monastery, Pillai taught and composed. Whenever the abbot was not conducting his own Sanskrit research and teaching, he insisted that Pillai hold Tamil classes in his presence. Disciples flocked

4. *The Poet Laureate,* T. C. Mīṉāṭcicuntaram Piḷḷaiyavarkaḷ (late nineteenth-century portrait).

to Pillai with textual queries, poets came to get their verses corrected and improved, admirers visited to hear his latest compositions or competed to give him the most costly gifts, and devout friends arrived to take him on pilgrimage. He also composed a number of poems (including several pillaittamils) in praise of the monastery or to laud various illustrious monks. He participated in the major annual festivals of the monastery, such as the celebration of founder's day and the annual anniversaries of past appointments of monastic abbots, events marked with fireworks, great feasts, and recitations of poetry. The monastery honored him on his sixtieth birthday with an elaborate ritual. Monks, musicians, and lay scholars mourned him deeply when he passed away in 1876.

Composition and Presentation

LIKE MOST LEARNED Tamil poets in this period, Pillai composed in highly conventionalized genres. For example, Pillai wrote many purāṇams, literally, "old stories," origin myths in verse about particular temple sites. To do so, he would first locate and read the Sanskrit collection of local legends about the temple, which told of the miraculous origins of the holy site and the marvelous deeds that the deity had performed there. Pillai then wove allusions to these events into the imagery of his poetry, using his verses as occasions for glorifying both the deity worshipped and the sacred site. Letters, words, and groups of words were governed by grammatical, metrical, rhetorical, and auditory prescriptions. An acclaimed poem combined an awareness of a genre's needs with attention to sound.

Two traits set Pillai apart from his fellow poets of the time: the intensity of his poetic inspiration and his ability to write poetry under varied circumstances and extreme time pressure. His biography abounds with anecdotes about his literary absorption. For example, one morning at dawn he journeyed to a nearby riverbank to perform his morning ablutions. In the midst of brushing his teeth with a twig, he suddenly became inspired with an idea for a poem. Villagers were astonished to find him five hours later still frozen in that spot, twig in hand, lost in inspiration (I:100/25). Equally impressive was his ability to compose verses in the morning that were to be recited before an audience that evening, as well as his common feat of carrying on a conversation and composing verse simultaneously.

Central to poetic composition of this period was recitation. This oral context accounts for the significance of a major literary ritual called the *araṅkēṟṟam,* a debut for the poem in which one presented the work for acceptance before a learned assembly. Such presentations served as the culmination of the composition process. Elaborate affairs, these events included recitation and explication of verses, defending the verses from criticism by Tamil savants, and receiving elaborate gifts and honors. An *araṅkēṟṟam* for a longer poem could continue night after night. Pillai's biography describes one such event in detail. For several months he had worked on a poem celebrating a particular temple, composing ten to fifteen verses daily. At his poem's debut, Pillai had just recited and was explaining a single stanza when a local expert complained that a poet should not incorporate allusions to other temples in a poem designed to praise a particular temple. Pillai first gave a theological reply, arguing that although God makes himself manifest in many sacred places, they are all forms of the One. Then he pointed to the precedent of another highly regarded poetic text that also contained references to sites other than the temple being lauded as the main focus of the poem. The critic was defeated, and the presiding dignitary wanted to throw him out. The poet argued for leniency, noting that such debate was a usual part of the protocol and made these public performances lively events (I:174–179/47).

Patronage played a large role in the process of composition. Usually a wealthy donor or temple commissioned Pillai to compose a poem. When it was complete and had received its public debut, the poet would receive a large amount of cash, as well as tokens of honor. For example, at the opening ceremonies of one *araṅkēṟṟam,* the palmleaf upon which he had inscribed the poem was placed in a canopied seat on the back of an elephant. Then some of the most distinguished men in the region carried the poet in a palanquin and they all went in procession (I:174–175/67). His biography records cash gifts of between Rs. 2000 and 5000 (equal to £200–£500 sterling in his day), the gift of a home, and sumptuous meals. In addition, patrons frequently bore the cost of publishing particular works of poetry, which were often preceded by the poet's verse in praise of his patron.

The story of how Pillai wrote his first pillaittamil demonstrates many features of his compositional process. One day he sat on a ferry with some friends, crossing the Kavery River to visit a temple to Goddess Akilāṇṭa Nāyaki. A friend noted that a previous poet on pilgrimage had composed a poem in the time it took to circumambulate a holy hill at the site of a temple. Could Pillai do the equivalent? The poet decided to try, spending much of the day writing and dictating. By the time his friends had finished their worship, his poem was complete. Then another friend urged him to write a pillaittamil to the same goddess and he took on the challenge. When this poem was complete, his friend considered it flawless and urged its publication, but Pillai could not afford the costs (I:45–55/13).[5]

Soon afterward when Pillai went to Madras, he visited one of the most famous Tamil scholars of the time, Maḻavai Mahāliṅkaiyar. When Pillai was asked to recite a verse, he chose one from the pillaittamil to Goddess Akilāṇṭa Nāyaki that he had just composed. The famous savant praised the poem lavishly, but was puzzled that he did not recognize it. Perhaps this was a poem famous only in the Tiruchirappalli area? With appropriate humility, Pillai owned up to authorship of the pillaittamil verse and Mahāliṅkaiyar, delighted, asked to hear more of it. In response to Pillai's recitation, the venerable scholar composed a verse on the spot in which he suggested that Pillai's poem had earned him the laurels previously allotted to the two most famous pillaittamil writers, Kumarakuruparar and Pakaḻikkūttar (I:62–69/16–17). As a result of this meeting, Mahāliṅkaiyar personally funded and oversaw the publication of Pillai's pillaittamil, ensuring that it was preceded by laudatory testimonials from respected poets of the day.[6]

Another of Pillai's pillaittamils remains notable for the witty remarks that took place during its *araṅkēṟṟam.* The poem was addressed to a famous past abbot of the Tiruvavatuturai Matha, Ampalavāṇa Tēcikar. In the protection paruvam, Pillai invoked the protection of illustrious earlier abbots for the Baby Abbot. This text's recitation took place in the monastery's shrine for an image of Śiva that was bent slightly forward. The shrine's legend recounts how a young girl, an ardent devotee of Śiva, wanted to place her garland around the icon's neck. Because she was not tall enough to reach it, the image leaned forward to aid her and has remained in that position ever since. This story emphasizes Śiva's graciousness: although an exalted and powerful deity, he deigns to lower himself for the sake of his devotee. Pillai refers to this legend in an oblique way, commenting that the past abbot, Ampalavāṇa Tēcikar, need not bend down so far to receive the garland of verse that Pillai has composed; this conceit emphasizes the past abbot's graciousness and the poet's humility. The poetic play greatly pleased the listeners, inspiring the current abbot to send for a garland of prayer beads and announce that he would "now bend forward a little and request that you lean forward a little," indicating his willingness to lower himself, due to Pillai's talent. The abbot then garlanded Pillai as a sign of his appreciation of his poetic abilities (I:222/54).

Pillai left his mark not only through poetic composition but also through his exegesis upon pillaittamils (and other texts) considered central to Śaivite monastic tradition. He spent much of his time at the *matha* expounding upon and elucidating texts that affirmed the Tamil Śaivite religious worldview. Pillai's pupils would bring their questions, and he would clear them up by giving word-by-word glosses on difficult passages as well as bringing out the inner meanings of the verses. Long after Pillai had left this world, his legacy to the Tiruvavatuturai Matha remained: his commentaries expounded to his students.[7]

Both during and after Pillai's lifetime, monasteries published many genres of religious texts, pillaittamils being notable among them. Research into their publication history reveals that, in addition to those published and sold by commercial presses, many Śaivite pillaittamils, especially ones composed by poets or edited by commentators associated with the famous Śaivite *mathas* in the Tanjore area, were published and presented gratis on special occasions. Distributed to dignitaries, devotees, and monks who attended various celebrations at the *mathas,* these texts served both as souvenirs of the event and resources for regular devotional reading. Religious texts dear to the monastic community were and are chosen again and again to be published as part of the celebration of the anniversary of an illustrious abbot's birthday or ascension to the abbotship.[8] As a result, both Pillai's pillaittamils and his pillaittamil commentaries have been periodically republished during the century since his death.

Praising a Saint

THE SUBJECT OF Pillai's final pillaittamil was Cēkkiḻār, author of the famous twelfth-century Śaivite epic *Periya Purāṇam.*[9] Writing *Cēkkiḻār Piḷḷaittamiḻ* was a labor of love for Pillai; he had studied and taught *Periya Purāṇam,* one of his favorite texts, over and over again at various stages of his life.[10] Once he turned his attention to composing, he completed the pillaittamil within a few days. Śaivite literary connoisseurs have showered praise on *CPT* as a well-crafted poem full of religiously auspicious and musically pleasing verse. Cultural historians will note other intriguing attributes, including its militantly Śaivite tone and its self-conscious identification with the Veḷḷāḷa community.[11] Both the poem's surface features and its choice of themes reveal much about the monastic milieu within which Pillai's poetry flourished.

Pillai's poetry is especially well known for its alliterative quality and use of the auspicious imagery, as *CPT* 26 demonstrates:

CPT 26 (lullaby 5)

All mathas are fragrant (maṇakkum) *with steaming rice.*
All minds are filled (maṇakkum) *with purity.*
All garments are filled (maṇakkum) *with gold.*
All shoulders are fragrant (maṇakkum) *with garlands.*
All fields are fragrant (maṇakkum) *with wet earth.*
All towers are filled (maṇakkum) *with riches.*
All balconies are fragrant (maṇakkum) *with the southern breeze.*
All poems are filled (maṇakkum) *with divine beauty.*
All foreheads are filled (maṇakkum) *with sacred ash.*
All curries are fragrant (maṇakkum) *with ghee.*
All Vedic altars are filled (maṇakkum) *with fire.*
All streets are filled (maṇakkum) *with affection.*

Lord of Kunrattūr, town filled (maṇakkum) *with festivals,*
talo, talelo.
Divine Śaivite teacher of all the Āgamas,[12]
talo, talelo.

Here Pillai creates a verse out of a series of parallel grammatical structures, all centered on the resonant verb form *maṇakkum.* It occurs in every line of the body of the verse and even in the first part of the refrain.[13] The *kum,* formally a future tense, marks the verb as habitual, indicating a state of affairs that is generally so and will continue to be so in the future. *Maṇa* can mean, among other things, "to yield a pleasing smell" (hence the translation "be fragrant") or "to be mingled or filled with." The poet uses both senses of the word to create a verse filled with auspicious sights. The repetition of the basic linguistic structure throughout the verse creates sonorous patterns, especially since the repeated words contain many resonant *m* sounds.

Furthermore, each scene described in the verse evokes an image associated with religious piety, along with material or natural prosperity. In these large Śaivite *mathas,* hundreds of people would be served rice: monks, monastic employees, and devotees who visited to express their piety. On special occasions, wealthy patrons made donations so that the poor could come to feast as well. *Mathas* exuding the smell of freshly cooked rice for all, foreheads covered with the ash sacred to Śiva and his devotees, and Vedic altars aflame with sacrificial offerings all suggest that devotees perform Śaivite rituals with care and that piety at the *matha* flourishes. In a similar vein, Pillai portrays the area around the monastery as partaking of the power and generativity of Lord Śiva: high towers enclose storehouses of riches, its inhabitants sport clothing made of gold thread, and its fields are moist from fructifying rains. Both the auspicious imagery and the mellifluous sounds in this verse delight the discerning listener.

Beneath their pleasant-sounding surface, a number of other verses in *CPT* attest to a self-conscious and militant Śaivism in this period. Pillai incorporates references to Cēkkiḻār's dislike of Jainism and his claims that Śaivite literature is superior. Back in the twelfth century, according to legend, Cēkkiḻār disapproved of his monarch's fondness for a Jain epic, suggesting that a king who administered hundreds of Śaivite temples should read Śaivite texts instead.[14] In response, the king then requested a comparable Śaivite epic to read. Cēkkiḻār answered that there was only Saint Cuntarar's song that listed Śaivite saints. The king commissioned Cēkkiḻār to write an epic based on the song and supported him while he composed it. Cēkkiḻār's *Periya Purāṇam* thus arose out of a situation where competing religious traditions sought kingly patronage for textual composition. Pillai's verse 86 from the little drum paruvam reflects the militancy of such composition, denigrating *Cīvakacintāmaṇi* by name and asking Baby Cēkkiḻār to "make your little drum roar, as if it were a funeral drum" for this Jain text and other texts like it.

Pillai also foregrounds Cēkkiḻār's vanquishing of his non-Śaivite foes in debate. The body of verse 54, for example, sets out major opposing views seen as competing with Śaivite tradition. Some of the *darśaṇas* (philosophic viewpoints) in this verse are readily identifiable. Among the *darśaṇas* he mentions in the poem are: those who place great value on sexual union with women (the doctrine of Lokāyata); those who identify religious liberation with the destruction of belief that the five *skandhas* constitute an eternal self (Sautrāntika Buddhists); those who identify release with the destruction of the *guṇas* (Jains).[15] The refrain culminates with praise of Cēkkiḻār for refuting these other philosophical viewpoints by means of his mastery of the Tamil language, lauding him as the jewel of his community.

Mention of Cēkkiḻār's specific community, the Veḷḷāḷa *jāti* (subcaste), recurs throughout the poem. A dominant non-Brahmin *jāti* powerful in paddy cultivation in the Tamil countryside, the Veḷḷāḷas had risen as high in the caste hierarchy as any non-Brahmins in South India could at that time. As Shulman notes, they and "allied agricultural castes had always provided the essential backbone for institutionalized Śaivism in the Tamil country."[16] Known for their wealth, patronage of temples, and support for religious education, Veḷḷāḷas played a major role in the development of Śaivite *matha* culture. Pillai took pride in celebrating illustrious members of his *jāti*, among whom the preeminent poet was Cēkkiḻār. Two of Pillai's verses translated below explicitly laud the Veḷḷāḷa lineage and the saint's connection with it.

The ideal of Veḷḷāḷa honor informs *CPT* 57, which centers on an ancient legend. According to the tale, one day, while a merchant was crossing the forest, the spirit *(pēy)* of his dead wife, whom he had murdered, began to follow him. Fleeing to Palaiyanur, a Veḷḷāḷa settlement, he took refuge with the village elders. When the ghostly spirit arrived, she convinced them to divest her husband of his sword. To convince the merchant to relinquish his weapon, they vowed that if any harm befell the man, each village elder would sacrifice his life. When the ghostly spirit then killed her prey, they all voluntarily entered the fire and gave up their lives, true to their vow. Thus, they reached the feet of Śiva in the heavenly world, while bringing honor in the earthly world to the Veḷḷāḷa lineage, of which both Pillai and Cēkkiḻār were proud.

Pillai even goes so far as to identify performance of the Veḷḷāḷa dharma (code for conduct, duties, proper actions) as that which maintains the order of the universe in *CPT* 60. The Veḷḷāḷa community owned large tracts of land, which they cultivated with a plough drawn by a bullock that they goaded forward with a small stick. A commentator writing about this verse describes its rhetorical strategy thus: "If the Veḷḷāḷas have a stick to drive [the bullocks] in their hands, all will do their duty. That is the idea."[17] Here Pillai foregrounds the eminence of the Veḷḷāḷa community and its importance to the functioning of the larger society.

Literary conventions, poetic inspiration, *araṅkēṟṟams,* and patronage all played significant roles in Pillai's literary milieu. He enjoyed the challenge of the pillaittamil's prescriptions and wrote many of them over the course of his life.[18] His love for pillaittamils written by great poets of the past also led him to develop learned commentaries on them. Both his compositions and his exegesis enriched the pillaittamil tradition. Pillai's *Cēkkiḻār Piḷḷaittamiḻ* was reprinted again and again; *mathas* reissued it on a regular basis and bestowed copies on those who attended important ritual occasions. The South Indian Saiva Siddhanta Publishing Works Society also kept the poem in print in an inexpensive, annotated, paperback edition. In the years since its first publication, *CPT* too has earned its share of commentaries that elucidate the excellence of its poetry.

CPT 37 (clap 6)

While Lady Umā watched, her shining breasts beautifully clad,
you stood before the Lord who dances in the lovely hall,
your heart melting and filled with sorrow.
The Lord who cares for you bestowed the first words.

Then the precious Brahmins, trusting in Śiva,
clasped their hands in amazement and showed their love
by giving you sweet fragrances right away,
adorning you with a garland,
and granting you the shining garment.

They knew without a doubt that you were
the One with shining matted hair, where the Ganges stays.
"Before you begin to compose," they said,
"gather and take some of the sacred ash."

With those hands that did obeisance,
received, and treasured the sacred ash,
clap your hands.

Eloquent One, Protector of victorious devotees,
clap your hands.

Umā: Here it refers to the temple icon of Śiva's consort.

lovely hall: Chidambaram, where Śiva performs his cosmic dance.

first words: Śiva revealed the first words of *Periya Purāṇam* to Cēkkiḻār in the midst of the awestruck Brahmins.

shining garment: Parivaṭṭam, clothing in which the icon is wrapped during worship. Afterward, it is bestowed on distinguished donors as an honor.

that you were the One: That Cēkkiḻār was a form of Śiva on earth.

CPT 54 (come 3)

Some say that union with a woman is enduring bliss.
Some say that destroying the five aggregates is lasting bliss.
Some say that destroying the three strands is complete bliss.
Some say that destroying the two kinds of karma is long-sought bliss.
Some say that destroying bonds is bliss.
Some say that immortality of the much-discussed self is bliss.
Some say that the arising of knowledge is bliss.
Some say that the destruction of the oft-lauded self is bliss.
Some say that the destruction of matter is bliss.
Some say that miraculous powers are bliss.
And there are others.

Since you know the value of rich pure Tamil
which defeats the skills of all these who come to debate,
Crown Jewel of the lineage of great devotees, come.

Master of Kuṉṟattūr, who worships the God
with a forest of matted hair adorned with koṉṟai flowers
in the temple hall, come.

---

aggregates: Sanskrit, *skandhas;* Pali, *kandas.*

three strands: The *guṇas: sattva* (purity), *rajas* (passion), *tamas* (heaviness).

two kinds of karma: Good karma and bad karma.

Kuṉṟattūr: Cēkkiḻār's birthplace.

God with the forest of matted hair: Śiva in his ascetic form.

CPT 57 (come 6)

Before the illustrious assembly of Palaiyanūr,
known for its unchanging goodness,
stood a merchant, trembling,
because he had seen terrifying Nīli.

The seventy Veḷḷāḷas of the assembly vowed,
"If death strikes this good man who lives on earth,
we will all bathe in the fire and forsake our lives.
Understand this."

They bathed in a pit of seven tongues of flame
and, living up to their word, won great victory.
Those seventy people attained the flower feet of the Lord
who dances in the forest to the north of the village.

Born of their lineage, O Cloud,
showering the rain of precious grace,
come, come.

King of Kuṉṟattūr,
where palatial buildings vie with mountains,
come, come.

---

assembly: Elders who settle conflicts and protect the honor of the village.

Nīli: The name of a woman whose husband murdered her. After her death, she tormented him as a ghost.

attained the flower feet of the Lord: Attained union with Śiva.

palatial buildings vie with mountains: Cēkkiḻār's birthplace is so prosperous that its dwellings compete with mountains in their height and majesty (hyperbole).

The Lord who dances in the forest to the north: Śiva in the cremation ground.[19]

CPT 60 (come 9)

So that Brahmā takes up the renowned stick
and Viṣṇu takes up the club of respected authority

So that all the resolute religious students
take up the jacktree sticks

So that those in the fourth stage of life
eagerly take up the bamboo stick

So that all the lineages of trustworthy merchants
take up their accurate weighing rods

So that all the kings with pure golden crowns
take up their righteous scepters

Cloud of grace, born into the lineage
of those who take up the small staff,
Come, come.

King of Ku<u>*ṉṟ*</u>*attūr,*
where palatial buildings vie with mountains,
Come, come.

---

fourth stage of life: Ascetics who have completed family life and gone to the forest to attain religious liberation.

CPT 73 (little house 2)

Is this the temple where Arukantan̲, the renouncer, lives?
Is this the monastery where resolute ones reside?

Is this the residence where people of other religions
live in a way that makes them despised as impure?

If you destroy with your feet
the little houses that we made so well,
will you earn merit or fame?

Lord of Toṇṭai, whose rich fields abound in good paddy,
growing so high and thick that it hides
even the uplifted trunk of a huge elephant
because it is watered by the swift swirling Pali River
which yields abundance,
don't destroy our little houses.

One from Kun̲r̲attūr, where wealth flourishes,
You are rich in grace.
Don't destroy our little houses.

Arukantan̲: A Jaina renouncer (Sanskrit *arahant*).

Toṇṭai: The name of one of the four main regions of South India, centered in the Chengalput area.

CPT 74 (little house 3)

Destroy the karma of unfortunate people
burdened with a desire for harmful other religions.
Destroy their entanglements completely.
Destroy their egotism utterly.

If you destroy all three bonds,
both your fame and merit will increase day by day.
But destroying our effort is ridiculous.

Eminent man from Taṇṭaka country
where red sugarcane that astonishes the world,
bunches of bananas, green areca nut trees,
and coconut trees shining with tender fruits
grow so high that they adorn the court of Indra,
don't destroy the little houses
of us little ones.

One from Kun̲r̲attūr where wealth flourishes,
You are rich in grace.
Don't destroy our little houses.

---

karma, entanglements, egotism: The three bonds to be overcome before attaining religious liberation, according to Saiva Siddhanta.

Taṇṭaka: Another name for Toṇṭai, the region of South India in which the powerful Pallava kings ruled.

where red sugar cane . . . court of Indra: Hyperbolic phrase suggesting that plants there grow so tall that they reach the celestial realm where the gods dwell. This phrase emphasizes the prosperity of Cekkil̲ār's native place.

CHAPTER SIX

A PILLAITTAMIL TO MUHAMMAD

BY CHOOSING TO write in the pillaittamil genre, Tamil poets within the Muslim tradition located themselves in relation to the Islamic culture of southeastern India, while simultaneously broadening the scope of the pillaittamil tradition. Seyyitu A̱napiyyā Pulavar (henceforth A̱napiyyā), deployed the pillaittamil genre in his nineteenth-century poem, *Napikaḷ Nāyakam Piḷḷaittamiḻ (A Pillaittamil on the Foremost of the Prophets)* in order to praise the Prophet Muhammad. The requirements of the paruvam structure shaped the way he portrayed the Prophet. Conversely, the influence of Islamic theology, which prohibited regarding God as a baby or addressing the Prophet Muhammad as a divine being, subtly transformed the emphases within particular paruvams in distinctively non-Hindu ways. This poem, and others like it, thus helped the pillaittamil genre to develop in new directions.[1]

Muslim Poets and Tamil Poetic Genres

ISLAMIC LITERATURE IN Tamilnadu has a long and diverse history.[2] While some Muslim writers chose to express themselves in Arabic and Persian,[3] others wrote in Tamil. Among the latter, some composed in Middle Eastern genres, but others chose to compose in Tamil literary genres. Among those who chose Tamil genres, some adopted primarily narrative poetic genres, while others were attracted to poetry composed of discrete verses.[4] The pillaittamil genre offered Islamic poets who wanted to use a Tamil literary genre composed of discrete verses a distinctive framework within which to express praise and veneration.

When Islamic poets used the genre, they did not compose pillaittamils to the divine. The Hindu pillaittamil involves envisioning the poem's subject in a particular form, an enterprise contrary to the spirit of the Qur'anic verse, "No vision can grasp Him" (Sura 6). More specifically, Sura 112 of the *Qur'an* says, "He did not beget, nor was he begotten," which excludes representation of the divine in the form of a baby. Given orthodox Muslim repugnance to anthropomorphizing the divine, the absence of pillaittamils to God is not unexpected.

Islamic poets did use the genre, however, to praise a number of those venerated within the faith, most notably the Prophet Muhammad, but also members of his family and various *walis* ("friends of God") whose tombs are revered in Tamilnadu.[5] The earliest four Islamic pillaittamils date from the eighteenth century, and Islamic pillaittamils continue to be written today. At least twenty extant Islamic pillaittamils are known to scholars at present; two were written to females (one to Fatima and another to Ayisha),[6] while the rest were addressed to males. Six are addressed to the Prophet Muhammad. Scholars of Islamic Tamil literature recognize *Napikaḷ Nāyakam Piḷḷaittamiḻ (NNPT)* as an excellent example of a pillaittamil to the Prophet Muhammad.

Adherents of Islam have long considered Muhammad's birth a momentous occasion; at least since the thirteenth century Muslims have celebrated the birthday of the Prophet. For example, among the genres for praising the Prophet in Sindhi, a language used in the Sindh province of modern-day Pakistan, one finds the genre *maulud,* which celebrates the Prophet Muhammad as a "newborn child." One such verse, for instance, tells of how Lady Amina smiled when she gave birth to the Prophet. Ali Asani comments that poetry celebrating the Prophet's birth is widespread throughout the Islamic world but notes that in such poetry emphasis "tends to be on the event itself and/or extolling the noble qualities of the newborn child," rather than celebrating events throughout early childhood.[7]

In addition to genres celebrating the Prophet's birth, there exists a long tradition of venerating the life of the Prophet as extraordinary, as reflected in the devotional poetry of Islam. Among other scholars, Annemarie Schimmel has called attention both to the scholarly neglect of this tradition of veneration and to its central role in Islamic piety.[8] Its centrality led to the composition of myriad poems venerating the Prophet, composed in many genres, in languages ranging from Arabic and Persian to the regional languages of Asia and Africa. In these poems we find not the austere, "stripped down" figure of Muhammad portrayed both by certain Muslim reformers and by some Western scholars, but the "mystical" Muhammad of popular piety and literary tradition. Poetry about the Prophet Muhammad in this vein tends to share a number of recurring features: reference to his primordial light and status as the perfect man, mention of the special attention lavished upon him (such as the opening of his chest and cleansing him of sin), celebration of miraculous deeds he performed (such as the splitting of the moon), praise of his great victories in battle, identification of his deeds as models of action for believers, and inclusion of many special names and epithets for him.

The wide-ranging emphasis on veneration of the Prophet in the Islamic world also played a major role in the Tamil Muslim communities in South India and Ceylon (later called Sri Lanka). A compendium of Muslim theology and jurisprudence written by Mapillai Alim (d. 1898), roughly contemporary with the life of A<u>n</u>apiyyā, gives a sense of the religious ideals of Tamil-speaking Muslims from the geographical area where A<u>n</u>apiyyā was born and reared. This work demonstrates that veneration of the Prophet was a major emphasis in the piety of this community. Mapillai Alim compiled a guide to proper religious behavior for those whose main language was Tamil but who could read Arabic script. This work made available to them a digest of the works of earlier Muslim writers.

In Mapillai Alim's discussion of "Priority in Dignity," he says, "It is necessary for a *Mu'min* [person of faith] to know that of all things Allah created, our beloved Prophet Muhammad *(Sal.)* holds the highest position in dignity and honour." One section of his work identifies "bearing love towards His [God's] Prophets" as the third most important prerequisite of *īmān* [faith], superseded only by bearing love toward God and His Angels, respectively.[9] The compendium clearly identifies veneration of the Prophet as a major form of Muslim piety in this particular community.

Schimmel has noted, "... although the basic forms of praise are everywhere and always similar, the elaborations and the shifts of emphasis around this or that peculiar aspect of the Prophet result in a surprisingly multicolored picture."[10] The comment applies well to the authors from the Tamil Muslim community who chose pillaittamils to express their veneration for the Prophet. A<u>n</u>apiyyā, in adopting a Tamil literary genre indigenous to the region, the pillaittamil, became part of a development in pillaittamil history that fostered a number of what Schimmel has called "shifts in emphasis," within the context of a highly conventional poetic genre.

Cultural Milieu and Publication History

THE FIRST EDITION of the *Napikaḷ Nāyakam Piḷḷaittamiḻ* is a thin pamphlet dated 1883.[11] Although our knowledge about A<u>n</u>apiyyā, his text, and his motivations in writing the poem is limited and fragmentary, it does indicate something of the cultural milieu in which the text was composed and the role of the text in the life of the Islamic Tamil community. The author's own name, Seyyitu A<u>n</u>apiyyā Pulavar, reflects the blending of traditions representative of his community. "Seyyitu A<u>n</u>apiyyā" is a Tamil transliteration of Arabic "Sayyid Hanafiya." "Sayyid" suggests that the person is a descendent of the Prophet Muhammad, an inherited status by which a family traces its lineage back to the founder of the Muslim community. "Hanafi" is the name of one of the four schools of Islamic law in Sunni Islam. "Pulavar," however, is a Tamil word for poet; this honorific appears at the end of names of respected Tamil poets and is not limited to members of any particular religious community. Thus, A<u>n</u>apiyyā's name indicates a pan-Tamil status among connoisseurs of literature, while simultaneously identifying him as a prominent member of the Muslim community.

Our historical knowledge about A<u>n</u>apiyyā must be gleaned from a few self-referencing comments that appear in verse 3, part of a prefatory section that precedes the ten standard paruvams. In it, the poet tells us that he is the son of Caitu (another Tamil transliteration for Sayyid) Mī<u>r</u>a Leppai. "Leppai" (Anglicized as Lebbai) is used to identify groups of Muslim merchants, and those connected to them, who settled in and around the port towns on the southern coast of Tamilnadu. Aṉapiyyā describes himself as son of a devout father who never failed to live according to religious law and lovingly taught the faithful in the town of Vadakarai.[12] This information locates the poet religiously in a family known to others for orthodoxy and knowledge. It also locates him geographically in the area of Tamilnadu known as a center of Islamic learning in South India.

Aṉapiyyā identifies his patrons in verse 12 of the protection paruvam. For the sake of Muhammad, the mystical Prophet who existed even before creation, the poet asks that God protect the enterprises of his patrons:

NNPT 12 (protection 9)

For the sake of the Prophet,
who was born in beautiful human form
on the earth surrounded by wave-filled oceans
and existed as a precious Prophet
even before the creation of the first prophet,
to Mēttar Muhiyittīṉ Rāvuttar,
who was born for excellence
in Tirunelveli region,
surrounded by fertile rich rivers
and cool groves,
and to good Muhammad Nayiṉār Rāvuttar,
from that same place,
who never deviates from justice,

give graciously from the beginning,
so that their honest trade will flourish
and make their wealth abundant.

Primordial source who possesses
rare and great fame!
God, Eternal One, Allah!

Here Aṉapiyyā asks God to protect the business of merchants Muhiyittīṉ Rāvuttar and Muhammad Nayiṉār Rāvuttar. Again the composition of these names reveals some cultural information. At the end, both men have the subcaste identifier "Rāvuttar," a Hindi term *(ravat)* meaning "horsemen" or "troops." In districts of Tamilnadu where these two patrons lived, this name is used by groups who claim that they were converted to Islam by the teaching of holy men such as Nathar Wali and those who claim descent from soldiers, officials, and literati attached to Muslim courts in the Deccan.[13] In verse 12 A<u>n</u>apiyyā identifies both patrons as coming from Mettar, an area in Tirunelveli district in which many Muslim Tamils lived. A<u>n</u>apiyyā asks that God bless them in such a way that "their honest trade will flourish and make their wealth abundant." These two merchants probably supported the poet while he composed the poem, as was the customary relationship between a poet and a patron in Tamil society of this time. Unfortunately, no information has been preserved about the first recitation of *NNPT.*[14]

The fairly recent republication of A<u>n</u>apiyyā's poem reveals its current place in the life of the Islamic Tamil community. The second edition of *Napikaḷ Nāyakam Piḷḷaittamiḻ* appeared in 1975 in Colombo, a culmination of a joint effort growing out of concerns about Tamil literature, education, religion, and political identity in Sri Lanka. The book's preface relates how a number of eminent Tamil Muslims were instrumental in getting this book edited, published, and accepted into the curriculum as a textbook for Sri Lankan government examinations in Tamil literature.

Yet organizers of this publication effort knew that the language and concepts of this nineteenth-century poem would not be easily accessible to either Muslim or non-Muslim readers. They therefore enlisted the aid of the noted scholar and educator C. Nayinar Mohamed, who was at that time teaching in the Tamil department of the Jamal Muhammad College in Tirucchirapalli, South India. He wrote an introduction to the piḷḷaittamil genre to explain each paruvam. He also accompanied each verse with an extensive commentary explicating the meaning of obscure terms, as well as the Islamic stories and doctrines that the verse took for granted. His labors mediated between a modern audience and a text written in an earlier literary and religious milieu for Muslims. The book was released on the auspicious occasion of the birthday of the Prophet and made available to Tamil Muslims in India and Sri Lanka. Thus, its publication was a way of participating in a religious celebration linked with the Prophet's birth and also a way of making a text venerating the Prophet's infancy part of the official Sri Lankan educational curriculum.[15]

Protection Reconfigured

MUSLIM POETS DEPLOYED the pillaittamil genre to praise the Prophet and other devout people within their religious tradition. In adopting the genre, however, they also subtly modified the use of particular paruvams to make them more appropriate to Islamic beliefs. Of particular interest, theologically, is how the protection paruvam undergoes certain changes in emphasis and composition. As we have seen, the paruvam contains a series of niches in which various powerful beings can be invoked, praised, and asked to insure the welfare of the infant. In the majority of Hindu texts, the poet calls upon a different god or goddess in each verse of the paruvam. In the Muslim context, there is only one God, Allah, so A<u>n</u>apiyyā alters the focus and extends the scope of the paruvam. A number of the protection verses ask Allah to protect the Prophet, but these verses invoke God's protection in a way that does not anthropomorphize him.

For example, in the first protection verse A<u>n</u>apiyyā lauds God for creating all beings, but especially Muhammad, for whom praises continue to arise, like a groundswell. Not only described as possessing clear knowledge, the quality of grace, and incomparable reason, the Prophet is also the best of all that can be perceived by the senses—most fragrant of fragrances and luminous as the sun. He acts as a haven for the meritorious and a well-earned refuge for the faithful.

The verse's refrain expresses trust that God will protect what he has created. As the refrain reminds us, God made all creatures and their destinies, saying *laulaka.* This pronouncement is found in an extra-Qur'anic revelation (hadith) in which God told Muhammad, "If you had not been [i.e., but for your sake], I would not have created the spheres."[16] For the sake of Muhammad, he did create the world, and A<u>n</u>apiyyā lauds God's majesty and creative power as fruitful and generative.

The protection paruvam in *NNPT* ranges from the all-encompassing praise in this first verse to verses that focus on particular scriptural figures of significance in Islamic tradition. For example, in verse 8, translated below, the poet builds a protection verse around the story of the sacrifice of Ishmael (Tamil: Icumāyīl). The verse depicts how Allah protected Ishmael, and then requests the same kind of protection for the Prophet. Here A<u>n</u>apiyyā utilizes a poetic pattern characteristic of the protection paruvam, namely, recounting a story central to the identity of his community of listeners. The poet tells of Ishmael, the son of Abraham who, according to Muslim accounts, settled in Mecca. Since Ishmael is identified as the progenitor of the Arab nation, Allah's act of protecting Ishmael remains absolutely central to Muslim sense of lineage and origins.[17] This verse commemorates care for the Muslim community in the distant past and asks for the same kind of protection for the newly born Prophet.

Unlike earlier protection paruvams, which only ask for the protection of the little baby, we saw that in *NNPT,* A<u>n</u>apiyyā requests that God look after the fortunes of his patrons' businesses as well. Linking the patrons with the Prophet, the poet asks God to make their businesses flourish for the sake of the Prophet. Also in keeping with the motif of praise so central to the paruvam, the poet lauds the personal and mercantile abilities of his patrons, designating the first patron "born for excellence" and the second as "adhering to justice," praising both of their businesses as "honest trade." In *NNPT,* thus, the poet fills some of the niches provided in the protection paruvam according to a rationale that differs substantially from that of traditional Hindu pillaittamil poets.[18]

Multireligious Poetic Patterns

In selected verses from *NNPT,* poetic patterns that we have encountered in earlier pillaittamils recur, with different dramatis personae. A<u>n</u>apiyyā uses familiar rhetorical strategies, but instead of drawing upon mythological materials as a Hindu poet would, he draws upon traditions about the life of the Prophet and his family, as well as other elements of Islamic belief. Consider for comparison a verse from each of the following paruvams: sway to and fro, clap, and kiss.

Like other sway to and fro verses we have seen, *NNPT* 15 interprets the swaying movement associated with the paruvam as dance. The verse's structure emphasizes the link between the swaying movements and the rejoicing that occurs throughout the creation of Allah (who is referred to with the epithet "the Deathless One"). The verse, thus, makes the Prophet Muhammad's gentle undulating movement the center of a cosmic celebration. It begins in the paradisal realm, where celestial women with large, dark, round eyes rejoice, angels dance, and the earlier prophets celebrate. Next comes the jubilation of the heavenly bodies: the moon (called "ambrosial luminary" because it is said to be filled with the sweet elixir of immortality) and the sun riding in its dancing chariot. The primordial light which emerged from the depths of the Unseen, dances, as do the stylus and tablet, upon which are written all that has happened and all that will happen. The divine throne and footstool also dance. Then, the poet descends to the level of the jinns (spirits) and creatures on earth; since the Prophet has been born on earth, he can provide a model for them, so they too dance with joy. In this verse, both the contents and the ordering of exultant beings have a significance, attesting to the joy in the cosmos, from heaven to earth, caused when Baby Muhammad sways to and fro.[19]

This verse resembles another sway to and fro verse, addressed to Mīṉāṭci (*MMPT* 18), which revolves around many forms of dancing. Both the verse to Goddess Mīṉāṭci (see chapter 4) and this one to the Prophet Muhammad share a fundamental poetic pattern. In the Hindu verse, each line describes a piece of jewelry that adorns the body of the goddess and tells how it dances, along with her smile, her feet, and her waist. Since the goddess holds the entire universe within her, when she dances all creatures move as well. In *NNPT,* when the Prophet sways to and fro, all of creation does so as well. Both extraordinary children bring about a cosmic dance, as they gently move back and forth, but the respective classification systems of the creatures in the cosmos differ.

In Aṉapiyyā's treatment of the *NNPT* 36, we find a clap verse oriented around a story in which the hero's hands play a major role. The verse refers to a time when the heavy rains had damaged the Ka'ba, and difficulty arose about putting the sacred black stone (called Hajar al-Aswad) back in its proper place. According to some traditions, Meccans from various tribes were unable to agree about who would receive the honor of restoring the black stone to its place. They decided to ask the next person who entered the gate to mediate their conflict. As Muhammad passed they asked for his aid; he placed the stone on a cloth and had a person from each tribe lift it into position collectively.[20] *NNPT* 36 does not mention all the details of the situation; it simply attributes to Muhammad's hands the completion of the task. Muslims who visit the Ka'ba during the pilgrimage to Mecca revere and kiss this ancient precious stone which rested in the Ka'ba from before the time of the Prophet but was resanctified by the work of his hands.

We have seen how in the clap paruvam, Tamil poets commonly link the baby's hands with extraordinary deeds performed later in life. Once again the hands of the Prophet form the link between childhood and the deeds of adulthood. For example, in *CPT* 37 (see chapter 5), Baby Cēkkiḻār is asked to clap with the hands that accepted the sacred ash from the Brahmins in the temple at Chidambaram. In *MMPT* 37 (see chapter 4), Baby Mīṉāṭci is asked to clap the hands that held and bathed her son. Aṉapiyyā even uses the standard phrases, complimenting the Prophet's hands as "fair" and "like lotuses." "Fair" means his hands had an attractive hue, while the comparison to the lotus implies that the Prophet's hands were lovely, round, and finely formed. With the hands that carried the stone as a grown man, Baby Muhammad is asked to clap. In all three verses, the poet links a deed an adult will perform with his hands and a baby clapping those same hands; the poets share not only the poetic pattern but also the exact language used to praise the fine appearance of those hands.

The familiar pun on kiss and pearl also occurs in *NNPT,* but with yet an added resonance to the already existing double meaning of the term *muttam*. *NNPT*'s verse 48 provides an especially good example of the way that the conventions governing an individual paruvam can resonate with Aṉapiyyā's desire to praise the Prophet Muhammad. There exists a pan-Islamic literary tradition linking the Prophet Muhammad to a pearl because of the similarity between the Arabic term for pearl and the term for orphan. Schimmel notes that Muhammad's "being an orphan, *yatīm*—as pointed out in Sura 93—was to inspire many later poets to compare him to a *yatīma,* a unique (literally, 'orphan') pearl."[21] That is, he is both an orphan, due to the death of his parents, and a pearl, due to his preciousness. Both Tamil conventions and Islamic traditions emphasize the uniqueness of the pearl they praise. This double tradition gives the familiar kiss/pearl imagery even more cultural and literary richness.

Aṉapiyyā's verse 48 concerns pearls and, also, literary practices dealing with pearls. The overall poetic strategy is familiar: he lists many items, then notes that none can compare with Muhammad's kiss. The first four items, however, are not pearls themselves, but items that poets have compared to pearls. The white tip of the peacock feather, the jasmine bud, the corner of a crane's eye, and the topaz are each so white and gleaming that they resemble pearls.[22] In the second half of the verse, Aṉapiyyā turns to the more familiar lists of pearls usually found in this paruvam. The verse resonates with the Arabic tradition of the Prophet as a pearl, makes use of the Tamil kiss/pearl pun, and provides an insider's comment on the metaphorical imagery of pearl descriptions.

These three verses show some of the many ways in which the paruvam structure remains open to material from non-Hindu religious traditions. The pillaittamil provides a framework suitable for the praises of the Prophet's deeds, appearance, and role in the cosmic structure. *NNPT,* like the other pillaittamils analyzed in this book, displays the creativity of an individual poet who fashions new poetry within the confines of the paruvam conventions.

De-eroticizing Little House Verses

In contrast to the verse just discussed, Aṉapiyyā's treatment of the little house paruvam incorporates radical changes required by Islamic tradition in the setting and characters of the paruvam. Aṉapiyyā minimizes certain traditional characteristics of the paruvam and deflects our attention away from some of its often erotic conventional language. To see how Aṉapiyyā brings about these changes, compare his treatment of the paruvam to that in Pakaḻikkūttar's *Tiruccentūr Piḷḷaittamiḻ* (chapter 3). Both Pakaḻikkūttar and Aṉapiyyā laud a heroic male for his strength in battle, handsome appearance, and extraordinary power. Yet each poet deals with the little house paruvam quite differently, due, at least in part, to different religious assumptions.

We saw earlier how an implicit eroticism coexists with the little house paruvam's attempts to persuade the boy not to destroy the little houses of the girls. In Pakalikkūttar's *TCPT* 87 (translated in chapter 3), for example, the girls try to convince the boy that he should attack the cities of enemies rather than the fragile playhouses of the girls. In the course of doing so, however, the girls describe their waists as "burdened with the support of our large breasts." This conceit—that their breasts are so buxom they overweigh their slim waists—is used frequently in hyperbolic descriptions of beautiful Tamil women to call attention to their voluptuousness and nubility.

When we turn to Aṉapiyyā's treatment of the little house paruvam, we find transformations in emphasis and tone. First, he shifts attention away from the girls and toward the heroic deeds of the Prophet. He provides us with almost no information about the girls' feelings, motivations, or appearance. Instead, the poet tends to use the girls' voice here primarily as a literary mechanism, and they appear in the refrain only as "we little ones" or "your servants." Consider, for example, the only description of the young girls in *NNPT* 91 (in the set of translations in this chapter): "don't destroy the little houses of your servants and believers."[23] Other than that they are his servants and believers, we learn little about them. In fact, were we not already familiar with the conventions of this paruvam, we might not even pay attention to whether the speakers were little, or even girls. Instead of focusing on the girls, the verse emphasizes the image of Muhammad as a victorious hero in battle.

Since it is not appropriate for Islamic poets to portray the Prophet Muhammad in a situation in which he would be identified as acting in a malicious or unfair way, this aspect of the paruvam is minimized as well. While the Hindu poets tell of the reproaches that the little girls pour upon the little boy, Aṉapiyyā depersonalizes them, or uses them as an occasion for religious instruction. For example, in *NNPT* 85 the actual thrust of the verse is less to reproach than to enumerate the enemies of the pious.

NNPT 85 (little house 2)

Don't you know the homes
of fools who ignore learned scholars' words
that elucidate the ocean of knowledge?

Don't you recognize the houses
of embittered men who refuse to give alms
for the sake of our precious God?

Don't you see the abodes
of treacherous people who plead legal suits
that violate justice?

Haven't you noticed the dwellings
of those who despise scholars
of God's scriptures?

This isn't the house of wicked people
who cause hardship and destruction,
is it?

Don't destroy the little houses
made by us little ones who play in the sand
with our little friends.
Noble Messenger Muhammad,
don't destroy our little houses.

Each stanza in this verse identifies and condemns persons considered to lack virtue in Islamic tradition—the ignorant, the miserly, the unjust, the denigrators, and the wicked. Although the verse contains a query about why the boy considers attacking the girls' playhouses, it concentrates on establishing that the houses of others are more deserving of attack because their inhabitants undermine true religious belief and practice.

On balance, Muslim pillaittamils are notable both for their continuities with pan-Islamic poetic tradition and for the ways they transform Tamil literary conventions so they are appropriate vehicles for Islamic literary expression. Aṉapiyyā's poem is filled with themes characteristic of wider pan-Islamic veneration of the Prophet. Verses retell the miraculous stories surrounding Muhammad's birth, allude to his victories in battle and to the cleansing of his breast, laud his compassion and wisdom, and proclaim him model and messenger. Refrains invoke his mystical names and epithets, refer to his special relationship with Allah, and praise his radiance.

Yet particular emphases and nuances are introduced into the veneration of Muhammad because of the pillaittamil genre's requirements. A<u>n</u>apiyyā places the childhood of the Prophet at the heart of the poem—not just the Prophet's childhood, but childhood as structured and shaped by the paruvam framework. The requirements of the paruvam conventions influence the episodes narrated and the literary conceits and imagery A<u>n</u>apiyyā uses. In addition to the examples we have discussed (the deeds of his hands, the pun on pearl), there are many other familiar strategies in the poem (the attiring of the baby for warfare in verse 57, the toy chariot). These themes are prominent in A<u>n</u>apiyyā's praise of the Prophet at least partially because of the pillaittamil's paruvam structure.

Nonetheless, A<u>n</u>apiyyā appropriates the pillaittamil in his own ways and for his own purposes. The comparison of his and Hindu treatment of protection and little house paruvams shows how A<u>n</u>apiyyā has subtly altered the import and tone of certain paruvams. Both Hindu and Muslim poets write according to the prescriptions for each paruvam, but poems differ at least partly because ways of praising Hindu deities differ distinctively from accepted ways of venerating the Prophet.

NNPT 4 (protection 1)

Praising God as the protector of the Prophet

Marvelous scripture, created things,
clear knowledge, recipients of sense knowledge,
undying life, pleasure,
delicious taste, clear ambrosia,
fragrance of fragrances, the essence of compassion,
the luminous tree, the rain cloud,
an eternal jewel, light of the sun,
peerless reason and undivided form
meritorious harbor—
praise rises and swells for these creations.

Eminent one,
embryo of embryos in heaven and earth,
you created the many creatures
according to their destinies
by thinking and proclaiming "Laulaka!"

Merciful One, you rule majestically
as fruitful protection.

---

laulaka: The words beginning a ḥadīth indicating that God told Muhammad, "If you had not been [i.e., but for your sake], I would not have created the spheres."

NNPT 8 (protection 5)

Asking God to protect Baby Muhammad

In those days Ipuṟahīm lived on the earth
along with his boy,
according to the religious path in fear of God.
Many religious teachers arose and came to him
in order to learn the right path.

Then, You told him, "Sacrifice your son."
As he began to cut his son forcefully with a sharp sword
according to his word,
You gave him a sheep,
quickly saving the boy from injury to his life.

Just as You protected Icumāyīl,
so that no harm came to him,
protect Seyyitu Irasūl Ahumat as the perfect Prophet,
O Lord filled with knowledge.

Ipuṟahīm: Abraham.

Icumāyīl: Ishmael.

Seyyitu Irasūl Ahumat: Sayyid Rahul Ahmad, name for the Prophet.

NNPT 15 (sway to and fro 2)

Lotus-faced houris with eyes like lilies
dance.

Celestials in heaven
joyously dance.

The prophets and their sons,
versed in revealed texts and commentary,
lovingly dance.

The sun's chariot,
pulled by seven lively horses,
dances.

The sun
dances.

The ambrosial luminary
dances.

The stylus and the tablet
dance.

The throne and the footstool
dance.

The heavenly city,
best of worlds,
dances.

The jinns
and the many living creatures,
produced by the great power
of the Deathless One,
take you as their principle
and dance.

Munificent jewel who returned
after bathing in the celestial waters,
sway to and fro.

Master Muhammad,
Lord of the holy light,
sway to and fro.

The sons, . . . heavenly city: There are some textual ambiguities here.[24]

bathing in the celestial waters: According to an early tradition about the life of Muhammad, the Prophet's breast was split open, his heart purified, and he journeyed to heaven.

Lord of the holy light: Refers to the mystical doctrine that before the creation of the universe Allah created the Prophet from the primordial light.

NNPT 24 (lullaby 1)

Your cradle's wheel
resembles the rich golden wheel of the sun,
so bright that it blinds the eye.

Your cradle
is like the sky chariot
that the lord of the star-filled sky
joyously rides.

Its frame is inlaid
with gems so full of color
that they radiate sunlight
as if lightning stolen from the sky.

The tips of the cradle's legs
are like vessels
made of shining green emeralds.

Its chains are of pure gold.

Celestial women sing you lullabies
while eminent celestial men praise you.

Prophet, Qāsim,
who sits rocking back and forth so wonderfully
that it overwhelms the eye,
talelo, talelo.

Ocean of mercy, talelo.
Friend full of wisdom, talelo.

Qāsim: A name for the Prophet meaning "Divider."[25]

NNPT 36 (clap 3)

In this world surrounded by water-filled oceans,
there live without anger
learned and ordinary people
both receiving the fruits of knowledge
and always-increasing wealth
without distress or poverty
in the land of victorious Mecca.

One day, there,
after the flooding rains ruined the Ka'ba,
when the Quraishis were renovating it,
even groups of strong men
were unable to pick up and move
the stone called Hajar al-Aswad.

But you picked up the stone
and carried it
to the southeast corner of the raised wall.

With those fair lotus-like hands
that picked up the stone as your own,
clap your hands.

Great teacher full of discipline,
Tāhā Muhammad, clap your hands.

---

learned and ordinary: In this great city not only the scholars but even the ordinary unlettered people possess the fruits of knowledge, are wealthy, and do not experience suffering.

Tāhā: A mystical name for the prophet whose exact meaning is unclear.[26]

NNPT 48 (kiss 5)

A peacock feather's white tip,
the fragrant buds of lustrous jasmine,
the eye of a determined crane,
radiant topaz,

the pearl the young lotus bears,
the pearl found in the mountains,
the moon's pearl with flawless luster,
the pearl grown in the elephant's tusk,
the pearl from sweet sugarcane—

We could list these pearls
from many sources,
but would it really be right
to compare them to the pearls
from your lips like lotus petals?

With your lovely mouth,
lustrous and ever-handsome,
grant us a pearl of a kiss.

With your lovely mouth
that spoke with the strong one,
grant us a kiss.

---

mouth that spoke: The lips with which little Muhammad is to give the speaker a kiss are the same lips with which the grown Prophet will speak with Gabriel during his heavenly journey.

NNPT 57 (come 4)

Come so I can bedeck, with anklets and bells,
your feet like day-blooming lotuses.

Come so I can put on, with delight, your warrior's anklets
that confound the enemies who battle you,
like the ocean that wars with the land.

Come so I can adorn you with tinkling jewels.

Come so I can anoint with attar, rosewater,
the four perfumes, and most fragrant sandalpaste
your shoulders and chest towering like mountains
and clothe you lovingly.

So I can place you in the cradle
and rock you happily,
come joyously.

Muhammad, who has the truth,
come joyously, come.

NNPT 67 (moon 4)

Look, you have a group of stars
but he has a group of luminary saints.

Look, you have a hare
but he has persevered in living
according to the word of God.

Look, in the wide sky you are powerful
but he's powerful in earth and sky.

Look, your light changes
but he uses the words of revelation
to change the infidels.

Look, you have the artful sixteen phases
but he knows all sixty-four arts.

Look, your space grows and then decreases
but he doesn't have the misery of decreasing.

Because he is the long-awaited one
with him, Moon, come to play.

With the Prophet from the Quraish lineage
praised by the whole world,
Moon, come and play.

---

luminary saints: It refers to the ḥadīth, "My companions are like stars," punning on the light given by a star, and alludes to the Prophet Muhammad's role as "pole," Tamil *kuttupu* (Arabic *quṭb*), around which all the bodies in the universe orbit.

Hare: Muyal can mean "rabbit" as a noun and "to persevere" as a verb.

sixty-four arts: A person who is talented, intelligent, urbane, and knowledgeable is said to possess the sixty-four arts *(kalai).* The moon, with only sixteen lunar phases *(kalai),* is outnumbered by Muhammad.

NNPT 79 (little drum 6)

The entire celestial world
totters.

The seven clouds
turn frenzied with terror.

Meru and the eight sky-scraping mountains
tremble.

The oceans
shake.

The whole earth
quakes.

The celestial serpent
reels.

The stunned elephants of the eight directions
stream with flowing rut.

The sky, so vast it overwhelms the eye,
is startled.

The moon and sun, disturbed, cannot keep their positions
and, along with their horses, they disburse.

With your true, strong, shapely hands,
beat your little drum.

Muhammad with the shade-giving parasol
of thick clouds, beat your little drum.

---

totters . . . terror . . . tremble, etc.: A description of judgment day.[27]

NNPT 89 (little house 6)

When the kings of the earth,
surrounded by wave-filled oceans
with roaring conches,
come and worship your lotus feet;
if the accomplished ascetic Abdul Muttalib
and the eminent Abu Talib
were to lift you up, give you kisses, and seat you
on their shoulders adorned with garlands,
wouldn't dust fall on their chests?

If Amina, royalty among women,
were to say "Come," pick you up,
and put you on her waist,
wouldn't the dust from your flower feet
soil her colorful, billowing silk dress?

Our fair hands suffered from sifting
the sand for careful building,
so don't destroy our little houses.

Noble Messenger Muhammad,
don't destroy the little houses
of us little ones.

Abdul Muttalib: Grandfather and guardian of the Prophet.

Abu Talib: The Prophet's uncle and guardian.

Amina: The Prophet's mother.

NNPT 91 (little house 8)

Thinking that there is one God who created
all the worlds filled with entities,
you confronted the sinful infidels
who lacked devotion.

You defeated and drove away those infidels
who came to raze beautiful houses
surrounded by pools and walls.

King who protected us by destroying
their houses like mountain fortresses,
if you have destruction on your mind,
to whom will we confide our misery?

Therefore, precious gem
who is light from the Great One,
don't destroy the little houses
of your servants and believers.

Muhammad, Prophet for the world,
don't destroy the little houses
of your servants.

NNPT 94 (little chariot 1)

The golden chariot spreads light
like the one with the never-ending wisdom of light.

The always-beautiful banner flutters
as if it were sweeping off dust with its hands.

The eruption of neighing among fiery horses
sounds like drumbeats saying to crowds of people,
and to kings whose fragrant lotus hands
hold gleaming spears like lightning,
"Leave the streets! Be gone!"

The fragrance emanating from the body
of the Lord of Prophets called "King"
is like a messenger announcing his arrival.

Riding lovingly on a seat decorated with nine gems
turning right to the south, turning left to the north,
and then west and east,
drive your little chariot.

Royal Messenger for the King of Heaven,
drive your little chariot.

---

banner flutters: This may be a reference to the green banner which will appear on the day of judgment.

South . . . east: Conventional language to describe the conquest of the lands in all four directions.

NNPT 103 (little chariot 10)

With the grace of the Primordial One,
long may the eternally excellent Prophet Ahmad live!

Long may the learned ones, the many believers,
and the companions of the Prophet live!

Long may those who recite music on earth
live by the precepts!

Long may avid listeners and generous people,
as well as their kin, prosper and live!

May the many people and other creatures who sing
gain riches and live!

With God's mercy, long may the celestials and houris
be free of distress and live!

To remove their manifold bad karma
and allow them to live,
drive your little chariot.

Victory, victory to the Prophet strong as a lion,
our Muhammad!
Drive your little chariot!

---

live . . . live: Verses in this form are called *mangalams,* auspicious ones, because they ask for blessings on all creatures, especially those who recite and listen eagerly to poetry and song.

CHAPTER SEVEN

ONE POET'S BABY JESUS

FOR CENTURIES THE image of Baby Jesus has played a crucial role in Christian tradition. Veneration of the infant Jesus began in the early Middle Ages and received a major boost in the twelfth and thirteenth centuries from the Cistercians and Franciscans. Thus, it seems natural that a Tamil Catholic would find the pillaittamil a particularly appropriate genre for expressing love of God. Several Christian pillaittamils have been composed since the mid eighteen-hundreds, one of which was written in 1985 by Aruḷ Cellatturai of Tirunelveli.[1] We are fortunate that he has given us his own account of writing the poem.[2]

In writing *Iyēcupirāṉ [Lord Jesus] Piḷḷaittamiḻ* (henceforth *IPPT*), Cellatturai self-consciously set out to compose a pillaittamil that would achieve several goals. Inspired by the beauty of ancient Tamil poetry, he wanted to write a poem in "Only Tamil" words, that is, excluding words and poetic imagery that came from Sanskrit, English, and other non-Tamil sources. Yet at the same time, he sought to make a place in the pillaittamil tradition for the world of technology.[3] As an engineer and a person fascinated by science, he wanted to praise the Lord as creator of the mysteriously complex and beautiful patterns of nature. Even though most of the commonly used words in his scientific training were English, in his poetry he translated them into Tamil as a way of displaying the richness of its linguistic resources.

Finally, he explicitly identified his pillaittamil as a way to teach the greatness of Lord Jesus to people of various religious persuasions. In consonance with the movement to indigenize expression of the

Christian faith in Tamilnadu, Cellatturai portrayed Baby Jesus as a Tamil child. In this way, he hoped to show people how Lord Jesus could enter their religious lives in a familiar form. Cellatturai's composition process and the circumstances of the poem's first recitation demonstrate how his pillaittamil sought to transcend conventional boundaries by bringing together lovers of Tamil literature in general, pious Christians, and those whose lives center on scientific and technical training.

How the Poem Came to be Written

DESPITE CELLATTURAI'S TRAINING and employment in the field of engineering, writing poetry has played a large role throughout his life. His father encouraged his son's education and, under the guidance of a literary guru, he studied selected classical Tamil texts and *Ta<u>n</u>ippāṭaḷ Tirattu,* an anthology of verses by various poets. He tremendously admired Sangam poetry, wishing that the poetry of his own time were more like the ancient verses. After studying thoroughly the techniques of poetic composition, he began writing poetry in the 1960s and showing it to his guru for correction. A turning point occurred in 1974 when, as Cellatturai describes it, his guru "was adorned with Po<u>nn</u>āḍai [a shawl of honor] on the public dais by the Bishop." Once his guru had attained public recognition as an outstanding poet, Cellatturai felt inspired to undertake more ambitious poetic enterprises of his own.[4]

Cellatturai was deeply influenced in his writing style by the literary magazine *Thenmozhi* (Words of Honey), in which various present-day poets wrote in the Sangam style. He recalls what an inspiration it was to discover the magazine; "I sighed with relief. I felt hopeful that it was possible to continue the literary work which had ceased to exist long back." From this point on, he sought to practice the principles set out in the Ta<u>n</u>ittami<u>l</u> Iyakkam (Only Tamil Movement), particularly as set out in the writings of G. Devaneya Pavanar.[5] That is, the movement sought to emulate the "unadulterated Tamil" of the ancient period, before it had been diluted by semantic borrowings from Sanskrit, Persian, and, more recently, English.

Cellatturai's motivation to write a pillaittamil arose from a religious vow. His children at the time consisted of two boys and a girl, but he and his wife deeply wanted another son and prayed daily for a little boy *(kuṭṭi tampi):* "I also made a personal vow that I would offer a pillaittamil to child Jesus if a male child was born," recalls Cellatturai. The parents, indeed, "were blessed by God" with a little boy whom they loved very much. So Cellatturai set out to write a pillaittamil to Baby Jesus. Since he now had a growing infant in his home, he observed his son closely as preparation for his pillaittamil writing: "God had given me a very good chance to study all the gestures and habits of a little child. I did so and was prepared to write." As a result, he felt comfortable assuming the voice of a mother: "Whatever she [his wife] feels as mother is known to me," he said.

His other preparation was to study every pillaittamil he could find, more than 228 pillaittamils at various libraries and private collections, the reading of which steeped him in the pillaittamil tradition. His highest admiration was reserved for the famous pillaittamil poet, Kumarakuruparar (see chapter 3), whose work he considered masterly. He was also impressed that Mi<u>n</u>āṭcicuntaram Piḷḷai could effortlessly write pillaittamils that flowed so sonorously (see chapter 5).

Cellatturai worked steadily on his pillaittamil. Every moment of free time was precious, so he used his daily forty-minute bus ride to the office for composition. The poem took him exactly ten months to write, the period that ancient Indian texts take to be the time between the conception and the birth of a child. When he finished his composition, he went to Mukkombu, the dam site on the river Kavery where it branches into three streams. Under a huge banyan tree there, from early morning to late evening, he gave the first recitation and explication of the full poem for two friends, one Hindu and the other Catholic. This, he said, was his version of the traditional *araṅke<u>r</u><u>r</u>am.*

At the time that Cellatturai completed the poem, he was attending Bible classes at St. Paul's Seminary in Tirunelveli. He asked his professor, Dr. Fr. Hieronymus, whether it would be possible to publish his work. The cleric convinced those in the seminary administration to act as patron for the poem's publication at a nearby Christian press. The publishers printed one thousand copies of the book, which were almost entirely sold out by 1990. Public libraries in Tamilnadu purchased three hundred copies, and the others were sold through direct orders.

The finished product received a book-releasing celebration, a type of ceremony often held for works of traditional poetry.[6] The ceremony welcomes a new book into the world and establishes it in a community of appreciative readers. Organizers of the ceremony accomplish these functions by inviting guests to witness the book receive honor from prominent people.[7] On a more mundane level, the ceremony also advertises the book, targeting appropriate markets. The ceremony for Cellatturai's book, organized by his publisher, took place in the city's Tamil Sangam, a statewide literary association that promotes traditional Tamil poetry. The audience of Tamil literary savants, members active in Catholic education and publishing, friends, and the poet's family members created a community for the new work of poetry and expressed their appreciation of its excellence by participating in the ritual. The book's reception thus began with a ceremony that helped it to cross boundaries of Tamil reading communities. Clearly the poem had a wider audience than just the Tamil Catholic community.

Why a Pillaittamil to Jesus?

CELLATTURAI CHOSE TO write in the pillaittamil genre for specific reasons that he had considered with care. In our interview he stressed that particular genres are appropriate for depicting certain kinds of activity and expressing particular emotions. Among the available genres, which was most appropriate for depicting the endearing activities of childhood and expressing the poet's love toward Jesus? Cellatturai quickly ruled out certain genres for the praise of Lord Jesus: "Other genres, like *ula, kōvai, kuṟavanci,* etc. are not acceptable to Christ because of their inclination towards sex."[8] Although he used the English term "sex" here, he glossed it with the traditional Tamil phrase *akapporuḷ,* a term dating from the ancient period of Tamil literature, meaning "the subject matter of love." According to the poetic taxonomy used by classical authors, poetry fell into two categories: *akam,* "inner," deals with the intimate feelings of lovers and families, and *puṟam,* "outer," deals with the public realm of court life, warfare, and praise of generous donors. Poems dealing with *akam* often possess an erotic tone that Cellatturai felt inappropriate for depiction of Jesus.

This tendency to avoid eroticism also shaped his decision to address his pillaittamil to Jesus rather than to Virgin Mary.[9] Although several Christian poets had written pillaittamils to Mary, Cellatturai felt that doing so would either compromise the image of Virgin Mary or the spirit of the pillaittamil genre. He noted, "In the church we make adoration to Mary because of her implicit obedience to the word of God and because she was the mother of Christ. We do not attribute to her personal beauties." He explained further that pillaittamils to females (especially in the last three paruvams) expatiate on the sensual beauty of the girls. In contrast, "There are limitations on *varṇaṉai* [description] regarding Mary Mother." He suggests that if one looks at the erotic description found in the *MMPT* (consult, for example, verse 47 in chapter 4), one can see why such material would not be appropriate for Virgin Mary.

Cellatturai wrote praise of Jesus as a *baby* because of the universal appeal of children, as he comments: "Everybody is fond of children and in every society there is a special place for children. Children amuse other members of the family." So he felt that a poem about a child would give particular pleasure to readers. Cellatturai also admired the creative scope of the pillaittamil genre. Commenting that it challenged his imagination to envision the childhood of Jesus in the Tamil land, he said, "If Jesus were born again in Tamilnadu, these are the feelings he would have."

Personal as well as poetic reasons led him to write to Jesus as a baby. He noted, "Adult Jesus is always kept in a high elevated position; [but] there is no fear to approach child Jesus." He could even address Lord Jesus as a baby with the nonhonorific grammatical forms used only for children or intimate friends.[10] He felt that the pillaittamil's focus allowed him the opportunity to share his life with Baby Jesus, describing his feelings about Jesus in terms of specific paruvams: "I wanted to walk hand in hand with him *(varukai),* I wanted to play with him *(ciṟṟil),* I wanted kisses from him *(muttam),* I wanted to put him in the cradle and sing for him *(tāla).* Altogether I wanted to enjoy the nature of Lord Jesus as baby." Note that in Cellatturai's "little house" verse (translated below) he portrays the little girls as inviting Baby Jesus to join them in play. Cellatturai thus sees the paruvams of the pillaittamil as a means of envisioning a close and loving relationship with his God.

Theology and Technology

CELLATTURAI'S RELIGIOUS AND professional experiences led him to an awareness of both the constraints and the freedom of writing a pillaittamil. Interestingly, some aspects of the protection paruvam irked him, because he found them theologically unnecessary. The paruvam might be appropriate for Hindu tradition, but it did not really square with Christian doctrine. As he put it, "I am convinced that the Son of God himself protects everyone." Further, he noted that the Father and the Son are one, and hence protection does not seem necessary, since the baby in his poem can surely protect himself.

Nonetheless, since pillaittamil tradition requires a protection paruvam, he set out to write one. Still, he felt a poetic tension between the multiple deities of Hindu pillaittamils and the monotheism of Christianity: "Regarding the first paruvam, namely 'kappu paruvam,' it is customary to pray to various gods according to Hindu mythology. There is a wider range of choice. But for me there was only one choice, to pray to God the Father, to protect the child Jesus. Since he is above all, I could not find anyone except the Father to protect him. This limitation was a constraint for me." One could say that as a poet he felt his style was constrained in this paruvam because he had only a single theological option for filling the protection niches.[11]

Such minor constraints, however, did not interfere with Cellatturai's overall sense of the elasticity of the genre. Although his extensive reading did not uncover any previous examples of pillaittamils that had dealt adequately with the marvels of modern technology, he took it for granted that he was free to focus on the topic. He recalls, "I found that the modern contemporary world of science and technology was not depicted in any of the literature I studied. There is no representative of my living, my world, in the [pillaittamil] literature." So in his poem he strove to encompass his daily work based on engineering technology, either by using familiar Tamil words or by coining his own Tamil words to describe various scientific terms, as this verse shows:

IPPT 52 (come 2)

Lamps burn because of water
and light shines inside the water.
Even wind cannot attack them.

All the sheets of paper turn into books
through linotype.
Tape recorders speak Tamil.

Speech comes from the sky
and favorite songs come.
Scenes spread on the wide screen.
Speedy arrow-boilers even touch the moon and return.

Night lamps burn without oil.
Spring water deep in the earth rises.
There is even artificial rain.
Medicine accomplishes transformations.

All sorts of machines develop
to calculate beyond the mind's ability
and change history.

Source of knowledge,
who encompasses all these things,
making people look to the sky in wonder,
to my rejoicing heart, come.

Practice balancing on your toddling feet,
like honey-dripping lotus petals.
Son of the loving God, come.

Cellatturai expresses a wonder at the miracles of modern science that remains deeply rooted in his belief in God, the God who made all these miraculous acts possible. The tone of this verse suggests that appreciation of these electrical and mechanical breakthroughs bears witness to the greatness of a supreme deity who is, simultaneously, a cute little boy balancing uncertainly on his feet, which resemble soft, shapely lotus petals.

Lest his audience miss the significance of some of the amazing inventions he describes in the verse, Cellatturai provides his own annotations at the end of the poem, which I have translated in full, complete with his additional remarks in parentheses and my own clarificatory remarks in square brackets:

lamps burn because of water: (connecting electricity with water [hydro-electric power]), electric lamps burn.
light shines inside water: at Anicut Dam, it shines unceasingly in the water that runs by the flower garden. [Anicut Park is lit by underwater electric lights.]
in linotype: as soon as you strike it, the letter is transformed into print (linotype).
tape recorders: tape which makes a sound recording (tape recorder).
scenes on the spreading screen: film (cinema).
arrow-boilers: rākkettu [rockets].
rising high from springs in the earth: water tube wells.
medical transformation: transforming, performing surgery (transplantation).
calculating machine: calkulettar [calculator], kampyūttar [computer].

These annotations act as a bridge between Cellatturai's world of engineering and the linguistic resources of Tamil. He has coined some of the terms he uses for mechanical devices, so he explains them in his notes. In other places, his annotations provide the widely used English term that has been transliterated into Tamil (e.g., *kampyūṭṭar* for computer), but he does not use those transliterated terms in his text because he has committed himself to writing in "Tamil Only." Rather than lose his reader, though, he will give the more familiar English term in his notes to show how the device can be expressed when he uses only Tamil words. The annotations also act as an educational device to inform or remind readers of the scientific advances that have been made in the last few decades. By incorporating verses accompanied by annotations into his poem, he brings his world of technology into the pillaittamil tradition.

Making the Poem Accessible

As Cellatturai himself admitted, his pillaittamil is written not for a popular audience but for literary connoisseurs: "I cannot expect a layman to read my book. Even general literary readers may not find it convenient to read." So he feels that the more he can aid people in reading his work, the more he can carry out his goal of providing religious education. He considers the composition of his poem "not only an act of devotion," but also "a way in which I pass on information [about Jesus] to non-Christians." He feels that this book will help others to appreciate Jesus, noting that all three of the Tamil savants who wrote forewords to his pillaittamil were non-Christians, and yet, "all the three have admired the good qualities of my Lord Jesus." Because Cellatturai knows of the diverse experiences that members of his audience bring to his poem, he provides readers with an elaborate explanatory apparatus: preface, introduction, and literary information compiled in charts.

Prefatory remarks written by admirers suggest particular ways to savor certain aspects the poem. For example, the Rev. Fr. Hieronymus' preface advises the reader to put Jesus in a local context, a perspective in keeping with recent trends to indigenize Christian symbols and practice in South India:

> The custom of Tamils is to rejoice and speak sweetly of a baby, praising its excellence, putting on ornaments, a tilak [an auspicious mark on the forehead], and collyrium [eye decoration]. The world knows that once upon a time Lord Jesus, the holy Son of God, who is capable of being born anywhere, was born in the country of Judea. . . . *Iyēcupirāṉ Piḷḷaittamiḻ* is an attempt through literary imagination to draw out, according to the tradition of *ciṟṟilakkiyam* and Tamil grammar, all the ways in which, if Jesus came and was born in our sweet Tamil country now, our mothers would adorn and praise him. (p. 3, frontmatter)

Extrapolating from the theological idea that an omnipotent God is capable of sending his son to earth anywhere, the Rev. Hieronymus takes the poem to be the author's attempt to envision Jesus born in Tamilnadu and nurtured as a Tamil infant.

After these comments come several appreciative essays, all providing "testimony" to the poem's worth from non-Christian Tamil literary scholars: a secular intellectual, a Hindu savant, and the secretary for the Tamilnadu Government Culture and Development Department. Cellatturai also presents his own guide to his work, including a concise description of the subject matter of each paruvam, classification of types of imagery used, a summary of electrical and technological subjects to which he alludes (e.g., rockets, remote control, orbits of electrons, velocity of light), as well as an enumeration of Biblical passages to which he refers.

After the front matter comes Cellatturai's introductory essay, in which he explains what he sees as the theological significance of his pillaittamil to Baby Jesus. Noting that every year on December 25th people celebrate the Lord's birth as a baby, he suggests that, in a sense, at Christmas time Jesus is born annually, again and again, all over the world. Cellatturai sees his pillaittamil as the logical outcome of this continuing celebration of Baby Jesus: "He [Jesus] continues to be born every moment in the mind of his devotees as they think of him, singing a pillaittamil." For this reason, Cellatturai argues that praising the Lord as a baby in a pillaittamil is quite an appropriate act of devotion (p. 10).

Some verses also come complete with the poet's footnotes and explanations, including Biblical references, as is shown by the following translations of verse 61 and the poet's own systematic gloss of the verse, exceeding the verse itself in length.[12] The moon paruvam is Cellatturai's favorite paruvam, so he sought to master "the tiger," saying, "I took it as a challenge and hope that I have overwhelmed others in this feat." In particular, he took pride in the fact that he had discerned an impressive number of similarities between Jesus and the moon: "To my own astonishment I have shown eight similarities in the first verse and five similarities in the second verse, thirteen in total, which is a record in the history of pillaittamil." The numerical organization of his exegesis of the verse highlights his quantitative triumph. As his quotation emphasizes, a mathematical approach provided one way for an engineer to master the tiger.

IPPT 61 (moon 1) *The Poem*

Since you receive light from another source,

since you rise high in the sky
while many people watch,

since you receive life again
even though your body dies,

since you remove the darkness of the world
with your light,

since you conceal your vast form
in a round white shape,

since you bear a blemish,

since those who read stars seek you,

since you are appropriate for supplicants/night blossoms,

and since the hero of my poem,
the Lord born of a virgin
who is conceived through the Holy Spirit,
is like you,

Moon in the beautiful sky,
you should quickly agree
to play joyously and happily
with the one who is entwined with Tamil poetry,
flowing like a waterfall.

Moon, come to play.

IPPT 61: *The Poet's Exegesis*

1. *Receiving light from another source*
moon: from the sun
Lord Jesus: from the Holy Father

2. Rising high in the sky while many people watch

moon: At the sea harbor many people watch each white moon rising on (full moon) day.

Lord Jesus: On the fortieth day after he returned to life, many people came to see him ascend into the sky (Luke 24:51; Mark 16:19).

3. Receiving life again even though the body died

moon: appearing again after the dark moon (new moon)

Lord Jesus: returning to life on the third day after death (Revelations 1:18, 2:8)

4. Removing the darkness of the world with your light

moon: removing outer darkness

Lord Jesus: removing inner darkness

5. Concealing your vast form in a round white shape

moon: making it appear that he has a round white form, when in truth his form is a large planetary sphere

Lord Jesus: hiding his large body in the round white wafer of communion

6. Bearing a blemish

moon: bearing the blemish called "hare"

Lord Jesus: his body bearing the stains (sins) of the world (1 Kings 2:24)

7. Those who read the stars seeking you

moon: Those who do celestial research for prediction (astrologers) seek to calculate the waxing moon and waning moon.

Lord Jesus: Those who watched the sky (shepherds) in the eastern direction sought him at birth.

8. Being appropriate for supplicants/night blossoms [pun]

moon: appropriate for making the night-blossoming lotus bloom

Lord Jesus: appropriate even for poor people

When asked why he added the extensive gloss at the end of his verse, Cellatturai answered, "I can't convey fully precisely what I want to convey if people don't understand." His extensive references to the Bible enable readers to find the exact passage to which he refers, if they would like to savor the ironies of his puns. Non-Christian pillaittamil fans can also appreciate how deftly he has packed his comparisons between the moon and Jesus into this short verse.

Cellatturai also makes his poetry attractive to readers by linking Christian imagery with the glories of the Tamil heritage. In addition to doing so by combining the moon topos with the idea of Christ as the light of the world in the Gospel of John, he also describes how the sounds of Tamil and divine compassion overflow with sweetness (verse 36). In another poem he even envisions a tottering Jesus clasping the hand of Mother Tamil, Tamil envisioned as a mother (verse 70). With such poetic strategies, he draws his reader into his religious vision by linking Jesus with Tamil literary culture.

Verse 31 provides the clearest example within the poem of "Tamilizing" the depiction of Jesus. This verse consists of a poetic conceit that idealizes play and the surprises of the natural world. The verse depicts Baby Jesus in a rural setting, observing the events around him. When he sees an irritated cock digging for pearls, the toddler rips his string of pearls from his neck and tosses them at the cock. The rest of the verse traces the result this single action sets in motion. One pearl hits a ripe mango, which plunges into the pond and throws up drops of water. When the peacock, which loves to prance about in the monsoon, sees the water, he mistakes it for rain and begins to dance. Baby Jesus views its performance with glee and claps his hands in appreciation.

The image that Cellatturai chose for the front cover of his book, based on this verse, may be seen as emblematic of his larger enterprise. It depicts a small baby dressed and bejeweled in the traditional Tamil style (necklace, a jeweled garland in his hair, tinkling anklets, arm bands, and an auspicious mark in the middle of his forehead), watching a cock and a peacock on a lush green bank near a mango tree. Cellatturai told me that he deliberately chose a Tamil landscape with Tamil features. Jesus looks Tamilian, not Mediterranean, Semitic, or European, and brings to mind Baby Kṛṣṇa. Even more striking, however, is the baby's resemblance to Murukaṉ—especially because a peacock stands prominently in the middle of the drawing. The peacock appears often in Tamil poetry as the vehicle of youthful Murukaṉ, a deity who is especially popular in South India. As Clothey notes, Murukaṉ is considered the quintessential Tamil deity.[13]

Cellatturai remarked that he placed Baby Jesus near the peacock because it would link his God with a familiar Tamil figure. This cover picture can be seen then as encapsulating a major motivation of Cellatturai's poem: to indigenize Jesus by envisioning him as a Tamil baby, through the use of a Tamil literary genre. To insure that his composition reached his intended audience, he made it accessible through annotation and familiar poetic conceits.

5. *Jesus and the Peacock*. Cover of *Iyēcupiran̲ Piḷḷaittamil̲* by Ci. Cantiran̲ (sketch by Brian Meggitt; original in the collection of the author).

IPPT 5 (protection 5)

Addressed to God the Father

Manna from heaven
and cool water from the mountain
you gave to people
as soon as they asked.

Descending from heaven
taking form on earth
Jesus was born
as the Son of Mary.

The Holy Child from heaven,
bless him with goodness in life
and the arts,
beautiful in form.

Shower from heaven
a rain of flowers,
O God worshipped
by all who live.

---

manna: The typological treatment of manna and Jesus implies that the coming of Jesus fulfills the Old Testament covenant. This verse follows a standard pattern in Christian exegesis of linking a salvific deed recounted in the Hebrew scriptures with the redemption through Jesus depicted in the Gospel.

a rain of flowers: The celestials in heaven are believed to send a downpour of blossoms when an especially auspicious event takes place on earth.

IPPT 31 (clap 1)

A cock pecks out pearls
from a heap of spilled emeralds.
Peering, he stands tall and dissatisfied,
scratching them with his feet.

Seeing this, you drive him away,
hurling the strand of pearls from your neck.
Then you happily clap your hands.

As the strand hits him, its pearls fly off
and snap the stalks of a bunch of ripe mangoes.
When the mangoes fall in the pond,
water scatters.

A peacock with brilliant eyes in its tail
stays in the cool grove.
He thinks the drops are rain from the sky
and dances.

Seeing his mistake, you clap your soft hands
and rejoice.

Our Lord the color of radiant burnished gold,
please clap your hands.

Our Lord, who is a storehouse that opens with a knock,
please clap your hands.

Seeing his mistake: According to Indian poetic convention, peacocks dance when monsoons come.
opens with a knock: Reference to Luke 11:9–10.

IPPT 36 (clap 6)

There are so many atoms in a fraction
of one eight-hundredth of a split sesame seed!

There are so many wide worlds far far away
that we cannot reach, no matter how we try!

How is it that the binding force of electrons changes,
and electricity flows?

How does the black bee live inside the oṭṭu *mango nut*
and still find food to nourish itself?

How does flowing water change state
into steam and snow?

How did the radiant ascetic
come here and live?
Is it easy to explain?

You, whose Father holds the wealth of flowing Tamil,
clap your hands!

You, whose sweet tender words of Tamil resonate,
clap your hands!

---

radiant ascetic: Kōlamātavan, literally, "handsome great ascetic," is a term for Lord Jesus. The suffering of Jesus on the cross is interpreted as a form of *tapas,* "penance." Acts of intense asceticism are said to generate an attractive glow from the heat *(tapas)* they produce so Jesus is called radiant.

IPPT 63 (moon 3): difference

You look like a pearl,
but a single smile from my Master surpasses that.

You rise high in the sky,
but have you ever crossed the sky
and seen lofty heavens like my Lord?

You get smaller when your form shrinks,
but my Master has never decreased like you.

You appear in one direction and disappear in the opposite one,
but he defeats you by going in all eight directions.

Only half of the time you wander
and then you remove the darkness outside,
but all the time, he remains inside us.

Don't you know his nature is superior to yours?
Why do you still hesitate?

With this young offshoot of God,
joined with budding and flowering Tamil,
Moon, come to play.

With the Son of God,
seated on the right side of Gracious God,
Moon, come to play.

---

eight directions: The eight compass points.

young offshoot of God: Literally, a leaf bud of God. The little child is compared to the tender, soft, beautiful bud of a leaf. The child is also linked with the tenderness and richness of the Tamil language, which has grown and flourished.

IPPT 66 (moon 6): giving

Curing the sickness that afflicts us,
driving out the demons who seize us,
destroying all our misery,
He is the Lord.

His touch cures the hunchback,
the blind, and the deaf.
Praising him enough
for the deeds he can perform is difficult.

A woman who suffered never-ending sickness was cured
the moment she touched the end of his robe.
With one hand, he raised the officer's daughter.

When you touch his body, he will remove your blemish.
Who will be your companion as you orbit?
Choose the company of the Pure One.

Is there any relish equal to the pleasure
of touching his radiant, shining body
treasured in the minds of the pure ones?

With the child of the Lord who gives eternal life,
come to play.

With the son of God,
seated at the right side of gracious God,
Moon, come to play.

Scriptural references provided by the poet at the foot of the page:

Casting out spirits—Matthew 8:28–34, Mark 5:1–20, Luke 8:26–39

Healing the hunchback, blind, and deaf by his touch—Luke 7:22

Ending the long illness—Mark 5, Luke 8

Raising the officer's daughter with a touch of the hand—Mark 5, Luke 8

The Lord who gives eternal life—John 6:68

IPPT 76 (little house 6)

Our Mother is your mother.
Our Father is your father.
You are our precious soul, right?
In our world, who else is kind?

You said you are the salt
in the surging ocean waters.
You declared you are the shining light.

We simple ones want to place
soft white rice in your mouth.

Come, we'll play in the little houses,
fixing them with fine sand from the Kavery River.

Our Lord and our King
with a straight scepter,
don't destroy our little houses.

Holy one who flows with clear honeyed Tamil,
don't destroy our little houses.

---

your father: Since Christians view God as father and the Virgin as mother, all people are children of these parents. So these girls tell Baby Jesus that he is their brother and should not knock down their little houses.

salt . . . shining light: Biblical references from Matthew 5:13–14 and the Johannine "I am the light of the world."

King with a straight scepter: In classical Tamil tradition, a king with a straight scepter rules fairly. A king's scepter is said to become crooked when he acts unjustly.

CHAPTER EIGHT

POETRY OF CULTURAL NATIONALISM

THE VAST MAJORITY of pillaittamils are religious texts composed by authors affiliated with established religious communities.[1] In the first quarter of this century, however, some poets wrote pillaittamils not to express institutionalized religious devotion but to articulate and praise selected "secular" political figures and ideologies. By 1925 a pillaittamil to Mohandas Gandhi appeared, followed by several others to him over the years. Then came a pillaittamil to Bharati, the nationalist Tamil poet, and another to C. Rajagopalachari, one of Gandhi's most influential supporters in South India. In an-other arena, as appeals for the assertion of regional, especially Tamil, identity won people's devotion, several poets composed pillaittamils to honor people and precepts connected with South Indian identity.[2]

This chapter presents translations and analyses of two such poems connected with what scholars have labeled "cultural nationalism," which I define as a social movement in which a particular cultural or linguistic group sees itself as a separate nation, even though legally it belongs to part of a much larger nation-state.[3] The first pillaittamil discussed below, addressed to Tamil (culture/language) personified as a mother, appeared in print on the occasion of a Tamil conference held in 1981. In the second pillaittamil, poet Mu. Singaravelu lauds E. V. Ramasami, the founder of the Dravida Kazhagam, an association that attacked brahminical privilege in Tamilnadu, preached social equality, and sought to undermine Hindu beliefs and ritual practices.

Although these poems demonstrate formal continuities with earlier pillaittamils, such as the theme of childhood and the ten-paruvam structure, they exhibit major ideological differences. The poem to Tamil as mother, I argue, reflects the conference's concern with glorifying and "classicizing" Tamil culture while simultaneously aiming to constitute an identity that includes Tamil-speakers affiliated with different religious and social communities. The second pillaittamil is addressed to "Periyar," a title of respect meaning "Great One" that was given to E. V. Ramasami. Although Ramasami advocated atheism and expressed contempt for religion, the pillaittamil's composer, Singaravelu, uses nonreligious equivalents to the religious features of other pillaittamils. For example, he depicts veneration of reason instead of deities, and lauds acts of political protest instead of worship. In the two poems discussed in this chapter, the pillaittamil has been appropriated as a frame within which to expound political messages.

A Conference and a Pillaittamil

Tamiḻ Aṉṉai Piḷḷaittamiḻ (henceforth *TAPT*), addressed to Mother Tamil, was commissioned, composed, and disseminated as part of the festivities for the Fifth International Tamil Conference, which took place in Madurai, South India, 4–10 January 1981. *TAPT* reduces the nuanced complexity of pillaittamil paruvams to a set of envelopes stuffed with praise for a highly selective picture of "Tamil culture." The motivation for assembling its verse, the criteria for publication, and intended audience reveal how the poem seeks to reconstruct Tamil culture through identification with a glorious and ancient Tamil past.

The Fifth International Tamil Conference combined a seminar, involving a small number of academics, with a cultural celebration of Tamil culture in which thousands of people from all over Tamilnadu participated. The scholarly papers given at the host institution, Madurai Kamaraj University, were only a tiny portion of an event that included elaborate illumination of public monuments, an exhibition ground filled with displays that extolled the glory of the ancient Tamil past, huge public debates, and an enormous parade filled with floats featuring cultural heroes and characters from Tamil epic narratives. Copies of the magazine that contained *TAPT* were freely distributed as souvenirs during the conference.

The unusual circumstances of *TAPT*'s composition grew directly out of its role in the Fifth International Tamil Conference, which

6. *Tamil Tay,* as a Child and with Palmleaf Manuscript. Souvenir, Fifth International Tamil Conference (photograph by Joseph Romano).

aimed to include as many, and as many kinds of, notables as it could. First, *TAPT* is the only pillaittamil known to me that was written as a joint venture. Eleven poets composed the work, with each one contributing two, three, or four verses. A number of these authors were relatively popular poets. Several had composed lyrics for film songs, and others had written poetry for political magazines. None of the poets had established reputations as pillaittamil writers. Instead, they mostly wrote so-called free verse, a kind of poetry quite different from highly stylized and metrically restricted genres such as pillaittamil.[4] Second, the compilers of the pillaittamil enlisted a woman, Saundara Kailasam, to compose the verses for one paruvam. Remarkably, these are the only pillaittamil verses that I have found written by a woman—despite the fact that most pillaittamil poetry is spoken in the maternal voice.

The overall format of *TAPT* also departs from the traditional norms. As we have seen, the "standard model" pillaittamil usually contains between 101 and 103 verses. According to the prescriptions for the genre, the protection paruvam usually contains nine or eleven verses (and may be preceded by a couple of prefatory verses). The vast majority of pillaittamils contain ten verses in each paruvam other than the protection paruvam. Even when a pillaittamil contains fewer than ten verses in each paruvam, usually each nonprotection paruvam contains the same number of verses: traditionally an auspicious odd number such as one, three, five, or nine.

In contrast, *TAPT* contains a peculiar number and grouping of verses: two verses in most paruvams, three in the lullaby paruvam, and four in the moon paruvam. In the introduction to the poem, the editors of the magazine *Tamiḻaracu* (Rule of Tamil), in which the poem appeared in time for distribution at the conference, wrote frankly about the reason for the unique number of verses. They claimed they lacked adequate space in their magazine for a pillaittamil of the usual length. In a striking departure from the layout of most pillaittamil publications, their text is profusely illustrated with drawings of Baby Tamil, the nursemaids who care for her, victorious kings from ancient Tamil history, and the banners of the three ancient Tamil kingdoms. At least two illustrations appear on each page. Thus, the decision of the magazine's editors seems to indicate that the need for visual images overrode the necessity for a pillaittamil of traditional length.

The poem's focus on Mother Tamil paralleled her major role in the conference. Narrowly conceived, Mother Tamil stands for the Tamil language, but the symbol has been broadened to stand for Tamil culture as a whole, represented as a maternal and nurturing female. Elaborate veneration of Mother Tamil figured widely in conference programs and culminated the events of the conference. As Norman Cutler notes, "The featured program for the last day was a spectacular procession of floats depicting legendary characters and authors of Tamil literature, some of the giants of Tamil scholarship, and finally Mother Tamil herself."[5]

Constructing Tamil through Poetic Design

THE POETS OF *TAPT* provide many (sometimes contradictory) visions of Mother Tamil. First and foremost, *TAPT* portrays her as mother of Tamilians. As Sumathi Ramaswamy's analysis of the development of the concept of Mother Tamil aptly puts it, Mother Tamil is the "apotheosis of the Tamil language as founding mother, sovereign queen, and guardian deity of the Tamil culture and its community."[6] Second, due to the requirements of the pillaittamil genre, the poets praise this mother as a young child. Third, the distinction between the Tamil language, specific works of Tamil literature, moral qualities attributed to Tamil society, and a Tamil "worldview" have been blurred. Given all of the maternal, infantile, linguistic, literary, historical, and cultural imagery, as well as the many poets who contributed to the text, it is not surprising that no consistent view of the extraordinary child emerges.

Or, it might be more appropriate to say that various poets envision this hybrid figure in a number of different, but related, ways. For example, in one verse, Mother Tamil is said to *be* Tamil literature and poetics: "You are the riches of grammar and literature" (verse 18). Another stanza of a different verse identifies her with Kaṇṇaki, the great Tamil heroine of the ancient epic *Cilappatikāram* (verse 12). Several verses portray Mother Tamil as a muse, inspiring Tamil poets to greatness (verse 3), and another verse addresses her as "Tamil who nourishes intellect and grace" (verse 21). In yet another place, she is identified with the goddess Sarasvatī, traditionally the patron of the Tamil arts, who is said to "walk on the tongue" of a poet (verse 22). Other writers give her a more active role as advocate and ambassador for Tamil literature, one declaring that she "searched out and bestowed literary texts" (verse 3), another that she "made many [Tamil] poets known to the world" (verse 7), and a third that she enabled the morality expounded in Tamil ethical texts to rule the world (verse 18).

A few verses relate directly to childhood and portray Mother Tamil as a young girl growing up under the protection of the poets who composed classical Sangam literature (verse 3)—a striking image, since this classical poetry is the earliest Tamil literature extant. Yet another verse notes that although many poets helped to rear her, religious writers enabled her to mature into a fully developed woman. This image expresses the idea that postclassical texts, most of which were religious ones, helped to expand the range and subtlety of the Tamil language. These images of the youth and development of Mother Tamil can be seen as part of the poets' efforts to envision tangibly the abstract entity Tamil as a little girl growing into a woman.

Although conceptions of Mother Tamil differ, all poets stress her special relationship to Tamil culture. It was during the late colonial period that the sociopolitical category of non-Brahmin was related to the notion of authentic Tamilness and a pre-Aryan civilization. With the selective reinterpretation and glorification of the incidents portrayed in ancient Tamil literature came the impetus to foreground a Tamil term that would convey the meaning of "civilization" and "culture." The term used to denote "culture," *paṇpāṭu*, seems to be a fairly recent usage; it does not appear as a noun in the index to classical Tamil poetry, the standard lexicon for Tamil, the dictionary of Dravidian cognates, or the dictionary by Fabricius.[7] Etymologically, the neologism derives from *paṇpu*, a noun with a wide semantic range, whose core meanings are "nature," "[good] quality," and "suitability." From these connotations, the related noun *paṇpāṭu* was coined to denote "culture" or "civilization."

Consider how one of *TAPT*'s poets, Nārā. Nācciyappaṉ, uses the term in the following verse to constitute what he believes to be the culture and civilization of Tamil:

TAPT 8 (clap 1): addressed to Mother Tamil

A poet advises an elder and younger brother
not to fight and shed blood on the battlefield.
That is your beautiful culture.

Donors lovingly bestow heaps of lavish prizes
upon impoverished poets who give rhythm and melody.
That is your culture.

If people have swerved into error
they give up their lives to set things straight.
That is your sweet culture.

Vibrant leader of that lineage,
clap your hands.

Tamil daughter famed as a virgin,
clap your hands.

The poet highlights several incidents and values which, to him, constitute the essence of Tamil "culture" *(paṇpāṭu)*, an essence characterized by refinement and actions of the highest moral tone. Addressing Mother Tamil throughout the verse, he begins by lauding her culture through which a bard is inspired to dissuade two brothers from going to war, thus encouraging the pursuit of peace. The famous classical poem to which he refers relates the bard's successful efforts to avoid war between royal brothers;[8] Nācciyappa<u>n</u> highlights that incident and identifies such attention to the bonds of kinship as a distinctive component of Tamil culture.

Tamil culture, according to Nācciyappa<u>n</u>, also includes the exemplary actions of the many patrons celebrated in classical Tamil poetry for their generosity to traveling bards. Dependent for their livelihood upon the largesse of royal donors, bards move from court to court, reciting and giving moral advice. In a good realm, if gifted poets write pleasing and creative verse, a king bestows large gifts upon them. So this stanza celebrates both the quality of bardic poetry and the generosity of kings as constituents of Tamil culture.

Even if a king unknowingly swerves from the path of honor, suggests Nācciyappa<u>n</u> in the third stanza, he will sacrifice to return to the honorable path. The poet refers to the narrative climax of the ancient epic *Cilappatikāram,* in which a Pandiyan king discovers that he has unfairly executed a man accused of stealing the queen's anklets. When the victim's wife confronts the king with clear evidence of his error, he gives up his own life to restore the honor of his dynasty. The foregrounding of this incident identifies honor as a key Tamil virtue. The refrain of the verse links the three examples of Tamil culture (avoiding bloodshed between brothers, giving generously to bards, and sacrificing one's life) to Mother Tamil, but does so in a multivocal way. The poet describes her as heroine or leader *(nāyaki)* of her family, suggesting that she embodies the values of Tamil culture so evident in ancient Tamil country, as perceived by the poet. The language of kinship evokes suggestive emotions. She may be Mother Tamil, but the pillaittamil presents her as a young child. The poet labels this "mother" *kumari,* which means both "virgin" and "youthful one." As virgin, she is the young, pure one fit for praise. The use of the term emphasizes how her sexual chastity protects the purity of her lineage. Her youthfulness reminds the reader that she has the potential to continue to make her lineage flourish.

The works cited in Nācciyappa<u>n</u>'s verse as proof texts all come from the corpus of what has been labeled "classical" (Sangam) literature, texts dated to the early centuries of this millennium and considered some of the finest Tamil poetry ever written. In assessing several literary texts about Mother Tamil, Ramaswamy notes how they participate in an "effort to construct the 'classicism' of Tamil."[9] In his analysis of the topics of the papers presented at the Fifth International Tamil Conference, Cutler notes the high percentage that deal with ancient Tamil civilization and suggests that this indicates that "Tamils are determined to prove to themselves and to others that their linguistic and cultural heritage compares favorably with the great civilizations of world history."[10] Also noteworthy is that Nācciyappa<u>n</u> refers to classical poetry from the sphere of "outer" (public, courtly, and war) poetry, as opposed to "inner" (love) poetry. From this literary corpus thought to define the political realm, he extracts a sense of exemplary behavior identified with Tamil culture for his reading public.

The conference organizers self-consciously defined "Tamil culture" as encompassing the many religious communities in Tamilnadu. This "ecumenical" spirit of the conference is mirrored in *TAPT.* Although some of the construction of identity in South Asia focuses on belonging to a single religious community, the organizers of the Tamil conference defined Tamil culture in a way that included all the major Tamil-speaking religious communities in the region. Thus, the conference emphasized the inclusive, rather than exclusive, nature of its intended audience.[11]

This desire for inclusiveness helps explain why a number of the *TAPT* poets focus upon Tiruvalluvar's *Tirukkuṟaḷ* (dated ca. 450–550 C.E.), a collection of couplets about how to live a virtuous life. Called an "ethical text" or "wisdom literature," and described as didactic, spiritual, or moral, it has no strong sectarian markers. Thus, it should not surprise us that the organizers of the Tamil conference paid special attention to the text. As Cutler comments, "perhaps the most representative emblem of the conference and of all that it stood for was the *Tirukkural,* a compendium of aphorisms on virtue in domestic and public life. While scholars generally favor the view that its author Tiruvalluvar was a Jain . . . this work is ecumenical in spirit. Consequently, modern day Tamils have adopted *Tirukkural* as *the* classical statement of Tamil cultural values."[12] Because *Tirukkuṟaḷ* is not seen as the exclusive property of any single religious community, as were many later Tamil religious works, the conference organizers could foreground it as an appropriate symbol for Tamils of all religious persuasions.

The conference as a whole, and this pillaittamil in particular, strove to project an inclusive definition of Tamil culture. Although the majority of Tamilians are Hindu Śaivites, in *TAPT* one finds specific mention of Vaiṣṇavite Hindu literature (verse 13), a famous Muslim patron of Tamil poetry (verse 11), and the Jain contribution to Tamil literature (verse 23). The pillaittamil carefully alludes to both male and female poets; even though the former dramatically outnumber the latter, *TAPT* makes a point of listing Auvaiyār and Āṇṭāḷ in prominent places. One also finds mention of the greatness of modern poets such as Bharati (1882–1921) and Bharatidasan (1891–1964) in contexts that stress the longevity and continuity of Tamil literature.

The pattern of appropriating "culture" as a symbol of identity reaches farthest when Tamil culture comes to be seen as encompassing the entire South Indian region. Many scholars argue that an old form of Tamil was spoken in three ancient kingdoms of South India. The kings of Chola country, sporting a tiger emblem on their war banners, ruled over the Thanjavur area. The Cheras, with their banners bearing the image of a carp, prevailed in southwestern India. The Pandiyan kingdom, whose banner emblem was a bow, was centered in Madurai. Frequent references to the three kingdoms and their banners occur throughout *TAPT,* as the rhetoric of the Tamil conference attempted to reappropriate Tamil's former dominance by identifying with these ancient far-flung kingdoms, instead of the limitations of the modern state of Tamilnadu.[13]

As one consequence of this encompassing tendency, the phrase "Tamil Culture" often becomes so broad that it fosters vagueness and even poetic banality. Consider, for example, verse 11, translated below. There the poet, Maturai Vāṇaṉ, asks Mother Tamil to heap kisses on him so arts will flourish, dreams will be fulfilled, Tamil Culture will be immortalized, and poets will receive inspiration; then flowers, rivers, waterfalls, and birds will all sing. This verse lacks both overall coherence and sophisticated maneuvering within the paruvam structure. Other than the mention of the banner emblems of the three ancient Tamil kings, the verse contains little specificity. Although the refrain identifies this verse as part of the paruvam asking for a kiss, the poet has done little more than use the pillaittamil structure as a frame in which to insert hackneyed sentiments that will sound universal and inclusive.

One notable exception to this pattern of blandness and overall poetic incoherence occurs in a moon verse using the threat of punishment *(taṇṭam).* For nearly half a century, large numbers of Tamil speakers united around a key ideological and political issue: they opposed the imposition of Hindi as the official national language of India in government offices, schools, and other public venues. In verse 17 (translated below) poet Pulamaippittaṉ likens the moon to the Hindi language because, he claims, Hindi speakers are so arrogant; like them, the moon continues to stay high in the sky, even though he has been invited to come play with Mother Tamil. The emotional center of the verse lies in the section that identifies the opponents of Hindi as Mother Tamil's young tiger cubs, who spilled their blood in order to save her. "They rose in anger, shaking the earth," says the poet, warning the moon that he will meet the same fate if he does not become a playmate for her. Stressing the passionate and fierce commitment of these young men to Mother Tamil, the poet envisions the moon's body riddled with holes unless he agrees to cooperate. The rhetorical momentum of this verse comes from uniting against an external threat, a threat to one's mother.

A Hero Inspires a Poet

BOTH PILLAITTAMILS ANALYZED in this chapter express antagonism toward North Indian culture, but *TAPT* celebrates Tamil culture in general, while the second pillaittamil celebrates a single figure within the movement for South Indian cultural nationalism. E. V. Ramasami, whose followers gave him the honorific title of "Periyar," meaning "Great One," is praised by this name in *Periyār Piḷḷaittamiḻ (PPT)*. E. V. Ramasami's admirers credit him with giving many non-Brahmins in Tamilnadu the ability to question accepted religious doctrines, as well as ways of developing forms of self-respect that transformed their lives. The author of *PPT,* Mu. Singaravelu, counts himself as one of the people touched by the ideas and charisma of Ramasami.

E. V. Ramasami, and several notable contemporaries in a series of sociopolitical movements in Tamilnadu, built an ideological framework upon colonial linguistic theories that identified two distinct families of languages, Dravidian and Aryan, functioning in India from ancient times. Extending the dichotomy from language families to cultures, ideologues condemned Aryan domination over Dravidians. They argued, with E. V. Ramasami as one of their most outspoken and well-known leaders, that Dravidians (that is, those who spoke the Dravidian languages of Tamil, Kannada, Telugu, and Malayalam) had been conquered and humiliated by Aryans, who came from the north to subdue them. Members of the Dravida Kazhagam (DK), the association that functioned as Ramasami's political and cultural base, claimed that Aryans had used Hindu religious prescriptions that upheld the privilege of Brahmin priests to denigrate Dravidians as low caste, impure, and despicable.[14] Ramasami encouraged his followers to embrace the path of Rationalism and study so they would not be dependent upon Brahmins for knowledge and so that they could raise their status to achieve independence and success.

Born in 1940, the composer of this pillaittamil, Singaravelu, grew up during the years when Ramasami drew huge crowds to his public speeches throughout Tamilnadu. In my interview with Singaravelu, he interpreted his own life according to the views of history, culture, and religion propounded by Ramasami.[15] Recalling that his father had purchased a house in an old Brahmin compound *(agrahāra)* of Coimbatore when Singaravelu was a young boy, he tells of how his neighbors denied him entrance to their homes, would not touch him, and called him "Shudra (low caste) boy." He emphasized that, in the school he attended, the teachers were Brahmins and they saw to it that all the scholarships went to Brahmin boys.

Singaravelu had no hope of changing the situation until he entered seventh standard (equivalent to junior high school in the United States) and took a Tamil class with a teacher who believed in the ideas of Ramasami. During language study period, his teacher said to the class, "All the Aryastanis (people of the Aryan land) and Pakistanis (people of the Pure [Muslim] land), go away! The remaining Dravidastanis (people of the Dravidian land), stay in class." So Brahmin students left to study Sanskrit and Muslim students went to Urdu class. Then the teacher explained to the remaining students that Periyar E. V. Ramasami had created a path for them to improve their situation in life and develop self-respect. He proclaimed that Ramasami was the only one who had an answer to the situation of the oppressed, suppressed, and depressed classes; arguing that the current social situation of Dravidians derived from the domination of Aryan outsiders, Ramasami urged Dravidians to liberate themselves through education, rejection of superstition, and demands for equal treatment.

Singaravelu testifies to the "miraculous effect" of Ramasami's views. He says that they helped him to do much better in his studies, and eventually he won first place in his class, usurping the position from a Brahmin boy who held it previously. Years later when Singaravelu was invited to attend the Poet's Symposium held in honor of E. V. Ramasami's Birth Centenary, he conceived the idea of writing a poem about Ramasami. Remembering how much he loved reading Kumarakuruparar's *MMPT* (see chapter 4 of this book) when he studied Tamil literature in college, he decided to write a pillaittamil. Now himself a college teacher, he returned home from work each day, drank his coffee, and wrote ten verses a day for ten days to produce *PPT*.[16]

Rationalism as Ideological Centerpoint

In addition to his Dravidian/Aryan theory of history, Ramasami also promoted "Rationalism." By this term he referred not to some Weberian sociological construct, but to views of religion embraced by thinkers such as Voltaire, Lenin, and Ingersoll. Ramasami attacked religion as a form of superstition and mystification that kept people dependent upon priests and ritual, rather than allowing them to develop their own intellect and power. Dismissing the idea of supernatural beings as something that only fools would accept, Ramasami proclaimed himself an atheist. In the context of his critique of religion, he lambasted Hindu religious texts such as the *Laws of Manu*—a Sanskrit compendium (compiled ca. 200 B.C.E. to 200 C.E.) of laws that sets out caste duties and tells of the punishments that befall those who deviate from prescribed rules.

A poet who writes a pillaittamil in honor of an atheist must decide how to treat the protection paruvam; filling the niches with requests to gods and goddesses would hardly be an option! Instead, Singaravelu chose to invoke protection for Baby Periyar from, respectively, Tamil, the sun, the moon, rain, the stars, the ancient poet Tiruvaḷḷuvar, nature, mankind, and Rationalism. Describing this choice to me, Singaravelu explained, "Since the hero of my pillaittamil is a Rationalist, we can't ask the gods to protect him. Everyone knows that the sun, moon, stars, and human beings are part of nature. Nature gave birth to us and nature protects us, so we must ask nature to protect him [Periyar]." As *pāṭṭiyals* testify, the identity of the first niche in the protection paruvam proves crucial. That the first "protection slot" in Singaravelu's poem falls to "Mother Tamil" proves significant, since traditionally this slot most often belongs to Viṣṇu, the deity characterized by the ability to preserve the baby, its devotees, and the larger world which sustains them.

Singaravelu also gave special attention to the final niche, which he saved for Rationalism, because he wanted to end the protection paruvam in an emphatic way. In this verse, conceptualizing Aryan culture as superstition and religious mystification, he contrasts it with Tamil culture, which he characterizes as fostering intelligent investigation. Praising such independent thinking, the poet identifies Periyar with intellectual bravery: ancient Tamil warriors defeated their foes with weapons on the battlefield, but victorious Periyar defeats his opponents, namely, brahminical orthodoxy and capitalism, by questioning the status quo and arguing that it should be reformed. The poem culminates, significantly, with a request that the Tamil people join their hands together in veneration of Rationalism. Thus, Rationality has become the functional equivalent of a deity for a piece of poetry in praise of an atheist.

According to Ramasami, in addition to rational inquiry, people need practical scientific knowledge to gain self-respect. Singaravelu cleverly foregrounds the importance of knowledge in verse 75 (translated below). As is usual in the paruvam, the girls scold the hero for trying to destroy their houses, but here they also remind Periyar that he was the one who taught them self-reliance. Nourished by the rain of his liberating knowledge, they have learned the rational way to build a house, so that they need not depend upon religiously imposed methods. Traditionally, a proper house for an orthodox Hindu family has a site and orientation dictated by religious prescriptions. In addition, construction must begin at an auspicious time chosen by an astrologer. In contrast, the little girls build their houses creatively and effectively; their enemies, the bastions of orthodoxy, feel threatened by their capabilities. Singaravelu explains, "The little girls have been brought under the system of Rationalism, so they know how to construct their houses. The constructed houses are symbols of Rationalism." Therefore, goes the logic of the verse, Periyar should not destroy them.

Singaravelu emphasizes another crucial aspect of Rationalism—that it empowers all in society, even those in the lowest strata. In verse 69, the poet addresses the moon, offering the gift *(tāṉam)* of Rationalism. Explaining why others have despised the moon, Singaravelu promises that Ramasami will happily share his knowledge and companionship with it. In contrast to others, Periyar evaluates each individual according to merit, rather than accepting social evaluations of certain groups as inherently "low." After carefully assessing the moon's intellect and seeing its wretched state, Ramasami bestows empowering knowledge upon it, for the moon too is entitled to the opportunity to attain self-knowledge through study of science (rather than superstition). Because Ramasami makes such generous and rational judgments, the moon should come and be his companion, argues the verse.

Extraordinary Deeds, Extraordinary Place

SINGARAVELU'S POEM LAUDS some of Ramasami's most notable achievements in the political sphere. If Rationalism functions as an equivalent of the religious belief systems structuring earlier pillaittamils, achievements of political leaders work as the structural equivalent of the mythic deeds attributed to the deities, prophets, and saints praised in religious pillaittamils. In verse 13, for example, Singaravelu notes Ramasami's early involvement in an organization dedicated to the welfare of South Indians (founded by Sir Tyagaraja Chettiyar in 1916); initial prominence in the Indian National Congress party, especially during the years in which its membership in South Indian states grew; later attacks on brahminical dominance within the Congress party; championing of English Rationalists such as Ingersoll; opposition to imposition of Hindi in government offices; and numerous campaigns for removing social inequities in society. In many verses from religious pillaittamils that belong to the sway to and fro paruvam, as does this verse, the poet lists the deity's great deeds that protected his devotees from demons and then requests that he or she sway to and fro (see, for example, *TCPT* 12). Singaravelu's verse lists Periyar's political activities that protect the Tamil masses from Brahmin domination, then asks Periyar to sway to and fro. The rhetorical structure remains the same, but Periyar replaces the deity.

Singaravelu viewed the punishment strategy in the moon paruvam as particularly appropriate to convey the force of Ramasami's liberatory actions. Because for centuries members of high castes had beaten, killed, or coerced those who refused to accept the low place allotted to them in the social hierarchy, Ramasami told his followers that they should carry weapons for protection. In Singaravelu's conversations with me, he stressed Ramasami's militancy and the leader's view that those who dominated the "low castes" should be punished; Periyar always suggested what Singaravelu wryly labeled *taṇṭam* (the term for punishment in the moon paruvam, here in the sense of retaliation) against degrading customs and superstitions, rather than passive acceptance. In keeping with this perceived link between Ramasami's views and the punishment strategy, Singaravelu's verse 70 compares Periyar to a washerman *(dhobi)*. Washermen were considered by high castes to be degraded and defiling, because of their polluting contact with dirt and exudations from the bodies of others. In contrast, Singaravelu praises Periyar for washing away hypocrisy and superstition, just as the washerman cleans away dirt. Singaravelu also notes, "The washerman cleans dirty clothes by beating them on a stone; Periyar beats society by bombarding it with language."[17] As the comic refrain reminds us, even celestial beings fear him because Periyar has shown that they are mere superstitious fictions.

Many religious traditions contain symbolic objects that evoke strong emotions in the hearts of adherents. Singaravelu uses the Dravidian Kazhagam banner as the functional equivalent of a religious visual symbol in verse 26. The black background of the banner symbolizes the oppression of the Tamils while the (auspicious) red *tilak* in its center symbolizes the hope of freedom from domination. The banner also stands for the ideal social and political state, which DK followers hope to attain. Singaravelu lauds the banner as a symbol of the chance for Tamilians to break out of their bondage, which was caused by deluded belief in religious superstitions. Because Ramasami raised the banner, he freed those stooped over from manual labor to stand straight. The banner thus symbolizes the ideal of self-respect.

Just as earlier pillaittamil poets praised the shrine of a deity or the birthplace of a saint (for example, Tiruccentur in *TCPT*), Singaravelu, in verse 83, praises Coimbatore in Kongu District as a place where people exemplify the ideals of Periyar. Coimbatore is known as "the Manchester of South India" because of its many successful cloth mills. Singaravelu celebrates the wonders of industrialism, which he sees as the consequence of Rationalism. He lauds the city as a barren land transformed into a thriving textile center through the adoption of scientific methods and a strong will to transform one's life—

both qualities encouraged by Periyar, the most famous of the sons of Kongu District.[18]

These verses show how Singaravelu uses the structural equivalents of religious beliefs, religious actions, and religious symbolism to praise Periyar's sociopolitical ideology. Praise for a deity has been replaced by praise for a cultural hero, who describes and calls for the end of Aryan oppression and asserts the right to Dravidian self-determination. Instead of a deity conquering a demon, we have a political figure attacking what he sees as superstition and caste oppression.

The two pillaittamils in this chapter contain the maternal sentiments and paruvam structure characteristic of the genre, but their poets have designed them for a different audience than the authors of the religious pillaittamils found in the earlier chapters in this book. Of the two poems, *TAPT* possesses fewer of the characteristics savored by pillaittamil connoisseurs. The lack of rhetorical depth in the use of the paruvam structure could be due to its multiple authorship, those poets' relative lack of familiarity with and commitment to the pillaittamil genre, or the pressure to get it finished before the conference began, among other factors. Its poets have drained much of the conceptual depth of the generic structure away, using the paruvams in a decidedly mechanistic way, so that in most cases only the wording of the refrain indicates their paruvam identity. In those verses, even if the refrain were omitted, it would not make a profound difference in the (minimal) effect the verse has on the reader. The poetry of *TAPT* takes a back seat to the clearly and repeatedly announced agenda of the poem. Therefore only a couple verses appear in the set of translations at the end of this chapter.

Pillaittamils gain their vitality from being rooted in a community of people with shared ultimate concerns: devotees who adore the same deity, followers of a single prophet, or disciples who all venerate a particular guru. By addressing an audience so diverse that it shares little except the ideology constituted in the verses, the poets of *TAPT* fail to do justice to the rich pillaittamil tradition; their poetry is bland and colorless. Singaravelu's pillaittamil to E. V. Ramasami, on the other hand, shows poetic depth and witty maneuvering within literary prescriptions; he has modeled his poem on religious pillaittamils, and he respects the paruvam structure and its conventions, as well as the genre's resources for expressing praise.

TAPT 11 (kiss 2): addressed to Mother Tamil

So that your devotees will rejoice and offer daily praise
to you who are a unique, luscious language
that we earned through asceticism,

so that the many arts will flourish,
so that we can fulfill our dreams,
so that we become immortal and towering,

so that poets will be inspired
with poetry in this beautiful world,
so that the epic will resound eternally,

so that the wave-filled ocean, the blooming flowers,
rivers, mountain waterfalls, birds, forests,
and all will sing a thousand songs,

you who have banners
bearing the bow, carp, and tiger,
heap kisses on me.

You who show the great munificence
of the donor who lay on the funeral pyre,
heap kisses on me.

---

the donor who lay on the funeral pyre: Sītakkāti, the patron, who supported the writer of *Cīṟāppurāṇam,* the great Tamil Muslim epic about the life of the Prophet.[19]

TAPT 17 (moon 4): about Mother Tamil

Even the water-filled clouds in the black sky
can't grasp you.
Why are you so arrogant before the entire world?

If the daughter saw that,
it would wound her heart.

Young warrior cubs of beautiful fair Tamil
watched the dominance of Hindi.
Their hearts throbbed.
The blood in their body boiled.
They rose in anger, shaking the earth,
and made war.

Today you don't know that history.
It's a bad time for you.

Unless you want your weak body
riddled with wounds everywhere,
like the holes in a piece of mesh,
get smart.

With that aṉṟil *bird whose excellence*
is praised by everyone who sees her,
Moon, come to play.

With the one who remains a virgin
even though she's old enough
to become a mother,
Moon, come to play.

If the daughter saw that: If Tamil Tay saw the moon's arrogance.

aṉṟil bird: Poetic name for a woman, like "turtledove" or "honey" in English.

virgin: Although Tamil Tay is viewed as the mother of Tamilians, she is also identified with the South Indian goddess Kanya Kumari, who remains a virgin rather than marrying Lord Śiva. In her virgin form, she is perceived as having great power because of her chastity and self-discipline.

PPT 11 (protection 10)

Asking Rationalism to protect Periyar

Rationalism tells us that asking "why"
is what elevates man.
Asking the question demonstrates
that the six senses exist.[20]

That question has destroyed the bondage
of those who were brought low
when many people called them "slaves."
We join our hands together and worship
the preeminent ideal of Rationalism.

He has destroyed the principle of orthodoxy
because he is committed to challenge,
vowing, "I will stand against it."
He destroyed the power of capitalism,
proclaiming that the principle of communism
will succeed in the universe.

We sing of this victorious one as "king."
This king's voice resounds
throughout Konguland.

May Rationalism protect
the baby with the white beard
who has Rationalism as his principle.

---

white beard: Periyar was known for his long, white beard, his black clothing, his circular glasses, and his walking stick.

PPT 13 (sway to and fro 2)

You were the courageous one
in the group that sought
the welfare of southern people.

Your firmness developed the Congress Party
that became prominent in the south.

You utterly destroyed
the fanatical dominance
of the party by those people.

You mastered and embraced
the British language
as the language of science.

You blocked the ascent of Hindi
that had gained a place
in the life of my people.

You are the king who rises up
if Tamils anywhere suffer.

You, who were enraged
at acts against downtrodden people
and reformed them,
sway to and fro.

You, who always think
about developing fair Tamil,
sway to and fro.

---

those people: Brahmins. They are so contemptible that Singaravelu does not even refer to them by name.

PPT 26 (lullaby 5)

In the sky, the black flag flutters
and the round tilak *at its center flutters.*

They consider this flag like the moon in sweetness,
symbolizing opportunity for the lineage
of ever-increasing Tamil people.

Those who pluck the stingers from scorpions
praise the flag each day, saying
"this flag gives us our courage."

The masses were born as hunchbacks and bonded slaves.
King, you raised the flag that made those stooped over
stand erect.

Great leader of the army of Self-Respect, O Jewel,
talo, talelo.

Enlightener of the deluded Tamils,
talo, talelo.

---

tilak: Round mark painted on the forehead of a respectable woman or child as a symbol of auspiciousness.

pluck the stingers from scorpions: Removing stingers from the scorpion's tail is dangerous because one may get stung in the process. But by removing the stingers, one makes everyone else safe from the scorpion's sting. DK members are likened to such pluckers because they courageously fight to make non-Brahmins safe from Brahmin oppression.

PPT 65 (moon 4)

As for you, moon with streaming light,
while rain clouds thunder
you don't cool things off at all.
But the famous king ignores the cold rain,
always sharing his cool ideals.

Lovely moon, you forget to give cool light
at nightfall one day each month.
But this reliable baby
never forgets to give cool light
each day of the month.

You have the fault of waning daily,
so they call you the moon who wastes away.
But his ideal of Rationalism is like a mountain
so his intellect never wastes away.

With he who calls you on Half-Moon Day,
Moon, come to play.

With he who makes the heavens
and all the other celestial worlds tremble,
Moon, come to play.

---

the famous king: E. V. Ramasami.

Half-Moon Day: According to Hindu tradition, it is an inauspicious day, so it would not be a lucky meeting time. Since E. V. Ramasami considers such beliefs superstition, the poet deliberately invites the moon to come on that inauspicious day, thumbing his nose at believers.

makes the heavens . . . tremble: Saying that a human being makes the heavens tremble means that he is more powerful than any gods. Since Ramasami teaches that belief in gods is just ignorant superstition, he undermines the whole concept of the existence of heavens.

PPT 69 (moon 8)

Periyar sees you, Moon, wandering around
without your own light
using borrowed light
and that handsome one,
who nurtures the world's masses,
gives light to you, saying
"knowledge is your own light."

Since he knows how you waver
and then fall into the dark precious sea
without even your little light,
he comes and even embraces you,
spreading the beloved light
of wonderful Rationalism.

He sees separated lovers
who reproach you as cursed light,
but he appreciates your intellect
on its own merits,
not thinking of you as low.

With one who has assessed your faults
in such ways and knows you,
Moon, come to play.

With the one who makes the heavens
and all the other worlds tremble,
Moon, come to play.

---

without your own light: The moon's light is reflected from the sun.

separated lovers who reproach you: When lovers plan a tryst they hope for a moonless night, so no one will see them as they steal out of their respective homes to meet each other.

PPT 70 (moon 9)

Once there ruled a king
of the virgin Tamil land
who made Kanaka and Vijaya
carry heavy stones on their heads.

Because this man is his descendent,
he quickly drove Hindi out.

He knew that the Aryans
were racial fanatics full of deceit,
so he hated that race.

Enduring all the insults
of the Brahmins who are here,
he steadfastly protected us.

Like a good washerman,
he began to cleanse our minds.

Picking a fight with this great hero
is not an intelligent act.

Before the handsome one beats you,
Moon, come to play.

With he who makes the heavens
and all the other celestial worlds tremble,
Moon, come to play.

---

heavy stones on their heads: This refers to an incident in *Cilappatikāram* where two North Indian kings, Kanaka and Vijaya, insulted two South Indian kings. As punishment, the remaining South Indian ruler forced the insulters to carry to Kerala huge stones for carving an image of Kaṇṇaki.[21]

PPT 75 (little house 4)

You, O cloud, rose in the sky.
From the rain of knowledge you showered
we learned many fresh ideals
and rejoiced.

After bathing in ghats
covered with fine black sand,
we have constructed our little houses
in every front yard
according to the new Rational method.

In the increasingly pervasive
tradition of Self-Respect,
we have tired ourselves
and perturbed our enemies
by constructing houses of sand.

Did we seek you and take refuge in you
in order to have you destroy them?
Don't destroy the little houses
of us little ones.

We have cut the fetters of slavery
and cast them off.
Don't destroy the little houses
of us devotees.

---

ghats: Steps leading down to a river.

PPT 83 (little drum 2)

In all eight directions they call it
the Manchester that brings renown to the south.
Because of Coimbatore's greatness, they praise it
as a desert that became a lush garden
due to the strong will of its people,
and as an industrial center
that astonishes the world today.

Isn't it so marvelous that
even people without respect show wonder?

Because of the Kongu people, full of strength,
precious wealth abounds everywhere
in the many cities of Konguland.

All these things are neither miracles
nor imagination, but modernity
produced by enthusiasm.

Venerated son raised in Konguland,
which people esteem highly,
beat your little drum.

You who came as a son
so fair Tamil could flourish,
beat your little drum.

PART THREE

REFLECTIONS ON PILLAITTAMILS

7. *The Reception of a Pillaittamil.* Sketch of a wall painting in the Mīṉāṭci Temple by Brian Meggitt (original in the collection of the author).

CHAPTER NINE

THE FRUITS OF READING PILLAITTAMILS

OVER THE CENTURIES the pillaittamil genre has attracted many writers and literary connoisseurs. When I asked practicing pillaittamil poets why they found the genre compelling, they recounted the pleasures of composing poems about children while maneuvering within particular paruvams. Their answers corroborate evidence about poetic practices in earlier centuries. Both suggest that the pillaittamil presents poets with a clearly circumscribed subject (the extraordinary child) and a well-articulated poetic structure (the paruvam framework), within which they find challenging opportunities to compose inventively. The paruvam structure offers multiple ways to express devotion to the winsome child, to invoke the aid of particular guardians in the protection paruvam, to plot the defeat of an opponent within the moon paruvam, to excel at sophisticated word play within the kiss paruvam, and much more. The subject matter and paruvams provide a capacious framework for poetic creativity.

In seeking to translate selections from the pillaittamil genre into English, the translator finds that providing an overview of the conventional ten-part structure aids in the process of helping the English reader cross over into the poetic world of the pillaittamil. The paruvam structure can function as a blueprint for both those who have not previously encountered Tamil literature and those familiar with aspects of Tamil literature but unfamiliar with the pillaittamil genre. Nonetheless many challenges remain for translator and reader, because the pillaittamil genre has produced such nuanced and varied poetry. The sampler of pillaittamil translations presented in this volume broadens our understanding of South Indian religiosity in several ways.

First, pillaittamil translations reveal how poets have incorporated the language of domesticity, traditionally identified with women's sphere, into religious poetry. Other genres of devotional poetry have used the language of eroticism to express love for the extraordinary being, imagining the deity as beloved and devotee as lover. In contrast, the poets represented in this book use, for the most part, the language of domesticity, envisioning the extraordinary being as child and the devotee as mother. In the pillaittamil, the imagery of domesticity is not denigrated or marginalized; instead poets deploy it to express a most elevated sentiment—devotional love for a god, goddess, saint, prophet, hero, or heroine. Because male poets express this devotional love by assuming a maternal voice, the genre promotes the phenomenon of cross-speaking, thus raising intriguing questions about the nature of gendered voice within the pillaittamil.

The genre also demonstrates how dramatically poetic structures can influence expressions of praise from different religious traditions. Poets from one community after another adopt the same pillaittamil literary conventions: the Chola court, Śaivas, Vaiṣṇavas, Muslims, Christians, and Tamil ideologues. Praise plays a major role in the cultural life of Tamil literature, and the ten paruvams provide poets with a structure to shape their praise. Thus, exploring pillaittamils prompts some reflections on the cultural construction of praise across community boundaries.

Finally, the translations show how different religious traditions inflect the genre in their own ways. That Hindus, Muslims, and Christians—with differing concepts of divinity, notions of virtuous behavior, and ideas of religious community—avail themselves of the same literary genre suggests the adaptability of a seemingly restrictive format. Viewing the pillaittamil as a multireligious genre suggests we should understand Indian religion as encompassing different traditions, many of which share certain literary modes of expression. Nonetheless, we must note how pillaittamil poets from different communities simultaneously affiliate themselves with other pillaittamil poets and differentiate themselves from other religious communities.

The Pleasures of Capacious Convention

WITHIN TAMIL LITERARY circles, two terms appear often in discussions of the history of poetic works: *pulavar* and *marapu*. The *pulavar*, or "traditional erudite Tamil poet," creates new poetry after immersing himself in the great works of the past. Through initial immersion in older poetry, a poet harnesses the power of *marapu*, "custom, convention, established usage, or practice," in order to create his own literary works. The two terms have been ubiquitous in the discourse of Tamil writers and connoisseurs over the centuries.[1]

Marapu guides the subject matter, the form, and the "arithmetic" of pillaittamil poetry. The subject matter of the poem encompasses both its topic and its addressee: the child. Pillaittamils not only celebrate the conventional phases of childhood, they laud a specific child. In a parallel way, pillaittamils not only possess a clear ten-part structure, the paruvam structure shapes the overall construction of the pillaittamil and forges links between individual verses and the poem as a whole. Conventions not only determine the arithmetic of each poem, the multiplicity of verses in each paruvam grants a poet numerous opportunities to depict, in varying ways, each childhood activity found in a pillaittamil. Finally, poets can call upon conventions even within particular paruvams, such as the niches of the protection paruvam and the four strategies in the moon paruvam.

In addition to the formal aspects (subject matter, poetic structure, numbers of verses, strategies for moon poetry) influenced by established practice, convention has also shaped the public performance and reception of pillaittamils. The legend of the first recitation of Kumarakuruparar's pillaittamil in the seventeenth century shows the extent to which Tamil literary tradition values the idea that pillaittamil poets address the extraordinary child directly. Not only was Goddess Mīṉāṭci the first audience for Kumarakuruparar's poem, but she took on the form in which she was addressed in his poem—a child—when she came to reward him for his superb artistry. Autobiographical evidence about Pillai's *araṅkeṟṟams* also emphasizes particular performance conventions, such as the exchange of witty wordplay, resolving of questions through exegesis, and frequent reference to other poems respected within the tradition. Even a relatively recent ritual, the book-releasing ceremony, displays its own conventions. The invitation to the ceremony indicates how shares of honor are apportioned among prominent guests, as well as how a community of readers formally welcomes a new book into its midst.

In the past, pillaittamil poets grew up in a milieu shaped by respect for the genre's traditions and history. For example, when Pillai's first achievements as a pillaittamil writer were recognized, praise for them took the form of his patron's likening his work to those of earlier pillaittamil poets: Pakaḻikkūttar and Kumarakuruparar. It was through memorization and recitation of past pillaittamils that the novice became steeped in the rhythms, words, and conceits of the genre. Pillai's own students in the monastery learned to savor the nuances of pillaittamils (and other texts) through Pillai's explication of verses. The very monastic calender encouraged periodic celebration of significant pillaittamils: To commemorate major anniversaries in the history of the monastery, monks would hold a feast and republish religious poetry, especially pillaittamils, thus keeping respected poetic texts in the forefront of literary life.

Even though the intensity of monastic patronage of poetry has waned over the decades, the impulse to steep oneself in past pillaittamils remains strong. Cellatturai searched private and public libraries to read every single pillaittamil that he could find, including more than 229 pillaittamils available in the early 1980s. In contrast to the monastic milieu of Pillai's experience, Cellatturai's pillaittamil reading indicates the increasing opportunities to read pillaittamils in addition to the ones composed in one's own religious community. Cellatturai considered it necessary to acquaint himself with every kind of pillaittamil text that had been published within any religious tradition.

Several pillaittamil poets have written self-reflexively about the desired effect of a pillaittamil on its intended audience. One such verse, from Kavi Vīrarākavar's seventeenth-century *Cēyūr Murukaṉ Piḷḷaittamiḻ,* presents the reception of a pillaittamil as a devotional act, as well as an aesthetic pleasure. The verse offers the moon a special gift if it agrees to be a playmate; it will receive the experience of hearing and reading devotional texts—including the author's own pillaittamil:

Cēyūr Murukaṉ Piḷḷaittamiḻ 69

You can recite the Tirumurukāṟṟupaṭai,
which eradicates obstinate cruel karma,
and you can chant the six-letter mantra.

You can attain salvation by praising
the rhythmic poetry of Aruṇakirinātaṉ's Tirupukaḻ
in the temple.

Because your merit has come to fruition
you can catch sight of the Lord of Kaḻukkuṉṟaṉ,
the munificent King of the World.

You can examine the ocean-like Skanda Purāṇa,
the source that recounts his battle with the fierce demon.

You can study the veṇpā *verses*
in praise of this Lord
in the sacred ulā *composed by Kavirāja.*

You can hear the verses of the kalampakam
and the piḷḷaittamiḻ *composed by Kavi Vīrarākavaṉ.*

You can enter the gleaming golden temple and play.
Come to play, Moon.

With handsome peacock-riding Skanda,
who comes from Ceyur, filled with bamboo groves,
Moon, come to play.[2]

The verse offers the moon myriad opportunities to savor the great deeds performed by Lord Murukaṉ, as artfully recounted in various conventionalized poetic genres. By learning to recite the *Tirumurukāṟṟupaṭai,* a guide to the six ancient shrines where Lord Murukaṉ made himself manifest, the moon will gain access to divine power available to devotees at each site. By hearing and lauding Aruṇakiri's *Tiruppukaḻ,* a poem that praises Murukaṉ as the eternally young lover and warrior, the moon will comprehend the true nature of the divine. If he visits Murukaṉ's resplendent shrine in Kaḻukkuṉṟaṉ, he will receive *darśan* (the auspicious sight of the divine that gives blessing to the viewer), thus realizing the consequences of his past good deeds. When he plunges into the vast *Skanda Purāṇa,* filled with stories of Murukaṉ's victories against demons, he will experience the power of the deity. If he immerses himself in the poetry of a pillaittamil, he can win God's ear by reciting mellifluous poetry. Quite specific textual benefits await the moon, according to a text from the very genre, the pillaittamil, mentioned and praised in this verse.

In a wider sense, this moon verse also addresses the connoisseur of Tamil poetry, suggesting that the best gift, not just to the moon but to anyone listening, is the chance to savor devotional poetry. The author even includes his own name and text, "the pillaittamil composed by Kavi Vīrarākavaṉ," among the poetic texts listed in his moon verse because, like the others, it contains descriptions of marvelous deeds of Lord Murukaṉ that prove precious to a listener and bring auspicious blessings.

Audiences and Translations

THE PROCESS OF translation across cultures remains fraught with complexity, especially when translating works from the "Third World" or "the Orient" for readers in the "First World" or "the West."[3] In addition, rendering Tamil into English provides its own particular set of obstacles, as chapter 1 demonstrated. Translation poses even more difficulties when poems draw upon non-Tamil as well as Tamil literary traditions. For example, in Muslim pillaittamils poets have skillfully integrated Persio-Arabic terms and scriptural references into their poetry; thus, translation into English can be seen, at least partly, as translation "once removed," to borrow a kinship term, since an initial process of translation from the Persio-Arabic tradition took place long ago.[4]

Despite these difficulties and others, much of the pillaittamil's character seems to come across in translation, at least partly because of the clarity of its paruvam structure. In order to initiate oneself into the pillaittamil tradition, one learns the paruvams and the conventional conceits and tropes found within them. After encountering them again and again, one feels like a connoisseur fairly soon. In a sense, one could argue that precisely because the structure of the pillaittamil remains so fixed, it facilitates crossing boundaries of audience and language.

Recently, the directors of a local poetry series in a small town in Ohio asked me to read some pillaittamil verses for an evening devoted to poems in translation. At first I demurred, fearing that the references, allusions, tropes, and epithets would make no sense to an audience with little background in Indian literature. When the directors suggested that I start the reading with a summary of the features of the pillaittamil genre and precede my selections by explaining phrases or allusions that would not be clear to the uninitiated listener, I agreed. Although the members of the audience were diverse, they all had experience in thinking about poems and poetics.

My selections came from the little house verses and the moon poetry. When the mother tries to convince the moon to come to earth or the little girls attempt to persuade the young boy not to knock down their sandcastles, listeners appreciated the playfulness of the poetry. The persuasive devices poets use are usually clever, but sometimes they are also fantastical, outrageous, or downright subversive. For example, the idea that a universe-preserving deity would find himself conned by a bunch of little girls into thinking that they only fear that he might dirty his feet, thereby soiling his divine parents' clothing, seems simultaneously amusing and absurdly charming. The notion that the moon's many flaws make it wise for him to submit to the mother's request may seem reasonable, until one realizes that the Lord of the Universe wants the moon to play children's games with him. During the reading, behavior suggested that members of the audience appreciated the witty ways in which different poets dealt with the same paruvam: they broke into laughter at each comic juncture.[5]

A few weeks later I received a poem that had been inspired by hearing translations of moon verses, written by the well-published poet June Goodwin, who had been in the audience on the night of my reading:

Wannaplay?

Yo, moon, have I got a deal for you.

I'm mama to a baby woman
who's got the body of the Buddha
and the cheeks of Betty Boop.
Her play with you would be its own reward.

Come see how my baby's eye-whites
are blue cool as you. Or,
if opposites attract, come melt
your razor rays on her skin
soft as hot solder.

As further inducement
I'll let you scrutinize
a quilt Britt built,
a slice of ocean on the nursery wall
with exotic aquatics unknown to you,

underwater plants, carnival fish
and waves that flutter
like sea anemone arms or
my baby's tongue still
tantalized by her last suck.

Descend soon or I'll trap her hungry howls
in a Pandora box
and pour them in your quiet craters
like an aural pox
of cacophonous peacocks.

Ah moon please,
come cavort with my baby,
come play piccolo and pointillism
on her eyelids, come whisper Melina
so she'll know early who pulls her tides.

Yo, moon, wannaplay?

In her note that accompanied her poetry, Ms. Goodwin made it clear that she did not seek to write in the pillaittamil genre. She did not have the linguistic training to draw upon the resources of the Tamil language for praising a child, nor did she place her poetry within the ten-paruvam structure. Instead, she turned to the moon verse as a situation within which to imagine a lunar playmate for her own extraordinary child, named Melina.

Her verse, filled with word play and alliteration, combines all four traditional moon strategies. After an aside that playing with her daughter should be so wonderful that no other reward need be offered, she makes cases for similarity and then difference. The whites of Melina's eyes and the orb of the moon have the same round shape and color, so they share certain qualities. Or, considering differences, she notes that the moon's cool rays could lose their chill if they warmed themselves on the baby's skin. The poet even makes the moon a special offer; he can savor the beauty of a baby quilt featuring inhabitants of an undersea world to which the moon has never before traveled.[6] If all else fails, the mother threatens the moon with that most exasperating of sounds, multiplied exponentially: the screaming of an angry infant. This verse bespeaks a determined and busy mother. She wants the moon to come, and fast, so she tries one strategy after another, to get a special playmate for her child.

Note, however, that Ms. Goodwin does not idealize her baby daughter. Some pillaittamil poets refer even to the naughtiest baby as charming. Pillaittamil verses sanitize even the drooling of the infant, calling it sweet ambrosia. Some elevate a child's noise to gentle prattle. Living with infants is not like that all the time, as anyone who has taken care of one twenty-four hours a day will know. That other side of childcare—the baby whose screaming, if amplified, could drive the moon crazy—finds its way into a moon verse in a pillaittamil, probably for the first time.

If those unfamiliar with Tamil literature seemed drawn to pillaittamil poetry at the first reading, those who self-consciously sought to preserve their Tamil culture responded with similar enthusiasm a few weeks later in Austin. The Tamil Sangam there, a cultural association composed of university students and Tamil families that have moved from India to the Austin area, invited me to give a reading in conjunction with a scholarly paper I had been invited to present at the university. Several people in the audience knew verses from famous pillaittamils by heart, many were generally familiar with the theme of pillaittamils, and a few had little background in the genre. Again, however, members of the audience were tremendously responsive to the poetry in English. They savored the beauty of Kumarakuruparar's devotional poems to Baby Mīṉāṭci, laughed at the insults in the verse that threatened to churn another moon, smiled at the clever ways the girls tried to outwit the boy in the little house paruvam, and generally relished hearing Tamil poetry through the fresh lens of translation.

The Ambiguities of Cross-Speaking

Many Tamil literati have credited the long popularity of pillaittamils to a fondness in Tamil culture for babies. Those who have seen paintings of infants in Tamil calendar art, shots of toddlers in Tamil television commercials, and affection shown toward offspring in many Tamil households would probably agree that very young children are celebrated in Tamil culture, not only as persons but as symbols of the continuity of family and lineage. The first translation in this book, where the mother calls the baby to nurse at her breast, does indeed suggest that certain pillaittamil verses delight in recounting the affection a parent feels for a child. But delight in children proves too simple an explanation for the complex history of the genre.

Some scholarly theories suggest that we could view the pillaittamil as the product of certain psychological projections based on childhood experiences, or as tools in the service of social pressure to keep women within domestic and subservient roles. For example, the Indian psychoanalyst and scholar Sudhir Kakar argues that certain kinds of devotional poetry create what he calls a "utopia of childhood," which he sees as "based on the assumption that poetic descriptions of the infancy and childhood of Krishna and Rama also contain certain desires that both relate to and derive from the period of childhood."[7] Or, one could argue that because pillaittamils feature mothers' voices, they could be seen as participating in essentializing women as mothers. Cultural critic C. S. Lakshmi has examined the idealization of the mother and the construction of the female body as womb for producing Tamil heroes, tracing the theme from classical Tamil literature to the Self-Respect Movement (begun in 1925 and continuing in various forms to the present day) in modern Tamilnadu.[8] Despite the cogency of each interpretation, however, neither theory proves particularly enlightening about the pillaittamil genre. Babies depicted in the pillaittamil do not usually practice the kind of mischievous acts credited to Baby Kṛṣṇa, and in fact Vaiṣṇava examples turn out to be surprisingly rare in the pillaittamil corpus.[9] Furthermore, most pillaittamils demonstrate relatively little glorifying of the Tamil mother, since the poetry focuses primarily upon the child, the moon, or the little girls. The mother's voice tends to function mainly as a generic literary device.

Furthermore, one would be mistaken to see the image of family life portrayed in pillaittamil tradition as a mirror of Tamil family life, even if such an "essentialized entity" were to exist. Mīṉāṭci's playhouse turns out to be the cosmos, Murukaṉ destroys world-threatening demons as child's play, Baby Muhammad's drum warns of the day of judgment, and Baby Jesus gives eternal life. The paruvam structure presents these cosmic events in a deceptively human-looking set of frames, but if God knocks down little houses, he demolishes more than just a sandcastle. These little babies wield salvific power. The cover of this book, a line drawing of the Śaivite divine family—Lord Śiva, his wife Pārvatī, his elephant-headed son, and Murukaṉ with his peacock, suggests the complex effects of projecting images of human family life upon extraordinary and sometimes awesomely unhuman deities. Their powers and peculiarities often go far beyond human limitations in both their magnitude and creativity.

Some poets seem to delight in the contradictions of certain pillaittamil scenarios. For example, consider the depiction of Tamil Tay, configured as Mother Tamil, in *TAPT.* The poem lauds a maternal construct turned into an infantilized construct, conceived as needing poets and ideologues to protect her from Hindi, perceived as a demonness![10] *MMPT* 37, in which the Baby Goddess rocks her infant son Murukaṉ on her voluptuous thighs, suggests other ambiguities. Is this an acknowledgment of infant sexuality? The result of the merging of childhood activities and adult deeds? Or, the outcome of an erotic component of Tamil poetry that is neither entirely explicit nor entirely absent in the pillaittamil genre? It is hard to determine on what basis one could definitively answer such questions.

To complicate things further, the problematic issue of voice must be acknowledged in interpreting pillaittamil poetry. Precisely whose voices speak in these poems? Initially what many people find so intriguing about the premise of the pillaittamil is male adoption of a maternal voice. In every paruvam except the little house paruvam, the poet assumes the voice of an adult female who expresses affection for a child.[11] In most Tamil families, as in most other cultures, many women are closely linked with the home and with the nurturing and house-maintaining chores that take place within that home. So by writing a pillaittamil, a male poet, at least temporarily, frees himself from writing solely within cultural constructions of masculinity. He can move conceptually across boundaries between male and female into the imaginative space of domesticity.

In a pillaittamil, thus, a male poet appropriates a culturally constructed "feminine" voice and speaks, in a stylized way, as a mother caring for her child. We might call this phenomenon "cross-speaking," using as a model the phrase "cross-dressing." Recently, scholars have begun to study cross-gendered verse as a literary and cultural phenomenon. Two recently commented: "the more we thought about it, the more daring some of its implications seemed. In crossing gender as they create their personae, poets dramatize gender itself."[12] In the case of the pillaittamil genre, however, poets have almost uniformly been male writers taking on a female voice, so the cross-speaking only goes one way. Furthermore, male adoption of an idealized maternal voice proves to be a complex phenomenon with many implications. Diverse facets emerge when one applies different critical perspectives, including the cultural construction of gender roles, the literary history of Tamil poetry, and theological analysis of imagery appropriate for the praise of the divine.

From the perspective of gender as a construct, this male adoption of the female voice can be seen as helping to reinforce societal roles, since males have conceptualized, defined, and preserved the ways in which they let the mother in pillaittamils speak. It is males too, and males only, who enjoy the rhetorical mobility that they attain by taking on a maternal voice. No parallel prestigious literary genre exists in Tamil that enables female poets to take on the voice of a father.

One might also see the genre as affirming the dichotomization of male and female activities because when the male poet takes on a "female" voice, he reiterates the ascription of domestic duties to women.[13] In addition, the genre replicates the hierarchical gender relations between men and women: the male presents his views of what a mother should be, which might explain why the portrayal of the mother in these poems is so generic, idealized, and highly stylized.

An additional perspective on the poet's assumption of a maternal voice emerges if we consider its historical roots in early Tamil literature. From the earliest stratum of Tamil poetry (with origins in ca. the first to the third centuries C.E. and influencing the subject matter of poetry for many centuries to follow), the convention of writing in the voice of a woman has been utilized as one of many rhetorical strategies among the poetic resources of Tamil.[14] Not only women, but all the characters in classical poems of love were portrayed in highly stylized ways, as were the activities in which they engaged. This corpus of poetry encompasses a whole set of dramatis personae, including poems written in the voice of the hero, the heroine, the heroine's girlfriend, the concubine, and the heroine's mother. In these classical love poems, the poet chooses among a number of personae to adopt. Thus, one could see the pillaittamil as a form of poetic specialization. That is, the pillaittamil genre focuses on just one of these dramatic personae, the mother, developing it into a full-fledged literary form.

Equally important is understanding the theological logic of the pillaittamil, which derives from a long tradition of adopting female voices in devotional poems—especially in the poetry to Kṛṣṇa. As one saying goes, in the presence of Kṛṣṇa (a male deity), all of humanity is female.[15] This line of reasoning rests on the assumption that Kṛṣṇa is different from human beings and may make himself manifest to them if he so desires. Within the logic of such a vision of divinity, if one envisions a male deity as one's beloved, then each devotee must imagine himself or herself as a woman. By this line of reasoning, taking on a maternal voice in a pillaittamil would be a way of expressing devotion to a male deity. This explanation makes sense for pillaittamils to Baby Murukan̲, but what about pillaittamils to female deities, of which there are many? Given textual evidence that the female paruvams developed later than the male ones, one could speculate that the convention of the poet taking on a female voice became established in early pillaittamils addressed to deities conceived of as males, turning into a fixed feature of the genre for poems to deities conceived of as females as well.[16] In light of the literary pattern of cross-speaking in pillaittamils, one could consider the adoption of the maternal voice to be a form of religious boundary crossing that enables male poets to draw closer to their object of devotion.

Whatever the theoretical stance one takes toward males assuming the voice of a mother, it is clear that the gender relations that a pillaittamil makes visible are uneven. The male poet has the privilege of temporarily assuming the female voice, without giving up the prestige or family status that he receives at his birth. That does not necessarily mean, however, that the genre prohibits female poets from writing in it. In fact, the pillaittamil may have the potential to subvert cultural constructions of femaleness, if used in a self-consciously canny way. Imagine, for example, a writer breaking down the idealizations of mother and child by using the ten paruvams to describe the boredom of repeated housework or to describe the process of adopting a child. Consider a mother making the ten paruvams a journal of her child's physical and mental development in the first years of its life. Such poetry would bear the distinguishing marks of a pillaittamil, both in subject matter and paruvam structure, but also contribute another perspective to a genre that has long proved capacious.

Praise as Cultural Construction

ESSENTIALLY, THE PILLAITTAMIL deals with two kinds of relationships: a relationship between a devotee expressing love for an extraordinary child, and a relationship between that piece of poetry and the community in which it is grounded. Although some Hindu theologians argue that the erotic relationship between devotee and deity is the most passionate, others see the relationship of parental love *(vātsalya bhāva)* as the most poignant. As one scholar put it, "*Vātsalya bhāva* would appear to represent the quintessence of disinterested loving devotion. The Supreme Lord of the Universe . . . , who inspires awe and fear in people's hearts is thereby concealed in the form of a helpless child who inspires the tenderest care and affection."[17] In a sense, the pillaittamil could be seen as providing the outward forms appropriate for expressing the most tender domestic sentiments. The relationship between the mother and child expresses intimacy and care, but the outward forms provided by the pillaittamil structure give the genre a distance or depersonalized nature that allow it to function as an expression of love not only for a mother of a child, but for all devotees who seek a way to envision their relationship to the ultimate, and extraordinary, child.

This expression of love between mother and child takes the form of a praise poem presented in a community. Even though pillaittamil writers address their poetry to a particular deity, they also write to please other devotees, their donors, and themselves. In order for a laudatory text to convey meaning to the poet's intended audience of devotees, its poetry must fit within cultural norms that define an effective paean. Anthropologist Arjun Appadurai has emphasized the negotiational aspects of praise:

> [P]raise is *not* a matter of direct communication between the "inner" states of the relevant persons, but involves the public negotiation of certain gestures and responses. When such negotiation is successful, it creates a "*community of sentiment*" involving the emotional participation of the praiser, the one who is praised, and the audience of the act of praise. Praise is therefore that set of regulated, improvisatory practices that is one route to the creation of communities of sentiments. . . .[18]

Essentially, to be successful, a pillaittamil must negotiate the involvement of author, addressee, and audience in a literary act of praise.

Appadurai's description of "a community of sentiment" describes remarkably well a visual image based on a central legend in the history of pillaittamils: the scene in which poet Kumarakuruparar recited his poem praising Goddess Mīn̲āṭci before his patron, Tirumalai Nāyakkar, surrounded by his courtiers, in the hall of the temple. As we have seen, while poet, ruler, and courtiers involved themselves in the mellifluousness of *MMPT,* the goddess herself joined the listeners, taking the form of a little girl. The painted image of that moment in which a "community of sentiment" was forged functions as a reminder to each worshipper who arrives at the shrine of Goddess Mīn̲āṭci today that he or she is a part of that ongoing and ever-increasing community defined by a work of devotional poetry.

Information presented about the reception of pillaittamils also testifies to a community's importance in the life of a pillaittamil. We have seen that the *aranke<u>rr</u>am* functions as a way of introducing a work of devotional poetry to people who care deeply about the extraordinary child it praises. The poet recites and explicates his poetry for a body of connoisseurs. At least in the *aranke<u>rr</u>ams* conducted in the monastic milieu (see chapter 5), the poet considers possible objections to his work and, if he refutes them satisfactorily, and if his audience deems his work to be of sufficient merit, his poem passes into the tradition of texts taught and preserved at the monastery. Even though the modern book-releasing ceremony does not have the same continuing power to keep the text in the forefront of a community of readers, it too functions to welcome a piece of poetry into a community of sentiment and put the book in the hands of those who care deeply about the extraordinary child whom the poem praises.

How does a pillaittamil draw upon, create, and reaffirm a "community of sentiment?" A pillaittamil poet who wants to write a sophisticated and resonant poem must be able to draw upon a deep reservoir of material. That reservoir may include (among other features) narratives about the extraordinary being, as well as consorts and relatives, information about the appearance of the extraordinary being, associations with particular sacred sites or family lineages, scriptural references to which the poet can allude, and a set of epithets and formulas of praise. These features, and others like them are "the nuts and bolts of praise."[19] For example, when A<u>n</u>apiyyā praises the Prophet Muhammad, he refers to the narrative of replacing the black stone in the Ka'ba, describes Muhammad's appearance as surrounded with light, calls attention to his identity as a member of the Quraishi lineage, alludes to passages in the Qur'an, and lauds him with epithets such as "the Perfect Prophet."

Within each community represented in Part Two of this book, there are equivalents for these features specific to that tradition. Among the narratives to which poets refer are Hindu stories of demons defeated in battle, Christian tales of Jesus raising the dead and healing the sick, and accounts of E. V. Ramasami challenging the power of the Hindi language. Poetic language about appearance ranges from refrains about Lord Murukaṉ riding astride a peacock vehicle to Jesus at the right hand of God, from depictions of the sacred ash on Saint Cēkkiḻār's forehead to descriptions of Goddess Mīṉāṭci's graceful gait. Poets celebrate the sacred sites of Tiruccentur by the sea, Madurai on the banks of the life-giving Vaigai River, Mecca with its learned and prosperous citizens, and even the industrial city of Coimbatore. Verses laud the Vēḷḷāḷa subcaste, the Quraishi lineage, and literary lineage of poets who nurtured the growth of the Tamil language envisioned as a mother. Quotations from or allusions to Śaivite texts, the Qur'an, the Gospels, and even Sangam poetry (conceived as textual classics at the center of Tamil culture) fill the translations in this book. Each pillaittamil builds upon traditional formulas of praise and creates its own.

The forms of praise just discussed function to make an extraordinary being seem accessible to members of a community of sentiment through an aesthetic strategy that literary critics have called "the verbal icon."[20] In such poetry, the writer uses descriptions of the appearance of an extraordinary being to create an image of the deity, forged out of words; experiencing the poetry thus becomes the textual equivalent of seeing an image of the extraordinary child. Pillaittamil poets of all ideological affiliations make use of this strategy. While Hindu poets may see this poetic practice as a form of making available an image of a deity or saint for the sake of worship *(darśan)*, other poets may view it as a means to venerate, commemorate, or imitate the life of an extraordinary being. A pillaittamil gives a verbal icon immediacy by praising attributes, characteristics, and marvelous accomplishments.

Politics of a Multireligious Genre

Two processes occur simultaneously in the communities of sentiment within which pillaittamils flourish: boundary-crossing and boundary-reinforcement. Such processes can occur at a several different levels, including those of genre, language, and religious or political affiliation.[21] At the level of genre, pillaittamils—and their intended audiences—share a literary heritage and set of poetic strategies. In that sense, pillaittamil poets constitute a kind of literary guild that can transcend the boundaries of ideological affiliation. From Oṭṭukkūttar, who wrote the first extant pillaittamil, through Pakaḻikkūttar, Seyyitu Aṉapiyyā Pulavar, and Aruḷ Cellatturai, all the way to the committee that composed a pillaittamil for a conference, as well as future pillaittamil writers, we find people who cherish poetry written in the Tamil language and who experience pleasure and challenges as they write within the paruvam structure of a pillaittamil.

As an example of how pillaittamil poets can share knowledge of the genre in ways that are not limited by affiliation with a particular religious tradition, consider the circumstances preceding the first publication of Aṉapiyyā's *Napikaḷ Nāyakam Piḷḷaittamiḻ*. The title page of the 1883 edition tells us that "Āṟumukacāmi [a literary savant] from Tiruvengadu, examined the text for errors."[22] Such examinations verify that paruvam structure, meter, and other stylistic features conform to literary prescriptions. Having another respected literary figure check one's texts for errors was a standard practice in literary circles of the time, but this statement attests to more than just attention to literary correctness; it shows that Hindu and Muslim pillaittamil writers shared a literary culture and a set of aesthetic standards that enabled them to act as "checkers" for each other. Consider as well the case of a Hindu poet named Mu. Caṇmukam, whose deep interest in Tamil literature led him to learn about Islamic tradition and read the work of Tamil Islamic poets. In 1978, he composed and published a pillaittamil to the Prophet Muhammad, a literary work that was welcomed by the Tamil Islamic community.[23]

That a modern pillaittamil writer might see himself as, to a certain extent, in conversation with past pillaittamil writers of all religious affiliations became clear in my interview with Aruḷ Cellatturai. By reading 229 previously written pillaittamils before he wrote his own, he put himself in touch with earlier practitioners within the genre, immersing himself in the pillaittamil tradition before making his debut. That he read these poems without regard to whether they were written by Hindus, Muslims, Christians, or those devoted to particular political figures suggests a sense of pillaittamil writers as part of an imagined literary guild.

This notion of poets bound by their shared commitment to a highly stylized set of literary conventions over a long period of time is not unfamiliar in the history of Tamil literature. Ramanujan, in conceptualizing the ways in which the classical Tamil corpus called Sangam *(caṅkam)* functioned in relation to a set of literary conventions about love, war, and public life, noted the appropriateness of the name given to the corpus:

> By a remarkable consensus, they all spoke this common language of symbols for some five or six generations. Each could make his own poem and by doing so allude to every other poem which had been, was being, or would be written in this symbolic language. Thus poem became relevant to poem. . . . The spurious name *Caṅkam* (fraternity, community) for this poetry is justified not by history but by the poetic practice.[24]

The pillaittamil tradition differs from classical Tamil poetry in many ways, but the notion that a literary consensus exists which enables poets with diverse visions to speak to each other through the common language of literary convention is similar. Note, for example, how Mu. Singaravelu takes an old pillaittamil refrain about the deity who makes all the other deities tremble and changes it in relation to E. V. Ramasami, slyly commenting that he makes all deities tremble because as an atheist he has discerned that they are all fabrications. The humor of this line becomes apparent only when seen within the lineage of pillaittamil poetry.

Although some poets have crossed boundaries as a result of their shared interest in pillaittamils, the pillaittamil poetry can also work to strengthen boundaries between religious communities. Evidence of this pattern becomes increasingly common in several significant pillaittamils written after the mid-1800s. For instance, several verses in T. C. Mīṉāṭcicuntaram Piḷḷai's poem to Saint Cēkkiḻār reify religious and social boundaries. In several places he celebrates Cēkkiḻār's writing because it induced the king to switch his allegiance from a Jaina epic to the Śaivite one written by Cēkkiḻār. Pillai lauds this achievement in a refrain where he asks the baby, "make your drum roar, as if it were a funeral drum" for the Jain text, while in another verse Pillai lauds Cēkkiḻār for vanquishing all other religious viewpoints in debate. Pillai's poem eulogizes a particular form of Śaivite monasticism, and especially the members of the Veḷḷāḷa *jāti,* who were prominent poets, ascetics, and donors within this regionally prominent monastic complex centered in Tamil-speaking country. Pillai makes repeated references to the perseverance, dominance, centrality, and honor of the Veḷḷāḷas, to which community both he and Cēkkiḻār belong. Such verses show how a pillaittamil can highlight boundaries between people of different religious and social affiliations.

A̲napiyyā's pillaittamil to the Prophet Muhammad shows a far more subtle tendency to showcase theological aspects of Islamic tradition that separate it from Hindu philosophical views. We have seen throughout Part Two of this book that the protection paruvam functions as an initiatory paruvam for a pillaittamil, indicating by the identity of those chosen to fill its niches what the poet sees as his ultimate concerns. Without any apologies or even discussion, Muslim poets simply refused to address their pillaittamils to Allah or even to characterize him in human form when they praised him in their verses. Furthermore, poets such as A̲napiyyā make a statement of affiliation when they transliterate into Tamil key Persio-Arabic terms, such as *laulaka* in *NNPT* 4, instead of using or coining Tamil words to replace the originals. When they introduce terms that would be unfamiliar to Hindu listeners (and even some Muslim listeners without extensive familiarity with Arabic or Persian), they differentiate themselves from other pillaittamil writers and limit their intended audience.

Even Cellatturai, whose book-releasing ceremony explicitly brings together a community of Christians and connoisseurs of classical Tamil literature, noted some specific political agendas in his reasons for composing a pillaittamil. As he told me in our interview, writing the pillaittamil was "not only an act of devotion but also a missionary activity," noting with satisfaction that the non-Christians who wrote forewords to his volume all "admired the good qualities of my Lord Jesus." At the same time, he sees the pillaittamil to Baby Jesus as a way of envisioning Jesus in a particularly Tamil way, so that Jesus becomes part of the literary fabric of Tamil poetry, rather than some outsider with a foreign set of characteristics. In a sense, he can be seen as negotiating a community of sentiment that will merge literary and religious affiliations and is self-conscious about doing so.

It is one thing to compose a pillaittamil within one or more already established communities of sentiment, but it is another kind of task to envision an extraordinary child *as a way* of uniting a community of sentiment. Of all the pillaittamils translated in this book, the two in chapter 8 seem to have had the least long-term impact on a community of readers. Singaravelu's pillaittamil to E. V. Ramasami attempts to give secular equivalents to the religious features found in other pillaittamils. The poem's relative neglect, however, resulted at least partly because no clearly circumscribed community of sentiment existed for it. E. V. Ramasami's followers splintered into a number of different parties and factions even during his life.[25] And, although E. V. Ramasami himself was a symbol of the fight for self-respect among non-Brahmins, his alternative ideology did not constitute an entire religious tradition. He dismissed myth, condemned ritual, and deconstructed the notion of religiously based social hierarchy. Moreover, Singaravelu's structural equivalents of religion (atheism, social reform, the notion of a Dravidian state) did not have the depth and history to equal the resources upon which a religious poet could draw.

More disappointing is the pillaittamil to Mother Tamil. Technically it follows the prescriptions for a pillaittamil. After all, it addresses a child and contains ten paruvams. But even in a genre where each verse can be seen as a separate piece of poetry, this poem's lack of overall coherence stands out. With its many poets in an artificial collective authorship, its inconsistent arithmetic (two verses in some paruvams, three verses in other paruvams), and its banal use of hackneyed sentiments, the poem echoes the intangibility of a community of sentiment that is devoted to Mother Tamil as its ultimate concern. The "nuts and bolts" of praise lack sophistication and resonance. Rather than building an image of the extraordinary child and demonstrating her greatness, the multiple poets seem largely content with identifying her with adjectives such as "great" and "ancient." This pillaittamil suggests how mere mechanical reproduction of the conventions of the genre fails both in aesthetic terms and in terms of the ability to negotiate successful praise in a community of sentiment.

If that particular pillaittamil to Tamil conceived of as a mother was as limited in its poetic effect as the conference was in the number of days it lasted, the most well-crafted and religiously evocative pillaittamils have continued to be meaningful among devotees in Tamilnadu and other places where Tamil-speakers live in established communities.[26] For example, the following anecdote reveals the influence of pillaittamil sentiments on a connoisseur of Tamil poetry. Recently V. S. Rajam, author of *A Reference Grammar of Classical Tamil*

Poetry and now a senior technical writer in the computer industry, recalled for me a Tamil poem that she had composed immediately after the moon walk had taken place in 1969. The poem assumed the voice of Neil Armstrong's mother, as she recalled his childhood and mused about his recent lunar stroll. She thought back to the moment when she had encouraged the infant to walk, envisioning him as a baby beckoned within the "come" paruvam of a pillaittamil. She had coaxed him to take a single step. Little did she know then that the one small step he took, on the moon, would turn out to be such a momentous action, for him, for his family, and for the world. Remembering this now-lost poem, she pondered the power of the pillaittamil's paruvam structure to shape perceptions of events.

By maintaining the sentiments of childhood and the paruvam structure, a poet gains a kind of imaginative freedom that accounts, at least in part, for the appeal, longevity, and diversity of the pillaittamil genre. With its highly conventionalized structure, the pillaittamil had the potential to turn rigid—formulaic, repetitious, and unsurprising. Instead it has remained lively, flourishing for more than seven centuries. For the pillaittamil's historical importance and continuing influence, its unwavering conventions and diversity of content, as well as for its significant place in both Tamil literature and the history of religions, this genre deserves a new generation of readers, encompassing a range from those who are fluent in Tamil to those who have hitherto been largely unaware of the richness of the Tamil language.

APPENDIX

DESCRIPTIONS OF PILLAITTAMILS IN TEXTS ABOUT POETICS

TAMIL LITERARY TRADITION includes a set of texts called *pāṭṭiyals,* whose name, appropriately enough, means "poetry's *(pāṭṭu)* essence *(iyal).*"[1] As works of indigenous poetic theory, *pāṭṭiyals* reveal how Tamil tradition concerns itself only with particular features of pillaittamils. They indicate which features are considered noteworthy in traditional literary circles. The issues *pāṭṭiyals* explore, and ignore, tell us much about the conceptualization, reception, and perpetuation of pillaittamils and other Tamil genres.

Tradition views *paṭṭiyals* as descriptive and explanatory, rather than prescriptive, texts. A *pāṭṭiyal* writer sifts through many poems to extract their essential formal characteristics. The process is likened to the pressing of sesame seeds to produce oil: the seeds represent individual examples from poems, and the oil stands for the descriptive essence that *pāṭṭiyal* writers extract.[2] Writers learned the formal conventions of a genre to compose poems in it; grammarians and commentators used their familiarity with the conventions to extract poetic patterns; audiences needed to know the conventions to savor poetry fully. Even though *pāṭṭiyal* writers did not intend to be prescriptive, *pāṭṭiyals* were likely to influence expectations about poetic genres over time. Or, to continue a metaphor, oil pressers can eventually influence the kinds of seeds planted.

Pāṭṭiyals take as their literary domain a set of ninety-six poetic genres known interchangeably as *pirapantam* or *ciṟṟilakkiyam. Pirapantam* (from Sanskrit *prabandha*) means "anthology" and indicates that the literary works under analysis all contain collections of poetry. *Ciṟṟilakkiyam* (from Tamil *ciṟu,* "small" or "short," and *ilakkiyam,* "literature") means "small" or "shorter" literature; the term distinguishes this poetry from longer poetic texts such as epics.[3] Scholars often define *pirapantam* in opposition to other literary categories or use it as a residual category. For example, Zvelebil contrasts it with anthologies of single discrete verses, emphasizing that *pirapantam* poetry consists of connected narrative and extensive description. He also identifies *pirapantam* texts as those remaining after "the solitary stanza *(taṉippāṭal)*, the didactic aphorism, the *bhakti* hymn proper, and the large epic-narrative forms" are removed.[4] If one looks at the ninety-six genres included under the rubric of *pirapantam*, it is difficult to determine what they all have in common, except that many of them share an origin in the medieval period and a high degree of literary convention that shapes their structure.[5]

Although writers disagree about precisely which genres belong in the *pirapantam* category, all include the pillaittamil as one of the most prominent *pirapantam* texts.[6] As S. V. Subramanian notes in his edition of a *pāṭṭiyal* text, *The Lamp of Pirapantam Literature*, "Among all the types of *pirapantams* which shine brightly, it [the pillaittamil] shines the most brilliantly."[7]

The first extant *pāṭṭiyal*, *Paṉṉiru Pāṭṭiyal* (henceforth *PP*), is the locus classicus for nearly everything that later *pāṭṭiyal* writers said about pillaittamils. According to tradition, *PP* was composed by *caṇkattuccāṉṟōr*, a collective term meaning "great men of the academy," referring to the legendary ancient literary circles. Tradition credits each section of *PP* to a different disciple of Agastya, the mythical grammarian. Present research dates the text around or before the twelfth century C.E., despite its own claims to origins in hoary antiquity.[8] *PP*, which deals more extensively with pillaittamils than any subsequent *pāṭṭiyal*, analyzes the contents of the pillaittamil by focusing primarily on three topics: (1) the span of a child's life covered in a pillaittamil, (2) the specific paruvams contained in a pillaittamil, and (3) deities to be invoked in the protection *(kāppu)* paruvam.[9]

The Ages of the Child in a Pillaittamil

ALTHOUGH INDIVIDUAL PILLAITTAMILS carry no explicit markers linking a specific paruvam to a specific age in a child's life, *pāṭṭiyal* writers attempt to develop schemes for determining such links. *PP* presents in sequence three differing opinions concerning the issue (verses 173–176).[10] The first viewpoint (anonymous, verse 173) sets out a scheme by which each paruvam is assigned to a two-month period in the life of the infant, beginning in the third month and ending in the twenty-first month.[11] For example, the protection paruvam would occur in the third to fifth months of life, whereas the request to the moon would take place when the child reached the fifteenth or sixteenth month of age. This developmental view assumes that the child performs increasingly complex tasks over the course of the poem, beginning with simple motions like swaying to and fro and building up to activities such as pulling a toy chariot. Thus, a pillaittamil would deal only with the earliest period in a child's life, before he or she turns two years old.

The next verse (attributed to Poykaiyār, verse 174) asserts one need not bar a poem from the genre even if it depicts the child from its first to fifth years of age.[12] This view avoids problems implicit in the first model, such as whether the paruvams are as strictly developmental as presented and whether all the activities included in the ten paruvams could really be accomplished by an infant of twenty-one months or less. For example, might it be difficult for a toddler to knock over girls' houses?

The last two verses (probably presenting the author's opinion, verses 175–176)[13] claim that pillaittamils may describe males up to sixteen years of age and females until the onset of puberty. In chapter 3 I discussed a classical Tamil love poem in which the hero knocks over the heroine's sandhouses as a prelude to wooing her. According to Sangam tradition, such a hero is thought to be sixteen and the heroine twelve, the age at which literary heroines attain puberty and respond to the advances of the hero. The author may have decided that, due to the motif of the boy destroying the girl's houses, the boy must be the same age as the boy in the Sangam poem.

The Paruvams

PP PROVIDES A list of the paruvams and establishes that some are apportioned to males, while others belong to females:

178. Poets who have attained divine goodness say that protection, sway to and fro [*ceṅkīrai*], tongue, clap, the well-constructed kiss, saying "Come," moon, little house, little drum, little chariot, and the trusted rest are spun to the extent.[14]

179. They say it is appropriate to talk first of father, mother, grandfather, and grandmother.

180. They say if it is for the perfect female child, remove the last three that stand.

181. All the rest except for little house, little drum, and little chariot are placed for women.

182. Poets say that those [paruvams for girls] are constructing little houses, cooking rice, beautiful young sons, swings adorned with jewels, requesting with a vow to beautiful Kāma in the twelfth year.

Although the first seven paruvams for both sexes and the remaining three for boys (verse 178) match usage in the pillaittamils analyzed in this book, the paruvams for girls largely diverge from poets' usage. For example, *PP* sets out not three but five paruvams for girls,[15] some of which are almost never found in extant poems. Of these five paruvams, only one, swinging, regularly occurs in pillaittamils addressed to girls. Furthermore, one paruvam that *PP* designates for girls shows up as a male paruvam: the little houses that the girls construct (verse 182) are threatened by little boys. Finally, with one notable exception, the paruvams of cooking rice, playing with young sons, and making a request to Kāma are not found in extant poems, so one can only speculate about their contents.[16] The "young sons" may be younger brothers or dolls. The vow to Kāma, the god of love, may refer to vows asking for good husbands.[17] These obscure paruvams suggest that pillaittamils addressed to females had not become as conventionalized as those for males at the time that *PP* was written.

Scholars have been intrigued by the statement that paruvams can be "spun to the extent" (verse 178). Indian texts often use the image of spinning to describe the creative process. Later writers have often interpreted this cryptic verse as meaning that additional paruvams may be created out of the poet's imagination: talented poets ("poets who have attained divine goodness") can "spin out" new paruvams. As the author of *Navaṉīta Pāṭṭiyal*, a fourteenth-century text, put it:

"They say the limit of the imagination is the limit of the poet."[18] Since two paruvams for girls—playing jacks *(ammāṉai)* and river bathing—do not appear in this *PP,* they must have developed later.

Although pillaittamils adopt a mother's voice and a few depict fathers in specific verses, grandparents play almost no role in extant pillaittamils, so verse 179 remains a puzzle. Nor are grandparents mentioned in subsequent *pāṭṭiyals.* One wonders whether pillaittamils now lost contained additional sections not present in extant texts and whether the content of a pillaittamil became more narrowly defined as the genre developed.

Deities to be Invoked for Protection

As we saw in chapter 3's discussion of the protection paruvam, specific guidelines determine the content of its niches. *PP* sets out in detail the deities to be invoked (verses 183–187). The first three are recognizable as members of the *trimūrti* (composed of three forms or aspects of divinity), with Brahmā responsible for creating the world, Viṣṇu for protecting or preserving it, and Śiva for destroying it. The protection paruvam begins with these three deities but presents them in a different order. The poet first invokes Viṣṇu, because his specialty is protection. Next comes Śiva, but he must be invoked in ways that avoid any mention of his role as destroyer of the universe; such inauspicious references are inappropriate in a paruvam specifically designed to portray the infant god as guarded from misfortune by a host of powerful gods. Invocation to Brahmā comes third, and that is not surprising since he plays a minor role in Tamil religiosity.

In *PP,* the deities specified for the remaining protection verses are listed without further comment about their manner of portrayal. *PP* identifies the following as appropriate for invocation in verse 183: Gaṇeśa and Murukaṉ (the children of Śiva and Pārvatī), Lakṣmī (the wife of Viṣṇu), Sarasvatī (the wife of Brahmā), Sāsta (or Aiyappaṉ, the issue of Śiva when he had intercourse with Viṣṇu, who had taken on the female form of Mohinī), the sun and the moon, the Vedic deities Indra (god of rain) and Kubera (god of wealth), the seven mothers (a group of Śaivite Tantric deities), Nīli (a venerated chaste wife from the village of Paḻaiyanūr), and Vaṭukaṉ.[19] The list ends with "the thirty-three gods" (see chapter 4).

This list contains a number of deities found in modern Hindu tradition. In addition to the *trimūrti,* we find the wives of Brahmā and Viṣṇu mentioned in *PP,* but not the wife of Śiva, perhaps because she (as Kālī or Durgā) often acts in malevolent ways in rural South Indian myths. The two sons of Śiva receive verses, as does the son of Śiva, by a female form of Viṣṇu. Nīli is among those chaste women from South India who were venerated after an untimely death. The seven mothers, often worshipped aniconically as a group of seven stones, receive offerings for protection. The remaining (mostly Vedic) gods, possess minor but clearly circumscribed functions: the sun and moon, the gods of rain and wealth, and the thirty-three deities to whom sacrifice was offered.

Repeated Concerns

AUTHORS CONTINUED TO compose *pāṭṭiyals* over the centuries, but their descriptions of the pillaittamil genre changed very little. The first extant *pāṭṭiyal* after *PP, Veṇpāp Pāṭṭiyal (VP),* written by Kuṇavīra Paṇṭitar, dates from the twelfth century.[20] Then, in an intriguing parallel to pillaittamil history, there appear to have been no further *pāṭṭiyals* until the fourteenth century, when *Navanīta Pāṭṭiyal (NP)* appeared. The famous author Parañcōti Muṉivar is credited with writing *Citamparap Pāṭṭiyal (CP)* in the sixteenth century.[21] By the seventeenth century, we have *Ilakkaṇaviḷakka Pāṭṭiyal (IP).*[22] Toward the end of the eighteenth century, the anonymous work, *Pirapanta Marapiyal (PM)* appeared.[23] Muttuvēṅkaṭa Cuppaiyar wrote *Pirapanta Tīpikai (PT)* in the nineteenth century.[24] These *pāṭṭiyals* contain verses that repeat, rephrase, elaborate upon, abridge, or slightly transform the description of *PP.*

As for the life-span issue, although all but one writer mention the twenty-one month scheme, they almost always provide an alternative as well.[25] This indicates increasing interest in other views of the time-span covered in a pillaittamil. Although the range of alternatives varies from text to text, each alternative involves auspicious odd numbers: one to five years *(PP),* five to seven years *(VP),* the third, fifth, and seventh years *(IP),* the fifth and seventh years *(NN).*

Over time, the treatment of the female paruvams became standardized. For example *IP* notes that, "Since the last three [male paruvams just mentioned] are not appropriate for women, the appropriate ones are *kaḻuṅku, ammāṉai,* and swinging" (verse 807). In pillaittamil texts themselves, these three occur frequently in poems addressed to female deities, but sometimes the paruvam "bathing in the river" is substituted. Apparently, paruvams for girls did not become as standardized as did paruvams for boys.

Finally, *pāṭṭiyal* discussions of the protection paruvam uniformly repeat that poets should invoke Viṣṇu first and then Śiva next, mentioning only his auspicious deeds. Most *pāṭṭiyals* dispense with listing deities for the remaining niches in the paruvam, but *IP* provides a full enumeration. Its slightly condensed list omits several of the more obscure deities and adds the wife of Indra to the list (verse 808).

Of the three topics considered by *pāṭṭiyals,* the discussion of age seems least relevant to the actual content of pillaittamils. The list of paruvams remained basically unchanged except for the gradual standardizing of the last three for girls. The discussion of those appropriate for invocation in the protection paruvam had the most effect on the composition of Śaivite pillaittamils and virtually no effect on Muslim, Christian, and political pillaittamils.[26]

NOTES

CHAPTER 1: EXTRAORDINARY CHILD

1. A. K. Ramanujan, "Where Mirrors are Windows: Toward an Anthology of Reflections," *History of Religions* 28, no. 3 (February 1989): 197.

2. The figure of sixty-nine million Tamil speakers is an approximation. Although the majority of Tamil speakers (about forty-eight million) live in the Indian state of Tamilnadu, many have also settled outside the state in the cities of Mysore, Bangalore, Bombay, Delhi, and Calcutta. Outside India, the largest community of Tamil speakers lived in the northern section of Sri Lanka (approximately four million), but in the past decade many of them have become refugees. Tamil-speaking communities also exist in Southeast Asia (about one million in Malaysia alone), the Americas, and the United Kingdom, with smaller communities elsewhere. See the discussion of Tamil in David Crystal, *An Encyclopedic Dictionary of Language and Languages* (Oxford: Basil Blackwell, 1992). For comparison's sake it is worth noting that there are more Tamil speakers than Italian speakers (approximately sixty-three million) in the world.

3. The secondary literature on pillaittamils remains relatively limited, except for short summaries found in the histories of Tamil literature that delineate the characteristics of medieval poetic genres (see appendix). One of the first book-length studies of the genre is *Ciṟṟilakkiyaccoṟpoḻivukaḷ—Iraṇṭāvatu Mānāṇṭu* (Tirunelveli: SISS, 1959), which contains the presentations from a Saiva Siddhanta-sponsored conference designed to foster an appreciation of the various genres of Tamil poetry. A number of such conferences were held, among which this one focused solely

on pillaittamils in the Śaivite tradition. A more recent Tamil critical analysis of selected examples of the genre focuses on pillaittamils to Hindu gods, goddesses, and cultural or political heroes. See Ku. Muttu-rācan̲, *Piḷḷaittamiḻ Ilakkiyam* (Chidambaram: Manivacakar Patippakam, 1984).

Surveys of Tamil literature tend to isolate Muslim pillaittamils, placing them in separate sections dealing with Muslim literature, thereby obscuring their links with Hindu pillaittamils. For example, the survey by Mu. Varadarajan, *A History of Tamil Literature* (New Delhi: Sahitya Akademi, 1980), deals with all Islamic literature in a separate chapter and all Christian literature in yet another chapter. The chapter called "Religious Works" does not, however, include any Muslim or Christian literary texts.

Similarly, in most cases when scholars focus on Muslim pillaittamils, they treat them separately rather than placing them in the context of Hindu and Christian pillaittamils. See, for example, the article on pillaittamils in Aptur̲-R̲ahīm, *Islāmiyak Kalaikkaḷañciyam,* vol. 3 (Madras: Yun̲ivarsal Papḷishars Aṇṭ Puk Cellars [Universal Publishers and Book Sellers], 1979), 559–560. A notable exception to this pattern is found in Cai. Pāttimā, *Napikaḷ Nāyakam Piḷḷaittamiḻ: Ōr Āyvu* (Madras: Amina Press, 1990), which compares literary features in pillaittamils addressed to the Prophet Muhammad with Hindu pillaittamils. To my knowledge, no comprehensive study of Christian pillaittamils exists in any language.

4. I have seen or found reference to more than 250 examples of pillaittamils (not all of them extant). The chart at the end of Ku. Mutturācan̲'s monograph lists sixty-six pillaittamils addressed to gods, fifty-five to goddesses, thirty-one to poets or learned men (including monastic abbots and venerated gurus), three to kings, and five to political leaders. A list of 227 pillaittamils is found in the editor's introduction to Vaittiyanāta Tēcikar, *Kamalālaya Amman̲ Piḷḷaittamiḻ,* ed. Vī. Cokkaliṅkam (Srirangam: Srī Vāṇi Vilāca Accakam, 1969), 18. Also see the list in the introduction to Mu. Caṇmukam Piḷḷai, *Ayyan̲ar Piḷḷaittamiḻ* (Madras: Cen̲n̲aip Palkali Kaḻakam, 1975), following p. 19. For a list of twenty-three Muslim pillaittamils, see Aptur̲-R̲ahīm, *Islāmiyak Kalaikkaḷañciyam,* vol. 3, 559–560.

5. For a discussion of these five modes of bhakti, see Edward C. Dimock, "Doctrine and Practice Among the Vaiṣṇavas of Bengal," in *Krishna: Myths, Rites, and Attitudes,* ed. Milton Singer (Chicago: University of Chicago Press, 1966), 49.

6. Notable works of scholarship have been written about *vātsalya* devotional poetry in Hindi literature, addressed to Kṛṣṇa. See, for example, John Stratton Hawley, *Krishna, The Butter Thief* (Princeton: Princeton University Press, 1983). Hawley explores connections between this Hindi poetry and Tamil pillaittamils on pp. 35–45. Also see Kenneth Bryant's *Poems to the Child-God: Structures and Strategies in the Poetry of Sūrdās* (Berkeley: University of California, 1978).

For a discussion of the nature and early history of the *vātsalya* tradition in Tamil literature, see Lynn Marie Ate, "Periyāḻvār's *Tirumoḻi*—A Bāla Kṛṣṇa Text from the Devotional Period in Tamil Literature" (Ph.D. diss., University of Wisconsin, Madison, 1978), 92–96. Periyāḻvār's poetry contains some tantilizing clues for a historian attempting to piece together the complicated prehistory of the pillaittamil genre. It includes four of the stylized kinds of poetry that would later appear as paruvams in all standard pillaittamils: lullaby, sway to and fro, clap, and the moon verses. Friedhelm Hardy's *Virāha-Bhakti: The Early History of Kṛṣṇa Devotion in South India* (Delhi: Oxford University Press, 1983), pt. 4 (especially 406–407, n21), provides useful historical analysis of several children's activities depicted in pillaittamils.

7. Other less frequently used names for the genre include *piḷḷaikkavi* (poetry of/for the child), *piḷḷaippāṭṭu* (songs of/for the child), and *piḷḷait-tirunāmam* (the sacred name of/for the child).

8. For a discussion of a modern pillaittamil in which a female poet composed a few of the verses, see chapter 8 of this book.

9. For examples of poets assuming the persona of a maternal figure, see *Naṟṟinai* 179, translated in A. K. Ramanujan, *Poems of Love and War from the Eight Anthologies and the Ten Long Poems of Classical Tamil* (New York: Columbia University Press, 1985), 65, 84–86.

10. Virginia Woolf, *A Room of One's Own* (New York: Harcourt, Brace, and World, 1965), 128.

11. Tillie Olsen, *Silences* (New York: Delacourt Press, 1978), 40–41.

12. The pillaittamil genre is one of the ninety-six genres classified as what in English has usually been called "minor literature." A bit of context shows, however, that this term both mistranslates and misleads. Tamil tradition tends to group literary texts into enumerated classes of literature. For example, one finds reference to the five great epics and the eighteen shorter works. Similarly, one set of literary works bears the title of the "96 *ciṟṟilakkiyam,*" a compound composed of *ciṟu* (small) and

ilakkiyam (literature). Although Tamil literary historians tend to translate the compound as "minor" works, evidence suggests that the term was used to distinguish these poetic genres from longer narratives of connected poetry. The term "minor" in this case has nothing to do with the domestic sphere. None of the other ninety-five genres included in the classification *ciṟṟilakkiyam* have as their main characteristic that the author takes on the voice of a mother. For a discussion of the ninety-six genres, see appendix.

13. Pakaḻikkūttar's *Tiruccentūr Piḷḷaittamiḻ* can be found in an edition with commentary by Pu. Ci. Puṉṉaivaṉanāta Mutaliyār in vol. 1 of *Piḷḷaittamiḻkkottu* (1957; reprint, Tirunelveli: SISS, 1979), sect. 3.

14. Kumarakurupara Cuvāmikaḷ, *Maturaimīṉāṭciyammai Piḷḷaittamiḻ,* in vol. 2 of *Piḷḷaittamiḻkkottu* (1964; reprint Tirunelveli: SISS, 1970), sect. 3.

15. See *Tamil Lexicon* (Madras: University of Madras, 1982), vol. 4, 2525, for both the general meanings of the term *paruvam* and the many specific or specialized meanings it takes on in particular discourses (e.g., astrology, anatomy, literature, life stages). The *Lexicon* derives the term from the Sanskrit *parvan,* "limb," "section [in a book]," or "period [of time]."

16. More than 80 percent of the pillaittamils I have seen possess one hundred or more verses, with ten verses in each of the post-protection paruvams, a kind of pillaittamil that I have labeled "standard."

17. Since one requests aid from the elephant-headed deity at the beginning of difficult enterprises so that obstacles to their completion can be overcome, some poets have asked for divine protection for the enterprise of writing a pillaittamil, invoking the deity at the very beginning of the poem, as well as in his assigned slot in the *kāppu* paruvam. See, for example, C. K. Cuppiramaṇiya Mutaliyār, *Tiruppukoḷiyūr Avināci Peruṅkaruṇaiyammai Piḷḷaittamiḻ* (Madras: Civakāmi Vilāca Publishers, 1926).

18. Kamil Veith Zvelebil, *Tamil Literature,* vol. 10, fasc. 1, of *A History of Indian Literature,* gen. ed. Jan Gonda (Wiesbaden: Otto Harrassowitz, 1974), 213 (hereafter *Indian Literature*), suggests the paruvam name comes from *cem,* "correct" or "proper," and *kīr,* "speech," defining the paruvam as one in which the child learns to speak properly. The view that the paruvam name refers to reddish-colored greens appears in J. P. Fabricius, *Tamil and English Dictionary* (Tranquebar: Lutheran

Publishing House, 1972), 432. The *Tamil Lexicon,* vol. 3, 1580, defines this paruvam as concerning the stage of childhood in which the infant lifts up its head and nods. Pillaittamil poets also have contributed their own views about what the paruvam portrays. One verse suggests that *ceṅkīrai* was a particular position in which the infant spread out its hands and legs on the ground, swaying and, perhaps, trying to crawl. For this description, see verse 15 of Civañāna Cuvāmikaḷ, *Kuḷattūr Amutāmpikai Piḷḷaittamiḻ* (Tirunelveli: SISS, 1939). Intriguingly, this lack of clarity about the precise contents of the *ceṅkīrai* verse has tended to make it a paruvam that encompasses a wider range of themes and topics than more circumscribed paruvams, such as the "clap" paruvam (see below).

19. This paruvam bears a name similar to the Tamil term for lullaby, *tālāṭṭu,* literally "moving the tongue" or "the tongue dancing." For a collection of Tamil folk lullabies known by this title, see Vi. Caracuvati, *Nāṭṭuppuṟap Pāṭalkaḷ: Camūka Oppāyvu* (Madurai: Madurai Kamarajar University, 1982). Although these folk lullabies do not usually contain the refrain "*tālēlō* " (or a similar phrase) in their refrain, the phrase occurs in some written lullabies. See, for example, Ā. Tarumaliṅka Mutaliyār, *Amirta Rāmāyaṇam* (Madras: B.N. Press, 1925) for such a lullaby to Rāma.

20. To distinguish between the two genders, texts on pillaittamil poetics use two separate terms: they call pillaittamils addressed to males *āṇpāṟ piḷḷaittamiḻ* (male-category pillaittamil) and pillaittamils addressed to females *peṇpāṟ piḷḷaittamiḻ* (female-category pillaittamil). This terminology to distinguish gender does not originate with analysis of the pillaittamil; it also occurs in grammatical analysis of gender markers in Tamil linguistics. See *Naṉṉul,* eds. various (Tirunelveli: SISS, 1978), verses 262–264, p. 212, for a discussion of the three grammatical classes *(pāl):* male *(āṇ),* female *(peṇ),* and plural.

21. While paruvams for males seem to be relatively fixed, there is variation among paruvams for females. In addition to the three paruvams mentioned here, one called *kaḻaṅku,* the name of another child's game somewhat similar to jacks, is found in some pillaittamils to goddesses. According to grammatical texts (see the appendix), there are several other paruvams for females, but they have not been found, with one notable exception: the anonymous pillaittamil believed to have been composed in the eighteenth century and addressed to Āṇṭāḷ. The text's author appears to have used the earliest grammatical work on pillait-

tamils *(Paṉṉiru Pāṭṭiyal)* as an exact guide, since it is the only pillaittamil known to scholars that contains four paruvams for females specified in that grammatical work, but found in no other extant pillaittamils: [building a] little house, [cooking] a little rice, swinging, and a vow to Kāma [for getting a husband]. See the edition by U. Vē. Re. Appuvaiyaṅkār Svāmikaḷ, *Āṇṭāḷ Piḷḷaittamiḻ* (Coimbatore: Presidency Press, 1904).

22. For reasons of space I have not been able to devote entire chapters of translation in this anthology to two older pillaittamils that are important largely for their early date rather than their influence upon the genre or their significance in an ongoing community. The earliest pillaittamil is a fragmentary one, but contains some complete verses (one of which is a moon verse translated in chapter 2). Furthermore, a large part of the poem includes lists of valorous acts of war performed by ancestors of the king, a kind of poetry that does not translate well into English. Those interested in the history of the pillaittamil genre can consult Oṭṭakkūttar, *Kulōttuṅkaṉ Piḷḷaittamiḻ,* T. S. Kaṅkātaraṉ, comp., Tañcai Carasvati Makāl Veḷiyīṭu, No. 154 (Tañcāvūr: Makārājā Carapōji Sarasvati Mahāl Nūl Nilaiyam, 1974). Epigraphical evidence indicates that Koṭikkoṇṭāṉ Periyāṉ Aticcatēvaṉ composed a pillaittamil titled *Kāṅkēyaṉ Piḷḷaittamiḻ* ca. 1230, but the text is not extant. See Zvelebil, *Indian Literature,* 213n52.

Another text not included in this volume of translations is the sole Jaina pillaittamil: the anonymous poem titled *Ātinātar Piḷḷaittamiḻ* (Madras: Ātinātar Patippakam, 1956), which deals with Ātinātar Vṛṣabhadeva, the first of the Jain *tīrtaṅkaras.* Zvelebil dates this text to ca. 1500 in Kamil Zvelebil, *Tamil Literature,* vol. 2, fasc. 1, of *Handbuch der Orientalistik,* gen. ed. Jan Gonda (Leiden: E. J. Brill, 1975), 213 (henceforth, *Handbuch*). As far as scholars know, this work neither won the praise of pillaittamil connoisseurs nor inspired the composition of any later Jain pillaittamils. No commentary was ever composed for it, and the text is virtually unknown in the Jain community today.

23. For an insightful discussion of the conventions of Tamil poetry that focuses on the battleground haunted by ghouls feeding on corpses, see David Dean Shulman, *The King and the Clown in South Indian Myth and Poetry* (Princeton: Princeton University Press, 1985), 276–292.

24. According to Hindu myth, the god Indra took the form of a sage and then seduced the sage's wife. When the sage returned and discovered the pair, he cursed Indra's body to be covered with a thousand vaginas.

Later, the vaginas are changed to eyes from which comes the epithet "the god with a thousand eyes."

25. I purposely keep the translation of the refrain for each paruvam as constant as possible throughout the volume. In that way I replicate in English the closure that it produces in Tamil, where the refrain functions in the same way as the final dominant note at the end of a piece by Bach. The treatment of the refrain closely follows the practice established by pioneer translator A. K. Ramanujan, who took the refrain as an unchanging phrase that anchors a piece of poetry. See his introduction to *Speaking of Śiva* (Baltimore: Penguin Books, 1973), 47, where he discusses "using them [refrains] constantly as a repetitive formula [so that] they will keep their chanting refrain quality."

CHAPTER 2: ASKING FOR THE MOON, TAMING THE TIGER

1. In this genre the moon is perceived as male and the stars are thought to be his wives, who orbit around him.

2. This saying is attributed to the female poet Auvaiyār. See Mutturācaṉ, *Piḷḷaittamiḻ Ilakkiyam,* 39.

3. The material synthesized in this section comes from my reading of Indian poetry and from articles that summarize Indian traditions about the moon in Vettam Mani, *Purāṇic Encyclopedia: A Comprehensive Dictionary with Special Reference to the Epic and Purāṇic Literature* (Delhi: Motilal Banarsidass, 1979), 171–172, and A. Singaravelu Mudaliar, *Abithana Chintamani* (New Delhi: Asian Educational Services, 1986), 578–579.

4. For a discussion of the moon and the Prophet in Islamic poetry, see Annemarie Schimmel, *And Muhammad is His Messenger: The Veneration of the Prophet in Islamic Piety* (Chapel Hill: University of North Carolina Press, 1985), 69–70.

5. For details of the story, see Cornelia Dimmitt and J. A. B. van Buitenen, trans., *Classical Hindu Mythology* (Philadelphia: Temple University Press, 1978), 96–98.

6. Hawley, *Krishna,* 249–251. Reference is also made to this incident in the *Kavitāvalī,* attributed to Tulsidas. See Raymond Allchin, trans., *Kavitāvalī* (London: George Allen and Unwin, 1964), verse I.4, 72.

7. Stuart Blackburn, *Inside the Drama-House: Rama Stories and Shadow Puppets in South India* (Berkeley: University of California Press, 1996), 205.

8. Recorded in Madurai, Tamilnadu, in January 1987 from a mother in a Śaiva Pillai family whose native place was Tirunelveli District.

9. Āṟṟalaracu and K. Ā. Turai, ed., *Nilā Nāṉūṟu* (Madras: Aracu Patippakam, 1973).

10. See Edwin Gerow, *A Glossary of Indian Figures of Speech* (The Hague: Mouton, 1971), 114, for a discussion of *śleṣa*. The Tamil transliteration of the term is *cilēṭai*.

11. *Muttukkumāracāmi Piḷḷaittamiḻ* in *Piḷḷaittamiḻkkottu*, vol. 1, sect. 2.

12. Mu. Singaravelu, *Periyār Piḷḷaittamiḻ* (Kovilpatti: Maṇimēkalai Patippakam, 1983), 63.

13. Lauding a king as an earthly form of Viṣṇu is an established and respected form of praising a monarch labeled *pūvainilai* in classical Tamil tradition. See Po. Vē. Cōmacuntaraṉār, ed., *Puṟapporuḷ Veṇpamālai* (Tirunelveli: SISS, 1978), *pāṭāṇ paṭalam*, 200.

14. T. S. Kaṅkātaraṉ, comp., *Kulōttuṅkaṉ Piḷḷaittamiḻ*, Tañcai Carasvati Makāl Veḷiyīṭu, No. 154 (Tañcāvūr: Makārājā Carapōji Sarasvati Mahāl Nūl Nilaiyam, 1974), 137. The pillaittamil praises King Kulōttuṅkaṉ II, who reigned from 1136 to 1146 C.E. The text is incomplete; for example, although the pillaittamil contains 104 verses, only four complete *tāla* verses have survived. For an analysis of the ways in which the text praises the Chola lineage, see V. R. Mahalingam, "Kulottungan Pillaittamil" (M.A. thesis, University of Madras, 1956), 65.

15. Cornelia Dimmitt, "Sītā: Fertility Goddess and Śakti," *Anima* 7 (1980): 19–30.

16. *Kuḷattūr Amutāmpikai Piḷḷaittamiḻ* in *Piḷḷaittamilkkottu*, vol. 2, sect. 3.

17. *Maturai Mīṉāṭciyammai Piḷḷaittamiḻ* in *Piḷḷaittamilkkottu*, vol. 2, sect. 2.

18. Ci. Nayinar Mukammatu, ed. and com., *Napikaḷ Nāyakam Piḷḷaittamiḻ* (Colombo: Publication Committee of the Sea Street Meelaad Committee, 1975).

19. Sāturām Svāmikaḷ, *Śrī Vaiṣṇavi Piḷḷaittamiḻ* (Madras: Śrī Vaiṣṇavi Illam, 1974), 32 (moon 3). The verse puns on two meanings of *mati:* "moon" and "intelligence."

20. Sometimes the distinction between a "giving" verse and a "punishment" verse is not completely clear, especially if the gift the extraordinary child gives is one of protection from danger or punishment.

21. *Tiruccentūr Piḷḷaittamiḻ* in *Piḷḷaittamiḻkottu,* vol. 2, sect. 3.

22. Aruḷ Cellatturai, *Iyēcupirāṉ Piḷḷaittamiḻ* (Tirucchirappalli: Aruḷ Vākku Maṉṟam, 1985.

23. According to legend, Kautilya was a contemporary of Chandragupta Mauriya. Most scholars believe, however, that the *Arthaśāstra,* as found in its present form, was put together some time ca. the fourth century C.E. The list of the four strategies comes from verse 47 in *Arthaśāstra* 2.10.47–56 as found in R. P. Kangle, *The Kautiliya Arthaśāstra* (Bombay: University of Bombay, 1972), pt.1, 50–51. The translation quoted below, which explains each strategy, comes from Kangle's English translation in pt. 2, 95–96, of the same work.

> 48: Among them, conciliation is five-fold, praising of merits, mention of relationship, pointing out mutual benefits, showing (advantages in) the future, and placing oneself at the (other's) disposal. . . .
> 54: Conferring benefits of money is making gifts.
> 55: Creating apprehension and reprimanding is dissension.
> 56: Killing, tormenting and seizure of property constitute force.

24. The moon paruvam in *Kulōttuṅkaṉ Piḷḷaittamiḻ* does not indicate that the author was familiar with or primarily guided by the four strategies, so they may have become influential to pillaittamil writers at a later date. The moon verses of Pakaḻikkūttar, in contrast, tend to be far more easily recognizable as fitting one of the four strategies.

25. For example, see the reference to the "four expedients" in the Laws of Manu: Wendy Doniger and Brian Smith, trans., *The Laws of Manu* (London: Penguin, 1991), sect. 7, verses 107–108, p. 139.

26. The chart below gives a schematic view of these differences: Do not be misled by the transliteration changes from Sanskrit to Tamil and the romanization system for Tamil, which account for the changes from *d* to *t, bh* to *p,* and *s* to *c.* Instead, note the difference in meaning (see the English translation) between the first two Tamil terms and the corresponding Sanskrit ones. Also note the order of the strategies.

ORDER	SANSKRIT	TRANSLATION	ORDER	TAMIL	TRANSLATION
1.	sāma	conciliation	1.	cāmam	similarity
2.	dāna	giving	2.	pētam	difference
3.	bheda	dissension	3.	tāṉam	giving
4.	daṇḍa	punishment	4.	taṇṭam	punishment

27. Aradhana Parmar, *Technique of Statecraft: A Study of Kautilya's Arthaśāstra* (Delhi: Atma Ram and Sons, 1987), 207.

28. In correspondence with David Shulman, he suggested that in the moon paruvam "the cosmos has now become a kind of *Arthaśāstraic* blueprint, with the moon taking on the role of enemy, the mother a clever strategist, the extraordinary child as the powerful agent, and the political strategies as divine play." Personal communication, June 1994.

CHAPTER 3: THE FLORESCENCE

1. This book focuses on lineages of pillaittamils written by poets belonging to (mostly religious) communities that generated several or more pillaittamils. Thus the single courtly pillaittamil of the twelfth century and the sole (extant) Jain pillaittamil lie outside the scope of this book. In contrast, *TCPT* influenced many pillaittamil texts that followed, so it receives close examination in this chapter.

2. Zvelebil surmises that he lived ca. 1375–1425 and dates *TCPT* to approximately 1410. See *Handbuch,* 216.

3. See, for example, Mu. Aruṇācalam, *Tamil Ilakkiya Varalāṟu, 15th century* (Tiruccirrampalam: Kānti Publishers, 1969), 296–297.

4. See Aruṇācalam, 297, and Es. Vaittiyanātaṉ, *Pirkālap Pulavarkaḷ* (Madras: Dr. U. Ve. Cāminātaiyar Nūlnilaiyam, 1986), 316–317.

5. G. Ramakrishna, N. Gayathri, and Debiprasad Chattopadhyaya, *An Encyclopedia of South Indian Culture* (Calcutta: K. P. Bagchi, 1983), 472. For a monograph on the manifestations of Murukaṉ in Tamil texts and material culture, see Fred W. Clothey, *The Many Faces of Murukaṉ: The History and Meaning of a South Indian God* (Mouton: The Hague, 1978).

6. For a bibliography of many of the known manuscript versions of *Tiruccentūr Piḷḷaittamiḻ,* consult K. C. Chellamuthu, T. Padmanaban, and P. V. Nagarajan, comp., *International Catalogue of Tamil Palmleaf Manuscripts* (Thanjavur: Tamil University, 1986), nos. 9389–9413. The

frequent reprinting of published versions, especially in the late nineteenth century and the first half of the twentieth century, is attested to in the list of books registered with the British colonial government, beginning with *Classified Catalogue of the Public Reference Library Consisting of Books Registered from 1867–1889 at the Office of the Registrar of Books, Old College, Madras* (Madras: By the Superintendent, Government Press, 1894). Supplements were reissued periodically, including in 1932, 1964, 1965, 1966, and 1971. See also John Murdoch, comp., *Classified Catalogue of Tamil Printed Books with Introductory Notices* (Madras: The Christian Vernacular Education Society, 1865), as well as the multivolume ongoing *Tamiḻ Nūl Vivara Aṭṭavaṇai* (Madras: Tamil Development and Research Press, 1962–). Even the edition of *TCPT* used here, published by SISS, testifies to continued republication. According to the publication information provided on the back of the title page, Ci. Pu<u>nn</u>aivana<u>n</u>āta Mutaliyār's edition of the text, accompanied by his commentary on it, was first published in 1889. The first SISS edition of *TCPT* came out in 1927 and was reprinted in 1941, 1957, 1963, 1969, 1972, 1974, and 1977. In addition, SISS created a collection of pillaittamils to Lord Muruka<u>n</u> in which the poem appeared, first released in 1957 and then reprinted in 1972 and 1979.

7. "Pakaḻikkūttar piḷḷaittamiḻ periya tamiḻ," quoted without attribution in Zvelebil, *Handbuch,* 217n80.

8. *Pāṭṭiyals* provide descriptions of a group of Tamil literary genres known as the ninety-six *prabandhas,* of which the pillaittamil is one. A large number of these *prabandhas* originated in the medieval period and are characterized by a high degree of literary convention. See appendix for further information.

9. Ra. Irākavaiyaṅkaḷ, ed., *Panniru Pāṭṭiyal* (Madurai: Madura Tamil Sangam, 1904), 21–22. Not all editions of the text number the verses in the same way, so in consulting another edition, care must be taken in locating the verses. The terseness of my translation echoes the terseness of the original. Terms in brackets are those that I have added because they are assumed in the original. Most scholars date *Pa<u>nn</u>iru Pāṭṭiyal* to the twelfth century. See K. Mutturāca<u>n</u>, *Piḷḷaittamiḻ Ilakkiyam,* for a detailed discussion of the scholarly controversies about the dating of *pāṭṭiyals.*

10. *Pa<u>nn</u>iru Pāṭṭiyal,* 22 ff.

11. Although these poetic sources for pearls are found in verse after verse, Tamil poets were well aware of the more conventional source for pearls. Another *muttam* verse (*MMPT* 47) deals only with specific locations on the Tamilnadu coast, where divers go for pearls.

12. See A. K. Ramanujan, *The Interior Landscape: Love Poems from a Classical Tamil Anthology* (Bloomington: Indiana University Press, 1967), 105–108.

13. Po. Vē. Cōmacuntaraṉ, com., *Kalittokai Nacciṉarkkiṉiyarurai-yum* (Tirunelveli: SISS, 1975), 66, verse 51.

14. Some poeticians say that the pillaittamil deals with the third to the twenty-first months of the child's life. Others say that later paruvams describe play of the male child up to age sixteen and females until puberty. See *Paṉṉiru Pāṭṭiyal,* verses 173–176, and my discussion in the appendix.

15. In Tamilnadu, babies often wear waiststrings and various ornaments, but Murukaṉ's ornaments are particularly elaborate because he is a divine baby.

CHAPTER 4: A TEMPLE AND A PILLAITTAMIL

1. Information about the life of Kumarakuruparar has been summarized from U. Vē. Cāminātaiyar, *Śrī Kumarakurupara Cuvāmikaḷ Pirapantattiraṭṭu* (1936; reprint, Tiruppanandal: Kasimatham, 1961), 19–20; S. Vaittiyanātaṉ, *Pirkālap Pulavarkaḷ* (Madras: Dr. U. Vē. Cāminātaiyar Publishers, 1986), 118–124; Ramakrishna, Gayathri, and Chattopadhyaya, *An Encyclopedia of South Indian Culture,* 254–255. Kumarakuruparar has himself been the subject of a pillaittamil. See Āṇṭavaṉ Piccai, *Śrī Kumarakuruparaṉ Piḷḷaittamiḻ.* (Madras: Pi. Tī. Pāṇi Company, 1953).

2. Kumarakuruparar then settled in Banares, learned Hindustani, and lectured on the excellence of *Kamparāmāyaṇam.* According to tradition, he received a gift of land from the Mughal emperor and established a monastery there. The sixth head of his monastery then returned to South India and established the Kasi monastery at Tiruppanandal, near the Dharmapuram monastery, where Kumarakuruparar had been educated. See Zvelebil, *Handbuch,* 230n167.

3. A. V. Jeyechandrun, *The Madurai Temple Complex (with Special Reference to Literature and Legends)* (Madurai: Madurai Kamaraj Uni-

versity, 1985), summarizes the political history of the temple as recorded in the two traditional accounts maintained by the priests and accountants of the temple. See p. 119 for the relationship between Tirumalai Nāyakkar and the Goddess Mīn̲āṭci. For a discussion of architecture and temple patronage in Madurai, see Susan J. Lewandowski, "An Historical Analysis of Madurai and Madras," in *Economy and Society: Essays in Indian Economic and Social History,* ed. K. N. Chaudhuri and Clive J. Dewey (Delhi: Oxford University Press, 1979), especially 306–309.

4. For a detailed account of the ways in which Tirumalai Nāyakkar shaped the worship of Mīn̲āṭci and her consort, see Dennis Hudson, "Śiva, Mīn̲akṣī, Viṣṇu—Reflections on a Popular Myth in Madurai," *The Indian Economic and Social History Review,* 14, no. 1 (January–March 1977): 107–118.

5. This well-known legend appears in a number of sources, including Jeyechandrun, *The Madurai Temple Complex,* 119.

6. The Pandiyan kingdom possessed renowned pearl fisheries, and its rulers sported pearl jewelry. See Indira Viswanathan Peterson, *Poems to Śiva: The Hymns of the Tamil Saints* (Princeton: Princeton University Press, 1989), 273.

7. For a more detailed discussion of Tamil meters, see V. S. Rajam, *A Reference Grammar of Classical Tamil Poetry,* vol. 1 (Philadelphia: American Philosophical Society, 1992), chap. 6, as well as George L. Hart and Hank Heifetz, *The Forest Book of the Rāmāyaṇa of Kampan̲* (Berkeley: University of California Press, 1989), 11–16.

8. David Shulman, personal communication, 31 July 1993.

9. The closest English equivalent to these terms, "mellifluous," turns out to be an appropriate choice because etymologically the word derives from Latin *melli,* "honey," and *fluens,* "flowing." In fact, Tamil connoisseurs laud well-crafted poems with praise of their "honeyed" words and their "flowing" rhythmic verses.

10. P. Mutharasu, *Life and Works of Saint Kumara Gurupara Swamigal* (Srivaikuntam: Kumaraguruparan Sangam, 1973), 13.

11. For an excellent analysis of the classical criteria for poetic beauty in Tamil poetry, see Rajam, *Reference Grammar,* 169–239.

12. Perāciriyār, as quoted in Rajam, *Reference Grammar,* 190n125. Also the chart of hard, soft, and middle consonants that follows is based on p. 43 in her chapter on phonology.

13. "Vocative" here refers to the situation in which the writer uses a distinctive form of a word in order to indicate a direct address to the intended audience. In older poems in archaic English, vocative phrases are often preceded by "O" or followed by an exclamation mark. Except for *MMPT* 61, I have not followed this practice in my translations, because it is usually clear from context that a particular phrase is vocative.

14. For the full story, see Na. Mu. Venkaṭacāmi Nāṭṭār, *Tiruviḷaiyāṭal Purāṇam,* com. (Tirunelveli: SISS, 1965), vol. 3, chap. 61.

15. Sometimes they are referred to as the thirty-three gods, sometimes the thirty-three crores of gods. These alternatives show the nonindividuality of deities in the group.

16. In the Indian *dūta* ("messenger") poem, a person asks a messenger to convey sentiments of love to a beloved. The most famous of these poems is the Sanskrit *Meghadūta* by Kalidāsa, in which an exile beseeches a cloud to carry a message of love to his wife. See Franklin Edgerton and Eleanor Edgerton, trans., *Kalidāsa: The Cloud Messenger* (Ann Arbor: University of Michigan Press, 1968). The Tamil name for the genre is *tūtu.* Like pillaittamil, it is another of *ciṟṟilakkiyam*'s ninety-six, in which according to prescription the poet writes a message of love to be sent through a companion with the purpose of bringing about communication or a reconciliation between two lovers. In this genre, among others, swans, peacocks, parrots, cuckoos, mynah birds, clouds, and the southern breeze are asked to carry messages. See Zvelebil, *History,* 205.

17. Jeyechandrun, *The Madurai Temple Complex,* 232–251. Also see Peterson's excellent discussion of scale types in the *ōtuvār* tradition in *Poems to Śiva,* 59–75.

18. This account is based on a performance that took place from 6:00 to 7:00 P.M. on 5 January 1987.

19. One commentator, Pu. Ci. Puṉṉaivaṉāta Mutaliyār, identifies the text as *Iṟaiyaṉār Akappoṟuḷ.* See p. 24 of the SISS edition of *MMPT.*

20. Puṉṉaivaṉāta Mutaliyār says the hair referred to is the short hair on the elephant's neck. See p. 155 of the SISS edition of *MMPT.*

21. The Tamil term *koṭi* means "vine" or "banner." In this verse, the poet demonstrates his semantic and metrical skill by using *koṭi* time and

time again in the same verse in different contexts. "Vine" has become a common term for a woman, referring to the woman who entwines herself around her lover, as a vine winds around a tree.

CHAPTER 5: THE HINDU MONASTIC MILIEU

1. His disciple was the famous U. Vē. Cāminātaiyar, a major force in the late nineteenth-century rediscovery of ancient Tamil poetry, who wrote the biography as a way of expressing his veneration for his guru. For an account of U. Vē. Cāminātaiyar's rediscovery of ancient Tamil texts, see A. K. Ramanujan, "Language and Social Change: The Tamil Example," in *Transition in South Asia: Problems in Modernization*, ed. Robert Crane. Monographs and Occasional Paper Series, no. 9 (Durham: Program in Comparative Studies on Southern Asia, Duke University, 1970), 61–84. For a discussion of the relationship between the disciple and his guru, see Francis Moraes, "Dr. Swaminatha Aiyar, Editor and Writer," *Tamil Culture* 4, no. 1 (January 1955): 40–53.

Cāminātaiyar wrote the first prose biography in Tamil. This work, *Śrī Mīṉāṭcicuntaram Piḷḷaiyavarkaḷin Carittiram,* 2 vols. reprinted as one (1938; reprint Tanjore: Tamil University, 1986), is the source from which I have drawn the evidence for my analysis of how Pillai composed pillaittamils in the context of monastic culture. Henceforth, page numbers in the biography will be referred to in the body of my chapter in parenthesis. The form is a roman numeral, indicating the volume, followed by a page number. After the slash is a page reference to the section in the very abridged version of text summarized in English for non-Tamil readers: Sridharam K. Guruswamy, *A Poet's Poet: Mahavidwan Sri Meenakshisundaram Pillai of Tiruchirappalli* (Madras: Dr. U. V. Swaminatha Iyer Library, 1976).

2. The biography abounds with stories of how Pillai convinced various monks or scholars to teach him texts that he wanted to master. In one case, he gave a potential guru gifts of hashish, to which the teacher was addicted (I:20/8); in another, he learned the appropriately obsequious form of veneration that a learned monk required before he was willing to teach the young scholar even a few verses of text (I:78/20).

3. *Tēvāram* is a collection of bhakti poems written by three of the foremost Śaiva *nāyaṉārs* (saint-poets): Appar, Campantar, and Cuntarar. *Tiruvācakam* is a particularly beloved devotional text to Śiva by Maṇikkavācakar, written as an allegory between the heroine and her lover.

4. For a celebratory account of the *matha,* see *A Short History of the Thiruvavaduthurai Adheenam of Thirukkailya Parambarai,* Publication Series No. 163 (Thiruvavaduthurai: Adheenam Press, 1979), especially 16, 23, 41. For analysis of the economic and social role of the *matha,* see C. J. Baker and D. A. Washbrook, *South India: Political Institutions and Political Change 1880–1940* (Delhi: Macmillan, 1975), especially 73–74.

5. One might wonder why Pillai could not pay the publication costs, since when he composed a poem for a patron he received costly gifts and cash. Even with such occasional gifts, a poet such as Pillai often had little cash in reserve, since he had to support his disciples, purchasing clothing and books for them on a regular basis. For a description of how traditional scholars earned their livelihood, see Kamil Veith Zvelebil, *Companion Studies to the History of Tamil Literature,* vol. 2, fasc. 5, of *Handbuch der Orientalistik,* gen. ed. Jan Gonda (Leiden: E. J. Brill, 1992), 170–171.

6. The edition consulted was Tiricirapuram Mīṉāṭci Cuntaram Piḷḷai, *Akilāṇṭavammai Piḷḷaittamiḻ* (n.p.: Śrī Maṭṭuvārkuḻalampāḷaccukkūṭam, 1892). This publication contains one full-page illustration of the goddess in her shrine with two spears flanking her.

7. For example, the great poet and ascetic Civañāṉa Cuvāmikaḷ was closely associated with the piety of the Tiruvavatuturai Matha. His *Kuḷattūr Amutāmpikai Piḷḷaittamiḻ,* accompanied by the commentary of Pillai, was published by the Tiruvavatuturai Matha in 1958; in 1960, the monastery published gratis another pillaittamil written by Civañāṉa Cuvāmikaḷ, *Kalicaicceṅkalunīr Vināyaka Piḷḷaittamiḻ,* with notes by Pillai; Pillai's commentary on *Kōmatiyampikai Piḷḷaittamiḻ* by Citamparanāta Pūpati appeared in 1971. This publication occurred as part of the celebration of the birth of Ampalavāṇa Cuvāmikaḷ, the abbot lauded in Pillai's own *Ampalavāṇa Cuvāmikaḷ Piḷḷaittamiḻ.* I found extensive information about the publication history of monastic pillaittamils in annual (and, as appropriate, quarterly) volumes of the *Indian National Bibliography* covering the years 1957 to 1978 (Calcutta: Central Reference Library, Ministry of Education and Social Welfare [Department of Culture]).

8. At the library of the Dharmapuram Matha I found a substantial number of pillaittamils published in honor of special monastic occasions. They were small in size, more like pamphlets than books. A few examples of their publication contexts demonstrate how closely these publications are tied to the ritual calendar of the monastery: In 1961 the

Kasi Matha published an edition of *MMPT* by Kumarakuruparar in celebration of the seventeenth year of the current abbot's ascending to his position of leadership. Tiruvavatuturai Matha published *Śrī Ñāṉacampantar Piḷḷaittamiḻ* in 1953 to commemorate its illustrious second abbot. A pillaittamil by Citampara Muṉivar titled *Cuppiramaṇiyakkaṭavuḷ Kṣēttirakkōvai Piḷḷaittamiḻ* was issued in 1955 to mark the fourth anniversary of the abbot's ascension to office. For a discussion of the publication history of pillaittamils, see Vai. Kaṇṇiyaṉ, "Pāvēntar Piḷḷaittamiḻ: Ōr Āyvu" (M.Phil. thesis, Madras University, 1981). Evidence indicates that monastic ritual celebrations have a long history in the Śaivite monasteries of Tamilnadu. Epigraphical remains attest that donors left money to *mathas* for the recitation and exposition of religious texts, which were held on a regular basis. See D. Natarajan, "Endowments in Early Tamil Nadu," *Bulletin of the Institute of Traditional Cultures, Madras* (July–December 1974): 101–118.

9. One of the epithets of the composer of *Periya Purāṇam* was "Vaṉ Tōṇṭar" (intense or harsh devotee). Narayana Chettiyar, the patron who requested that Pillai compose a pillaittamil to Cēkkiḻār, had also won the epithet "Vaṉ Tōṇṭar." Pillai replied to Narayana Chettiyar's request by saying that since the first "Vaṉ Tōṇṭar" (namely, Cēkkiḻār) provided the basis for the entire *Periya Purāṇam,* it was appropriate that another "Vaṉ Tōṇṭar" (Narayana Chettiyar) originate a poetic work on the author of *Periya Purāṇam* (II:184/109).

10. The edition I used was *Cēkkiḻār Piḷḷaittamiḻ* (Tirunelveli: SISS, 1977). This edition has been reprinted on a regular basis since 1958 by SISS. Also helpful was another edition with extensive commentary: Pālūr Kaṇṇappa Mutaliyār, com., *Cēkkiḻār Piḷḷaittamiḻ* (Tiruppōrūr: Sri Kantapperūmaṉ Tēvattāṉam, 1964).

11. Historically one noteworthy feature of *CPT* is Pillai's transformation of the protection paruvam. Instead of filling each niche with requests for protection to individual deities, he takes the words from Cēkkiḻār's poem listing the Śaivite saints and makes these quotations the basis of his request for the saints to protect Baby Cēkkiḻār. For a discussion of the ways in which later Hindu pillaittamils begin to take many other liberties in filling the protection niches with items including sacred ash, particular mantras, and divine weapons, see Mutturācan, *Piḷḷaittamiḻ Ilakkiyam,* 30–33.

12. The *āgamas* are religious treatises. Here Pillai refers to a set of Śaivite texts that set out proper Śaivite philosophy and ritual practices.

13. This verse exemplifies a type of Tamil poetic ornamentation called *col pi<u>n</u>varum nilai aṇi,* in which the same word occurs again and again with more than one sense.

14. The text was *Cīvakacintāmaṇi.*

15. For one commentator's identification of each of these philosophical schools, see Catāciva Ceṭṭiyār's discussion in the SISS edition, 67–68.

16. David Dean Shulman, *The Hungry God: Hindu Tales of Filicide and Devotion* (Chicago: University of Chicago Press, 1993), 20. For more on this community of paddy cultivators and their role in agrarian history, see David Ludden, *Peasant History in South India* (Delhi: Oxford University Press, 1989).

17. From the gloss by commentator Catāciva Ceṭṭiyār, p. 75, SISS edition.

18. U. Vē. Cāminātaiyar collected and published an anthology of his teacher's *pirapantam* literature titled *Śrī Mī<u>n</u>āṭcicuntaram Piḷḷaiyavarkaḷ Pirapantattiraṭṭu* (Madras: Vaijayanti Printers, 1910), which contains eight of the twelve pillaittamils Pillai wrote, including the three mentioned in this chapter.

19. The forest north of the village is Tiruvālaṅkāṭu, where, according to Śaivite myth, Lord Śiva dances in the cremation ground. See Norman Cutler, *Songs of Experience: The Poetics of Tamil Devotion* (Bloomington: Indiana University Press, 1987), 117–121.

CHAPTER 6: A PILLAITTAMIL TO MUHAMMAD

1. Shulman sums up the scholarship on this body of texts as follows: "The large corpus of poetic works in Tamil produced by the Muslims of Tamilnadu in South India could no doubt claim to be one of the least-known Muslim literatures in the world. Few compositions by Tamil Muslim poets have ever been popular beyond the boundaries of their community; nor have these works won the attention of scholars." David Shulman, "Muslim Popular Literature in Tamil: The Tamīma<u>n</u>cāri Mālai," in *Islam in Asia,* vol. 1: *South Asia,* ed. Yohanan Friedmann (Boulder: Westview Press, 1984), 174. For a set of key reference works on Islamic Tamil literature, see Ma. Mu. Uvaicu and Pī. Mu. Ajmalkā<u>n</u>, *Islāmiyat Tamiḻ Varalā<u>r</u>u,* 3 vols. (Madurai: Kamarajar University, 1986–1992) for a history, as well as their *Islāmiyat Tamiḻilakkiya Nūl Vivarak-*

kōvai (Madurai: Madurai Kamarajar University, 1991) for a bibliography. Also useful is Uvaicu's Tamil-Arabic lexicon, *Tamiḻ Ilakkiya Aṟapu Col Akarāti* (Madurai: Madurai Kamarajar University, 1983). His work in English includes M. M. Uwise, *Muslim Contribution to Tamil Literature* (Kandy: Tamil Manram Publishers, 1953).

2. Muslim communities have a long history in Tamilnadu—especially in the coastal areas. Studies in English include: Susan Bayly, *Saints, Goddesses and Kings: Muslims and Christians in South Asian Society* (Cambridge: Cambridge University Press, 1990), chap. 3–5; M. Abdul Rahim, "Islam in Negapatam," *Bulletin of the Institute of Traditional Cultures, Madras* (July–December 1974): 85–99; Mattison Mines, *The Warrior Merchants: Textiles, Trade, and Territory in South India* (Cambridge: Cambridge University Press, 1984).

3. See Muhammad Yousuf Kokan, *Arabic and Persian in Carnatic, 1710–1960* (Madras: Ameera Press, 1974).

4. Some Islamic Tamil poets chose to write in longer narrative forms. For example, Umaṟuppulavar wrote an epic on the life of the Prophet called *Cīṟāppurāṇam.*

5. Several holy men whose tombs have become pilgrimage sites in Tamilnadu have had pillaittamils composed to them, including Shahul Hamid (tomb in Nagore) and Nathar Wali (tomb in Kayilpatnam).

6. Part of the pillaittamil to Fatima is said to be extant in manuscript form. The pillaittamil to Ayishā, one of Muhammad's wives, was written recently: Mu. Sherīp, *Ayishā Nācciyār Piḷḷaittamil* (Madras: Cītakkāti Nūl Publishers, 1979). Interestingly enough, Sherīp told me that asking for a kiss from Ayishā, wife of the Prophet, did not strike him as a respectable request. It was for this reason that he slightly modified the traditional refrain for the kiss paruvam to ask that Baby Ayishā kiss the feet of Muhammad. Interview at the poet's home in Madras, 21 August 1986.

7. This statement is from Asani's correspondence to me dated 24 July 1995. He also said, "As far as I know, the manner and style in which Tamil poems address the baby Prophet is unique and an excellent example of the impact of local traditions." Ali Asani, personal communication.

Ali Asani, trans., "In Praise of Muhammad: Sindhi and Urdu Poems," in *Religions of India in Practice,* ed. Donald S. Lopez, Jr. (Princeton: Princeton University Press, 1995), 160–161, explains the characteristics of *maulud* poetry. For the example that celebrates the smile of Amina when she gave birth to the Prophet, see p. 163. For a description of *maulud* celebrations in the Turkish context, see Suleyman Chelebi, *The Mevlidi Sherif* (1943; reprint, London: John Murray, 1957). For more on popular Islamic poetry in South Asia, see Ali Asani, *Celebrating the Prophet: Images of the Prophet in Popular Muslim Poetry* (Columbia: University of South Carolina Press, 1995).

8. Schimmel, *And Muhammad is His Messenger,* 5–8.

9. *Fat-Ḥud-Dayyān Fi Fiqhi Khairil Adyān (A Compendium on Muslim Theology and Jurisprudence by Sayyid Muḥammad Ibn Aḥmad Lebbai ᶜAlim Al-Qāhiri Al-Kirkari),* trans. Saifuddin J. Aniff-Doray (Colombo: The Fat-Ḥud-Dayyān Publication Committee, 1963), 25, 22.

10. Schimmel, *And Muhammad is His Messenger,* 201.

11. The title page makes a vague reference to an earlier version (a handwritten copy?), but it has not been found. I am grateful to Dr. Uwise for bringing from Colombo and showing me his rare copy of the 1883 edition.

12. See Bayly, *Saints, Goddesses and Kings,* 80, 88, for a discussion of Lebbais and Hanafis and Vadakarai.

13. For a discussion of Rāvuttar (also transliterated by the British as Rawther), see Alf Hiltebeitel, *The Cult of Draupadī,* vol. 1: *Mythologies: From Gingee to Kurukṣetra* (Chicago: University of Chicago Press, 1988), 102. See also Bayly, *Saints, Goddesses and Kings,* 99.

14. We do have some information about the first recitations of several other Islamic pillaittamils. See Cai. Pāttimā, *Napikaḷ Nāyakam Piḷḷaittamiḻ: Ōr Āyvu* (Madras: Amina Press, 1990), 47–55.

15. Ci. Nayiṉār Mukammatu, ed. and com., *Napikaḷ Nāyakam Piḷḷaittamiḻ* (Colombo: Publication Committee of the Sea Street Meelaad Committee, 1975).

16. Furuzanfar, *Aḥādīth-i-Mathnawī,* no. 546, as quoted in Schimmel, *And Muhammad is His Messenger,* 131.

17. For an analysis of the diverse ways that the story of Abraham's sacrifice has been told in Islamic tradition and the conflation of Isaac and Ishmael, see Reuven Firestone, *Journeys in Holy Lands: The Evolution of the Abraham-Ishmael Legends in Islamic Exegesis* (Albany: SUNY Press, 1990), especially 135–151.

18. One Islamic Tamil poet asks for God's protection for Baby Muhammad in the first five protection niches, and in the next five niches notes that the prophets, the Ulama (the community of Islamic scholars), *wali*s (holy men), Hasan and Hussain (grandsons of the Prophet), and a wife of the Prophet also request that God protect Baby Muhammad. See Pāttimā, *Napikaḷ Nāyakam Piḷḷaittamiḻ,* 72–74.

19. The theme of the entire cosmos dancing is also important in the writings of Rumi. For a discussion of nature, the inhabitants of heaven, and other creatures dancing as part of a cosmic dance, see Annemarie Schimmel, *The Triumphal Sun: A Study of the Works of Jalāloddin Rumi* (London: East-West Publications, 1980), 219–222.

20. For a survey of information about this black stone, see *Encyclopedia of Islam, New Edition* (Leiden: E. J. Brill, 1978), vol. 4, 317–322.

21. See Schimmel, *And Muhammad is His Messenger,* 10.

22. Topaz can be white, as well as other colors.

23. Literally the phrase means "the servants who are in *tīn,*" a Tamil transliteration of the Arabic *dīn.* It is used here to mean a person who is a believer, a member of the religious community.

24. *Putal* (sons) might be used in a figurative sense here. It could refer to those considered to be the "heirs" of the prophets, since the Prophet Muhammad, for example, had no surviving sons. I have used "revealed texts" and "commentary" for the problematically vague Tamil terms *maṟai* and *kalai.* An equally plausible translation would be "scripture" and "arts." There are two possible interpretations of the phrase that occurs several lines later, *corkkapati. Corkka* (Sanskrit, *svarga*) means "heaven," and *pati* can mean, among other things, "lord" or "city." The commentator of the edition that I used, C. Nayinar Mohamed, avoided the idea of the Lord of the Heavens dancing, since it is unorthodox to anthropomorphize Allah. His alternative, that "heaven" can be taken to modify city, is also grammatically correct.

25. For a discussion of the history and meaning of this name for the Prophet, see Schimmel, *And Muhammad is His Messenger,* 257.

26. This name comes from the letters at the beginning of Sura 20. Schimmel, *And Muhammad is His Messenger,* 108–109.

27. For Qu'ranic descriptions of the day of judgment, see Suras 81, 82, 84, and 99. The seven clouds seem to come from Islamic tradition. It

is believed that Allah made many of the aspects of creation in groups of seven: seven planets, seven days, and seven actions in fasting. The elephants of the eight directions are standard features in Hindu cosmology. The language about the celestial serpent refers to Seṣa, the serpent upon which Lord Viṣṇu sleeps.

CHAPTER 7: ONE POET'S BABY JESUS

1. For example, for nineteenth-century Christian pillaittamils to Jesus, see Cāminātapiḷḷai, *Cēcunātar Piḷḷaittamiḻ* (Madras: Lyceum Press, 1864), and Pēkkuḷam Upāttiyāyar, *Meyññāṉa Piḷḷaittamiḻ* (Palaiyankottai: Church Mission Press, 1870). For another twentieth-century poem to Jesus, see I. Kuṟṟālam, *Yēcunātar Piḷḷaittamiḻ* (Nagercoil: Kavimaṇi Illam, 1965), which contains the imprimatur of the Bishop of Kottar on the back of the title page. For recent pillaittamils to the Virgin Mary, see S. Tāmas, *Mariyaṉṉai Piḷḷaittamiḻ* (Tañcai: The Author, 1972), and S. Tampurāṉ Tōḻapiḷḷai, *Kaṉṉimari Piḷḷaittamiḻ* (Kaliyikkavilai, Kanya Kumrai District: Reverend Fr. V. M. George, 1972).

2. On 27 July 1991 in Tirucchirappalli, I interviewed Aruḷ Cellatturai, who was accompanied by the Rev. Fr. Soosaimanickam from the Catholic press that published the book. In this chapter, all quotations without notes come from my conversations with the poet. Quotations in the text followed by page numbers in parentheses are taken from Aruḷ Cellatturai, *Iyēcupirāṉ Piḷḷaittamiḻ* (Tirucchirappalli: Aruḷ Vākku Maṉṟam, 1985). I am grateful to Thomas Thangaraj for his helpful reading of the first draft of my analysis of Cellatturai's pillaittamil to Jesus.

3. Mariyasusai, who writes under the pen name of Arul Cellatturai, holds diplomas in both mechanical engineering and technical teaching and is a registered senior technical member of the Institution of Engineers. After five years as an engineering instructor at St. Joseph's College in Tirucchirappalli, followed by three years at St. Joseph's Industrial School, he has worked for more than two decades at Bharata Heavy Electrical Limited as a foreman in the Human Resource Development Center.

4. In addition to the work under study here, some of his other writings include a *patikam* (a kind of poetry) on Mother Mary (1984); *Velaṅkaṉṉip Patirruppāṭṭu,* a guide to bards focusing on Mary as worshipped in the form of the Virgin (1987); and a poem in honor of his wife.

5. Author and cultural commentator G. Devaneya Pavanar (born 1902), called Tamil "the Primary Classical Language of the World." Along with Maraimalai Atigal, he was a major figure in the Only Tamil Movement and wrote widely about the glories of ancient Tamil.

6. For an analysis of the book-releasing ritual in Tamil culture, see Paula Richman and Norman Cutler, "A Gift of Tamil: On Compiling an Anthology of Translations from Tamil Literature," in *Between Languages and Cultures: Translation and Cross-Cultural Texts,* ed. Anuradha Dingwaney Needham and Carol Maier (Pittsburgh: University of Pittsburgh Press, 1995).

7. An analysis of the invitation to the ceremony indicates the key actors in the events. There it is announced that Bishop Rev. Thomas Āṇṭakai Avarkaḷ will release the first copy of the book. Thus, not only do Catholic titles of status (bishop, reverend) precede his given name, it is followed by Tamil literary titles of veneration (Āṇṭakai, "preeminent," and the honorific Avarkaḷ). The person deemed worthy of receiving the first copy was Aruḷ Thiru Lambert Miranda Atikaḷ, director of St. Joseph Theological College, Tirucchirappalli, an influential representative of the institution that supported the poet early in his career. Several people gave words of blessing, including the widely acclaimed poet Mariyatācu (the name means "Servant of Maria") and the secretary of The Three Tamils Sangam, an organization active in promoting classical and classically inspired Tamil literature.

8. The genres to which he refers fall under the rubric of *ciṟṟilakkiyam* (see appendix). The three genres he rejected have prescribed subject matter that he considers inappropriate for glorification of Jesus. For example, *ulā* is a genre in which, by poetic prescription, the poet describes the hero of the poem going in procession through a city. Upon seeing him, women of all ages fall in love with him. The poet should explain in detail, with a tone of eroticism permeating the poem, the sensual allure of these women and how they feel attracted to the hero. Cellatturai clearly rejected such genres. He mentioned one other genre from the *prabandham* classification that he did feel would be appropriate for the praise of Jesus: the *āṟṟuppaṭai,* in which the poet lauds holy places.

Not all Christian Tamil poets would necessarily agree with Cellatturai's attitude toward many *pirapantam* genres. For example, Vedanayaka Sastri wrote *Bethlehem Kuṟavañci* in the *kuṟavañci* genre, which possesses a notable erotic content. For an overview of these genres, see Zvelebil, *History,* chap. 5.

9. Note that Cellatturai is *not* claiming that it would be impossible to write a pillaittamil to Mary. In fact, there are several to her. He is, instead, saying that it would be impossible to write one to her that maintained traditions of erotic imagery that are associated with the pillaittamils to females that have earned the highest literary praise, while simultaneously staying within the constraints of Christian propriety.

10. As he said, "I can even call him in the single person [a grammatical form indicating familiarity and intimacy, rather than honor and distance], like *vā, nāta,* etc."

11. It is instructive to compare Cellatturai's treatment of the protection paruvam to that of A<u>n</u>apiyyā (see chapter 6), who also writes within the ideological framework of monotheism.

12. He labels it *pirippurai,* "gloss of separate [sections]." This label refers to the commentarial technique of dividing the poetry into components and then glossing words and explaining their meaning, as opposed to the opposite technique of focusing on the overall verse as a unit and providing exegesis of it in its entirety.

13. Frederick Clothey, *The Many Faces of Murukan,* 116–131.

CHAPTER 8: POETRY OF CULTURAL NATIONALISM

1. I use "religious" in the formal sense to refer to (1) belief in supernatural beings or a transcendent entity, (2) a set of ritual behaviors and guides to moral action, and (3) a community of adherents who share the same set of symbols. The case of *Kulōttuṅka<u>n</u> Piḷḷaittami<u>l</u>* remains ambiguous in terms of category. One might say it is a secular pillaittamil, since it is addressed to a king who is praised primarily in terms of the honor he brings to his lineage. On the other hand, the king is consistently envisioned as Lord Viṣṇu in human form. See note 13 in chapter 2 for a discussion of this use of religious imagery.

2. For Gandhi, see Rāya. Cokkaliṅka<u>n</u>, *Kānti Piḷḷaittami<u>l</u>* (Karaikudi: Ta<u>n</u>avaiciya Ū<u>l</u>iya<u>n</u> Accukkūṭam, 1925), and Ti. Iḷamuruku, *Kāntiyaṇṇal Piḷḷaittami<u>l</u>* (Kōvai: Kōvai Kānti Ma<u>nr</u>am, 1964); for C. Rajagopalachari, see Kō. Irāma<u>n</u>, *Irājāji Piḷḷaittami<u>l</u>* (Kumbakonam: Makāpāratam Press, 1951); for Bharati, see Ta. Vētarāca<u>n</u>, *Perumpāvalar Pārati Piḷḷaittami<u>l</u>* (Nidamangalam: Valarthamizh Pathippagam, 1982); for Maraimalai Atigal, see Ci. A<u>n</u>pānantam, *Ma<u>r</u>aimalaiyaṭikaḷ Piḷḷaittami<u>l</u>* (Madras: Meyyammai Publishers, 1978). For political figures in Tamilnadu, see

Ponmāri, *Aṇṇa Piḷḷaittamiḻ* (Cinnalapali, Madurai District: By the Author, 1972), and Cumāca, *Peruntalaivar Kāmarācar Piḷḷaittamiḻ* (Erode: Vi. Ka. Patippakam, 1982). See Pulavar Vētā, *Em. Ji. Ār. Piḷḷaittamiḻ* (Madras: Em. Ji. Ār. Muttamiḻ Maṉṟam, 1969) for M.G.R., the movie star who became a politician.

The two pillaittamils in this chapter are Mu. Singaravelu, *Periyār Piḷḷaittamiḻ*, and various authors, *Tamiḻaṉṉai Piḷḷaittamiḻ*, *Tamiḻaracu*, 11, no. 13 (1 Jan. 1981): no page numbers.

3. For one of the formative discussions and illustrations of the term "cultural nationalism" as it applies to South India, see Marguerite Ross Barnett, *The Politics of Cultural Nationalism in South India* (Princeton: Princeton University Press, 1976).

4. The information about the eleven poets in this paragraph is based upon conversations with several people knowledgeable about the Tamil literary scene in the early 1980s, as well as S. V. Subramanian and N. Ghadigachalam, eds. *Tamil Writers Directory* (Madras: International Institute of Tamil Studies, 1981).

5. Norman Cutler, "The Fish-eyed Goddess Meets the Movie Star: An Eyewitness Account of the Fifth International Tamil Conference," in *Cultural Policy in India*, ed. Lloyd Rudolph (Delhi: Chanakya Publications, 1984), 117.

6. Sumathi Ramaswamy, "En/gendering Language: The Poetics of Tamil Identity," *Comparative Studies in Society and History* 35, no. 3 (July 1993): 686.

7. For the noun *paṇpu* in older texts, see Fabricius, *Tamil and English Dictionary*, 655–656; *Index des mots de la litterature tamoule ancienne*, vol. 3 (Pondichery: Institut Français D'Indologie, 1970), 962; and *Tamil Lexicon*, vol. 4, 2454. Also of interest is T. Burrow and M. B. Emeneau, *A Dravidian Etymological Dictionary* (Oxford: Clarendon Press, 1961), 262–263. For the noun *paṇpāṭu* in contemporary Tamil usage, see the recently published dictionary, *Kariyāviṉ Taṟkālat Tamiḻ Akarāti* (Madras: Cre-A, 1992), 669. Note also a related verb, *paṇpaṭu*, with the meaning "to become refined," "to fit," "to adapt," "to till the land." The idea of cultivation makes the verb appropriate to refer to both agriculture and societal culture.

8. These two Chola brothers are Nalaṅkiḷḷi and Neṭuṅkiḷḷi. See *Puṟanāṉūṟu Mūlamum Uraiyum*, ed. U. Vē. Cāminātaiyar (Madras: Madras Law Journal Press, 1935), verse 45, 122–123.

9. Ramaswamy, "En/gendering Language," 696.

10. Cutler, "Fish-eyed Goddess," 120.

11. This tendency conforms to the findings of Ramaswamy, "En/gendering Language," 706, who notes that in one set of materials about Mother Tamil, "Great pains are taken to distance it from any kind of overt religious affiliation." She refers here to a strand of imagery about Mother Tamil that deliberately does not make her into a Hindu goddess figure, to insure that she will be an image that goes beyond religious boundaries among Tamil speakers.

12. Cutler, "Fish-eyed Goddess," 123.

13. Not surprisingly, among present-day South Indians, virtually only Tamilians, mostly ideologues, seem to find this "expansionist" idea desirable.

14. For an overview of secondary literature on E. V. Ramasami, see Paula Richman, "E. V. Ramasami's Reading of the *Rāmāyaṇa,*" in *Many Rāmāyaṇas: A Narrative Tradition in South Asia* (Berkeley: University of California Press, 1991), 176–181, 196–198.

15. The quotations from Mu. Singaravelu in this chapter come from my interview with the poet on 29 December 1991 at his home in Kovilpatti.

16. Singaravelu precedes his protection paruvam with a verse in praise of E. V. Ramasami's disciple and (in some sense) successor, C. N. Annadurai.

17. Traditional washermen in India take dirty clothes to the river, soak them, and then beat them on a rock to take out the stains.

18. The poet lauds the link between scientific knowledge and industrialism even though E. V. Ramasami's interests lay not primarily in championing factory work but in attacking the socioeconomic hierarchy, as expressed in dominant landholding castes and governmental job ranks. Singaravelu extrapolates from those emphases to industrialism, which he sees as an expression of the work ethic articulated by Ramasami.

19. According to a popular legend, during Sītakkāti's lifetime, whenever poets came to him, he honored them with great gifts. As his dead body lay on the funeral pyre, a poet came asking for gifts. Miraculously there appeared as a gift for the poet a flower and a gold ring on his finger.

20. Mention of the six senses is not accidental here. Traditionally Tamil philosophical texts enumerate the six senses as taste, smell, hearing, sight, touch, and intellect/discernment. The term for this last sense, *pakuttaṟivu,* came to be used as the Tamil equivalent of Rationalism. Singaravelu also puns on the Tamil word *puraṭci* (from *puraḷ,* to roll), a term coined to translate "revolution," in verse 93 of the little chariot paruvam, where he asks E.V.R. Ramasami to roll his chariot over the Laws of Manu, the caste system, and the concept of widowhood.

21. See V. R. Ramachandra Dikshitar, trans., *The Cilappatikaram* (Tirunelveli: SISS, 1978), 351 ff.

CHAPTER 9: THE FRUITS OF READING PILLAITTAMILS

1. Rajam, *A Reference Grammar of Classical Tamil Poetry,* 115.

2. Antakakkavi Vīrarākava Mutaliyār, *Cēyūr Murukaṉ Piḷḷaittamiḻ* (Madras: Minerva Press, 1902).

3. Terms such as "Third World," "the Orient," and so forth are in quotation marks because they refer here to marketing categories. For an anthology of articles about the difficulties and challenges of cross-cultural translation, see the essays in Anuradha Dingwaney and Carol Maier, eds., *Between Languages and Cultures: Translation and Cross-Cultural Texts* (Pittsburgh: University of Pittsburgh Press, 1995).

4. Paula Richman, "Prospects for the Study of Islamic Tamil Literature," *Sri Lanka Studies: A Newsletter of the Sri Lanka Studies Group* (November 1994): 1–5.

5. Main Street Readings, directed by Matt Cariello, Lynn Powell, and Jessica Grim, was a three-year series of poetry and prose readings, with an annual session on translation.

6. Just as Kumarakuruparar alluded to figures that would be well known to his audience, Ms. Goodwin alluded to figures well known in her town. Britt Friedman, a local quiltmaker, makes modern quilts of brilliant colors and patterns.

7. Sudhir Kakar, *Indian Childhood: Cultural Ideals and Social Reality* (Delhi: Oxford University Press, 1979), 20.

8. C. S. Lakshmi, "Mother, Mother-Community and Mother-Politics in Tamil Nadu," *Economic and Political Weekly* (20–29 October 1990): WS 72–83. For a discussion of Lakshmi's argument, also see M. M. S.

Pandian, S. Anandhi, and A. R. Venkatachalapathy, "Of Maltova Mothers and Other Stories," *Economic and Political Weekly* (20 April 1991): 1059–1064.

9. The rarity of Vaiṣṇavite pillaittamils in general is noteworthy, but the fact that there are few to Baby Kṛṣṇa seems even more puzzling, since the earliest text to use some of the pillaittamil paruvams is addressed to Baby Kṛṣṇa (see chapter 1, note 5, for information about this text). The few Vaiṣṇava pillaittamils that exist are addressed to Viṣṇu, Rāma, or Hanumān. For Viṣṇu in his form of Aḻakar, brother of the Goddess Mīṉāṭci, see Nārāyaṇaiyaṅkār, *Aḻakar Piḷḷaittamiḻ* (Madurai: Madura Tamil Sangam, 1919). Pillaittamils to Rāma and to the Lord of Vaikuṇṭha (Viṣṇu's heaven) are included in T. Chandrasekharan, *Pillai-T-Tamil-K-Kottu (With Notes),* Madras Government Oriental Manuscripts Series, No. 50 (Madras: Government Oriental Manuscripts Library, 1956). For Hanumān, see Cīrkāḻi Aruṇacāla Kavirāyar, *Anumār Piḷḷaittamiḻ* (n.p.: Aḻvār Tirunakar Tiruñāṉa Muttitirai Piracurālayam, 1960).

10. Ramaswamy, "En/gendering Language," 683–725.

11. In fact, the little house paruvam provides the adult male poet with even greater rhetorical mobility. There he speaks both as a female (or females) and as a child (or children).

12. Alan Michael Parker and Mark Willhardt, *Cross-Gendered Verse* (London: Routledge, 1966), 2. This point is elaborated on p. 196. For a genre of cross-gendered poetry in Urdu, see Carla Petievich, "The Feminine Voice in the Urdu Ghazal," *Indian Horizons: Indian Council for Cultural Relations* 39, no. 1–2 (1990): 25–41. For more contemporary discussions about men writing in ways that take on women's voices in theoretical terms, see the collection of essays edited by Alice Jardine and Paul Smith, *Men in Feminism* (London: Methuen, 1987).

13. See Caroline Bynum, "Women's Stories, Women's Symbols: A Critique of Victor Turner's Theory of Liminality," in *Anthropology and the Study of Religion,* ed. Robert L. Moore and Frank E. Reynolds (Chicago: Center for the Scientific Study of Religion, 1984), for a comparative study of the issue of reversal and gender.

14. For discussion of classical Tamil love poems where the poet assumes the persona of a woman, see Ramanujan, *Poems of Love and War from the Eight Anthologies and the Ten Long Poems of Classical Tamil,* 248–249.

15. John Stratton Hawley, "Images of Gender in the Poetry of Krishna," in *Gender and Religion,* ed. Caroline Bynum, Stevan Harrell, and Paula Richman (Boston: Beacon Press, 1986), 235.

16. See Caroline Bynum, *Holy Feast and Holy Fast: The Religious Significance of Food to Medieval Women* (Berkeley: University of California Press, 1987), 94–112, for a discussion on gender and imagery of subordination. For a discussion of male devotees of Rāma who take on the personae of Sīta's female friends, see Philip Lutgendorf, "The Secret Life of Rāmchandra," in *Many Rāmāyaṇas: The Diversity of a Narrative Tradition in South Asia,* ed. Paula Richman (Berkeley: University of California, 1991), 222–223.

17. Peter Bennett, "In Nanda Baba's House: The Devotional Experience of Pushti Marg Temples," in *Divine Passions: The Social Construction of Emotion in India,* ed. Owen M. Lynch (Berkeley: University of California Press, 1990), 190–191.

18. Arjun Appadurai, "Topographies of the Self: Praise and Emotion in Hindu India," in *Language and the Politics of Emotion,* ed. Lila Abu-Lughod and Catherine Lutz (Cambridge: Cambridge University Press, 1990), 94. For related discussions of the cultural shaping of emotional expression, see the other essays in *Language and the Politics of Emotion* and Owen Lynch's introduction to *Divine Passions: The Social Construction of Emotion in India,* 3–34.

19. Appadurai, "Topographies of the Self," gives a few equivalent "nuts and bolts" in his discussion of the praise prefaces of Sanskrit inscriptions. There one of the main forms of praise is genealogical and chronological statements. We find the dominance of such forms of praise in the early courtly pillaittamil to the Chola king Kulōttuṅkan.

20. Bryant, *Poems to the Child-God,* 72–112.

21. In formulating my discussion of the political aspects of pillaittamil writing I am indebted to members of the panel "Language, Genre, and Discourses of Plurality in South Indian Literature" for the Association for Asian Studies in Washington, D.C., in 1995, especially Indira Peterson and Martha Ann Selby.

22. Nayinar Muhammad, ed. *NNPT,* back of title page (ii).

23. Mu. Caṇmukam, *Napikaḷ Nātar Piḷḷaittamiḻ* (Tanjavur District: Nāccikuḷattur Press, 1978).

24. Ramanujan, *The Interior Landscape,* 115.

25. Eventually the D.M.K. split off from the D.K., and several factions have evolved since then.

26. At least two pillaittamils were composed in praise of Śaivite religious sites outside of India. The temple at Kathiragama, the pilgrimage site in Sri Lanka, was praised in Civañ Karuṇālaya Pāṇṭiyar, *Katirakāmap Piḷḷaittamiḻ* (Colombo: Roberts Press, 1937), reprinted by the Department of Hindu Affairs in Colombo in 1983 with several pictures of the temple included. A pillaittamil to Goddess Mariyammaṉ as manifest in Kuala Lumpur also exists. See Vā. Mu. Cēturāmaṉ, *Kōlālampūr Makāmariyammaṉ Piḷḷaittamiḻ* (Madras: Kaviyaracaṉ Patippakam, 1983).

APPENDIX

1. Traditional Tamil literary discourse makes a crucial distinction between literary texts, *ilakkiyam,* and the works that provide commentary upon and analysis of those literary texts, *ilakkaṇam. Ilakkaṇam,* a Tamil transliteration of the Sanskrit *lakṣaṇa,* denotes a defining characteristic. In Tamil literary tradition, these *ilakkaṇa* texts set out the defining characteristics of literary texts and their constituent parts. An *ilakkaṇa* writer is conceived of by the tradition as a grammarian, but "grammarian" must be taken in its broadest sense, as a person who charts the systems that structure a given discourse. Such writers provide a "grammar" for producing words, syntactical units, and poems. Tamil tradition assumes that clear patterns of textual usage can be elucidated for all three areas through careful textual analysis. *Pāṭṭiyals* provide a "grammar" for the content of poetry. Although the content of *pāṭṭiyals* overlaps at times with that found in literary criticism, literary prescription, and literary history, *pāṭṭiyals* have their own goals, presuppositions, terminology, and discourse conventions.

2. For a discussion of the Tamil aphorism explaining the relationship between the seed and the oil, see Zvelebil, *Companion Studies to the History of Tamil Literature,* 129–131.

3. *Ciṟṟilakkiyam* is often translated as "minor literature" in English histories of Tamil literature, but it actually describes the *form* of texts, rather than rendering some *evaluative* judgment (see chapter 1, note 12).

4. Zvelebil, *Indian Literature,* 194.

5. See Shulman, *The King and the Clown,* for analysis of three other *pirapantam* genres: *ulā* (303–324), *nonṭikanāṭakam* (379), and *paraṇi* (278–292). For a description of the *kuravañci* genre, see Indira Viswanathan Peterson, *The Play of the Fortune-teller and the Birdcatcher: Discourses of Identity in an Eighteenth Century South Indian Literary Genre* (forthcoming).

6. Tamil literary tradition recognizes the existence of a set number of *pirapantam* genres, but the actual number changes over time; the earliest texts enumerate forty *pirapantams*, while later texts discuss ninety-six (although writers disagree about which ninety-six genres belong in the category). The number ninety-six may have been adopted partially for its symbolic value. Cf. the ninety-six components *(tattvas)* of the human body, according to certain philosophical texts.

7. S. V. Subramanian, *Pirapanta Tīpam* (Madras: International Institute of Tamil Studies, 1980), 67.

8. Na. Vī. Ceyarāman, *Cirrilakkiyac Cēlvaṅkaḷ* (Chidambaram: Manivacakar Publishers, 1967), 12.

9. Since this appendix focuses upon *pāṭṭiyals'* discussion of pillaittamil content, I do not discuss *PP* verses on meter and metaphor here. See N. V. Jeyarāman, *Pāṭṭiyalum Ilakkiya Vakaikaḷum* (Madras: Mīnāṭci Putaka Nilaiyam, 1981).

10. Irākavaiyaṅkāl, *Panniru Pāṭṭiyal,* 20. Note that not all editions of the text number the verses in the same way.

11. That odd numbers are more auspicious than even ones partially accounts for emphasis on the third and the twenty-first months in the life of the child.

12. By citing an earlier authority, the author shows his knowledge of the tradition and veneration for his predecessors.

13. We can infer that these verses may present the views of the author since he omits reference to "they," a code word for "previous grammarians," and does not cite a previous authority for his statement.

14. Seemingly superfluous adjectives such as "well-constructed" and "trusted" are sometimes added due to metrical requirements.

15. Or six paruvams, depending upon the way the verse is construed.

16. Discussion of this exception can be found in chapter 1, note 21.

17. On these vows, see Norman Cutler, *Consider Our Vow: An English Translation of Tiruppavai and Tiruvempavai* (Madurai: Muttu Patippakam, 1979).

18. S. Kaliyāṇa Cuntaraiyar and S. G. Kaṇapati Aiyar, eds., *Navanītap Pāṭṭiyal* (1944; reprint, Madras: Dr. U. Ve. Caminathaiyar Library, 1961), 25.

19. The identity of this deity is obscure.

20. Ko. Irāmaliṅkat Tampirā<u>n</u>, commentator, *Veṇpap Pāṭṭiyalum Varaiyaṟutta Pāṭṭiyalum* (Tirunelveli: SISS, 1976). For an overview of the *pāṭṭiyals* mentioned in the following notes, see Cēyarāma<u>n</u>, *Ciṟṟilakkiya Cēlvaṅkaḷ*, 11–14.

21. Ki. Irāmā<u>n</u>ujaiyaṅkār, ed., *Citamparappāṭṭiyal* (Madurai: Madura Tamil Sangam, 1932). The author of this *pāṭṭiyal* wrote both grammatical works and literary texts, including *Tiruviḷaiyāṭal Purāṇa*.

22. Ti. Vē. Kōpālaiyar, ed., *Ilakkaṇa Viḷakkam: Poruḷatikāram Pāṭṭiyal* (Tanjore: Tanjore Sarasvati Mahal Library, 1974). Vaittiyanāta Tēcikar and his son, Kumārarā<u>n</u>a Tiyākarāca Tēcikar, wrote this work.

23. The verses on pillaittamils in this text are cited in the appendix to *IP*.

24. Ca. Vē. Cuppiramaṇiya<u>n</u>, *Pirapanta Tīpikai* (Madras: International Institute of Tamil Studies, 1982).

25. *Pirapanta Tīpikai* is that exception.

26. In poetic practice, those invoked in the protection paruvam vary widely in ways that do not conform to *pāṭṭiyal* descriptions, partly because *pāṭṭiyals* only consider Hindu pillaittamils. The translations in this book demonstrate that Muslim, Christian, and political pillaittamils need not adhere to what the *pāṭṭiyals* say. Even Hindu pillaittamils, however, added Kālī/Durgā to the list of deities invoked for protection early in pillaittamil history. After the poet laureate Pillai filled the protection paruvam of his *Cēkkiḻār Piḷḷaittamiḻ* with invocations to Śaivite saints, later pillaittamil poets felt free to invoke a wide range of protectors in the paruvam.

BIBLIOGRAPHY

Tamil Sources

Note: Since the usual conventions of "first" and "last" name do not fit many South Indian names, I have used the initial standing for a village name or the father's name as the bibliographical equivalent of a "first name" in most cases. Also note that pillaittamils may be listed under the name of the author or under the name of the editor or compiler.

A̲npānantam, Ci., *Maṟaimalaiyaṭkaḷ Piḷḷaittamiḻ*. Madras: Meyyammai Publishers, 1978.

Antakakkavi Vīrarākava Mutaliyār, *Cēyūr Murukaṉ Piḷḷaittamiḻ*. Madras: Minerva Press, 1902.

Āṇṭavaṉ Piccai. *Śrī Kumarakuruparaṉ Piḷḷaittamiḻ*. Madras: Pi. Ṭī. Pāṇi Company, 1953.

Appuvaiyaṅkār Svāmikaḷ, U. Vē. Re., com. *Āṇṭāḷ Piḷḷaittamiḻ*. Coimbatore: Presidency Press, 1904.

Apturṟ-Ṟahīm, *Islāmiyak Kalaikkaḷañciyam*, 3 vols. Madras: Yuṉivarsal Paplishars Aṇṭ Puk Cellars [Universal Publishers and Book Sellers], 1979.

Āṟṟalaracu and K. Ā. Turai, ed. *Nilā Nāṉūṟu*. Madras: Aracu Patippakam, 1973.

Aruṇācalam, Mu. *Tamil Ikakkīya Varalāṟu, 15th century*. Tirucciṟṟampalam: Kānti Publishers, 1969.

Ātinātar Piḷḷaittamiḻ. Madras: Ātinātar Patippakam, 1956.

Cāminātaiyar, U. Vē., ed. *Śrī Kumarakurupara Cuvāmikaḷ Pirapantattiraṭṭu*. 1936. Reprint, Tiruppanandal: Kasimatham, 1961.

———, ed. *Puṟanāṉūṟu Mūlamum Uraiyum*. Madras: Madras Law Journal Press, 1935.

———, ed. *Śrī Mīṉāṭcicuntaram Piḷḷaiyavarkaḷin Carittiram*, 2 vols. reprinted as one. 1938. Reprint, Tanjore: Tamil University, 1986.

———, ed. *Śrī Mīṉāṭcicuntaram Piḷḷaiyavarkaḷ Pirapantattiraṭṭu.* Madras: Vaijayanti Printers, 1910.

Cāminātapiḷḷai, *Cēcunātar Piḷḷaittamiḻ.* Madras: Lyceum Press, 1864.

Caṇmukam, Mu. *Napikaḷ Nātar Piḷḷaittamiḻ.* Tanjavur District: Nāccikuḷattūr Press, 1978.

Caṇmukam Piḷḷai, Mu. *Ayyaṉar Piḷḷaittamiḻ.* Madras: Ceṉṉaip Palkali Kaḻakam, 1975.

———. *Ceḻiyataraiyaṉ Pirapantaṅkaḷ.* Tanjavur: Tamil Palkalai Kaḻakam, 1986.

———. *Ciṟṟilakkiya Vaḷarcci.* Madurai: Manivācakar Nūlakam, 1981.

Caracuvati, Vi. *Nāṭṭuppuṟap Pāṭalkaḷ: Camūka Oppāyvu.* Madurai: Madurai Kamarajar University, 1982.

Cellatturai, Aruḷ. *Iyēcupirāṉ Piḷḷaittamiḻ,* Tirucchirappalli: Aruḷ Vākku Maṉṟam, 1985.

Cēturāmaṉ, Vā. Mu. *Kōlālampūr Makāmariyammaṉ Piḷḷaittamiḻ.* Madras: Kaviyaracaṉ Patippakam, 1983.

Cēyarāmaṉ, Na. Vī. *Ciṟṟilakkiya Cēlvaṅkaḷ.* Madras: Nāval Art Printers, 1967.

Chandrasekharan, T. *Pillai-T-Tamil-K-Kottu (With Notes).* Madras Government Oriental Manuscripts Series, No. 50. Madras: Government Oriental Manuscripts Library, 1956.

Cīrkāḻi Aruṇacāla Kavirāyar. *Anumār Piḷḷaittamiḻ.* No place: Aḻvār Tirunakar Tiruñāṉa Muttitirai Piracurālayam, 1960.

Ciṟṟilakkiyaccoṟpoḻivukaḷ—Irantāvatu Mānāṭu. Tirunelveli: SISS, 1959.

Citampara Muṉivar. *Cuppiramaṇiyakkaṭavuḷ Kṣēttirakkōvai Piḷḷaittamiḻ.* Tiruvavatuturai: Tiruvavatuturai Adheenam, 1955.

Citamparanāta Pūpati. *Kōmatiyampikai Piḷḷaittamiḻ.* Commentary by Ta. Ca. Mīṉāṭcicuntaram Piḷḷai. Tiruvavatuturai: Tiruvavatuturai Adheenam, 1971.

Civaṅ Karuṇālaya Pāṇṭiyar. *Katirakāmap Piḷḷaittamiḻ.* Colombo: Roberts Press, 1937.

Civañāṉa Cuvāmikaḷ. *Kuḷattūr Amutāmpikai Piḷḷaittamiḻ.* Tirunelveli: SISS, 1939.

Civañāṉayōki, Mātava [Civañāṉa Cuvāmikaḷ]. *Kalicaicceṅkalunīr Vināyaka Piḷḷaittamiḻ,* edited with notes by Mīṉāṭci Cuntaram Piḷḷai, Tiricirapuram. Tiruvavatuturai: Tiruvavatuturai Adheenam, 1960.

Cokkaliṅkaṉ, Rāya. *Kānti Piḷḷaittamiḻ.* Karaikudi: Taṉavaiciya Ūḻiyaṉ Accukkūṭam, 1925.

Cōmacuntaraṉ, Po. Vē., com. *Kalittokai Naccinarkkiṉiyaruraiyum.* Tirunelveli: SISS, 1975.

Cōmacuntaraṉār, Po. Vē., ed. *Puṟapporuḷ Veṇpamālai.* Tirunelveli: SISS, 1978.

Cumāca. *Peruntalaivar Kāmarācaṟ Piḷḷaittamiḻ.* Erode: Vi. Ka. Patippakam, 1982.

Cuntaraiyar, S. Kaliyāṇa, and S. G. Kaṇapati Aiyar, eds. *Navanītap Pāṭṭiyal.* 1944. Reprint, Madras: Dr. U. Ve. Caminathaiyar Library, 1961.

Cuppiramaṇiya Mutaliyār, C. K. *Tiruppukoḷiyūr Avinâci Peruṅkaruṇaiyammai Piḷḷaittamiḻ.* Madras: Civakāmi Vilāca Publishers, 1926.

Cuppiramaṇiyaṉ, Ca. Ve. *Pirapanta Tipikai.* Madras: International Institute of Tamil Studies, 1982.

Iḷamuruku, Ti. *Kāntiyaṇṇal Piḷḷaittamiḻ.* Kōvai: Kōvai Kānti Maṉṟam, 1964.

Irākavaiyaṅkaḷ, Ra., ed. *Paṉṉiru Pāṭṭiyal.* Madurai: Madura Tamil Sangam, 1904.

Irāmaliṅkat Tampirāṉ, Ko., commentator. *Veṇpap Pāṭṭiyalum Varaiyaṟutta Pāṭṭiyalum.* Tirunelveli: SISS, 1976.

Irāmaṉ, Kō. *Irājāji Piḷḷaittamiḻ.* Kumbakonam: Makāpāratam Press, 1951.

Irāmāṉujaiyaṅkār, Ki., ed. *Citamparappāṭṭiyal.* Madurai: Madura Tamil Sangam, 1932.

Jeyarāman, N. V. *Pāṭṭiyalum Ilakkiya Vakaikaḷum.* Madras: Mīṉāṭci Putaka Nilaiyam, 1981.

Kaṅkātaraṉ, T. S., ed. *Kulōttuṅkaṉ Piḷḷaittamiḻ.* Tañcai Carasvati Makāl Veḷiyīṭu, No. 154. Tañcāvūr: Makārājā Carapōji Sarasvati Mahāl Nūl Nilaiyam, 1974.

Kaṇṇaiyaṉ, Vai. "Pāvēntar Piḷḷaittamiḻ: Ōr Āyvu." M.Phil. thesis, Madras University, 1981.

Kaṇṇappa Mutaliyār, Pālūr, com. *Cēkkiḻār Piḷḷaittamiḻ.* Tiruppōrūr: Śrī Kantapperūmaṉ Tēvattāṉam, 1964.

Kariyāviṉ Taṟkālat Tamiḻ Akarāti. Madras: Cre-A, 1992.

Kōpālaiyar, Ti. Vē., ed. *Ilakkaṇa Viḷakkam: Poruḷatikāram Pāṭṭiyal.* Tanjore: Tanjore Sarasvati Mahal Library, 1974.

Kumarakuruparar. *Muttukkumāracāmi Piḷḷaittamiḻ.* Tiruppanandal: Kasi Matha, 1969.

Kuṟṟālam, I. *Yēcunātar Piḷḷaittamiḻ.* Nagercoil: Kavimaṇi Illam, 1965.

Mīṉāṭci Cuntaram Piḷḷai, Tiricirapuram. *Akilāṇṭavammai Piḷḷaittamiḻ*. No place of publication given: Śrī Maṭṭuvārkuḻalampāḷaccukkūṭam, 1892.

———. *Ampalavāṇa Cuvāmikaḷ Piḷḷaittamiḻ*. Notes and com. by Mīṉāṭci Cuntaram Piḷḷai, Tiricirapuram. Tiruvavatuturai: Adheenam, 1961.

———. *Cēkkiḻār Piḷḷaittamiḻ*. Tirunelveli: SISS, 1977.

Mutturācaṉ, Ku. *Piḷḷaittamiḻ Ilakkiyam*. Chidambaram: Manivacakam Patippakam, 1984.

Naṉṉul, eds. various. Tirunelveli: SISS, 1978.

Nārāyaṇaiyaṅkār. *Aḻakar Piḷḷaittamiḻ*. Madurai: Madura Tamil Sangam, 1919.

Nayiṉār Mukammatu, Ci., ed. and com. *Napikaḷ Nāyakam Piḷḷaittamiḻ*. Colombo: Publication Committee of the Sea Street Meelaad Committee, 1975.

Pāttimā, Cai. *Napikaḷ Nāyakam Piḷḷaittamiḻ: Ōr Āyvu*. Madras: Amina Press, 1990.

Pēkkuḷam Upāttiyāyar. *Meyññāṉa Piḷḷaittamiḻ*. Palaiyankottai: Church Mission Press, 1870.

Piḷḷaittamiḻkkottu, 2 vols. 1964. Reprint, Tirunelveli: SISS, 1970.

Ponmāri. *Aṇṇa Piḷḷaittamiḻ*. Cinnalapali, Madurai District: By the Author, 1972.

Pulavar Vētā. *Em. Ji. Ār. Piḷḷaittamiḻ*. Madras: Em. Ji. Ār. Muttamiḻ Maṉṟam, 1969.

Puṉṉaivaṉanāta Mutaliyār, Pu. Ci., com. *Tiruccentūr Piḷḷaittamiḻ*. 1957. Reprint, Tirunelveli: SISS, 1979.

Sāturām Svāmikaḷ. *Śrī Vaiṣṇavi Piḷḷaittamiḻ*. Madras: Śrī Vaiṣṇavi Illam, 1974.

Sherīp, Mu. *Ayishā Nācciyār Piḷḷaittamiḻ*. Madras: Cītakkāti Nūl Publishers, 1979.

Singaravelu, Mu. *Periyār Piḷḷaittamiḻ*. Kovilpatti: Maṇimēkalai Patippakam, 1983.

Singaravelu Mudaliar, A. *Abithana Chintamani*. New Delhi: Asian Educational Services, 1986.

Śrī Ñāṉacampantar Piḷḷaittamiḻ. Tiruvavatuturai: Tiruvavatuturai Adheenam, 1953.

Subramanian, S. V. *Pirapanta Tīpam*. Madras: International Institute of Tamil Studies, 1980.

Tāmas, S. *Mariyaṉṉai Piḷḷaittamiḻ*. Tañcai: The Author, 1972.

Tamiḻ Nūl Vivara Aṭṭavaṇai. Madras: Tamil Development and Research Press, 1962– .

Tamiḻaṉṉai Piḷḷaittamiḻ, Tamiḻaracu 11, no. 13 (1 Jan. 1981).

Tampurāṉ Tōḻapiḷḷai, S. *Kaṉṉimari Piḷḷaittamiḻ.* Kaliyikkavilai, Kanya Kumari District: Reverend Fr. V. M. George, 1972.

Tarumaliṅka Mutaliyār, Ā. *Amirta Rāmāyaṇam.* Madras: B.N. Press, 1925.

Uvaicu, Ma. Mu. *Tamiḻ Ilakkiya Aṟapu Col Akarāti.* Madurai: Madurai Kamarajar University, 1983.

Uvaicu, Ma. Mu., and Pī. Mu. Ajmalkāṉ. *Islāmiyat Tamiḻ Varalāṟu,* 3 vols. Madurai: Madurai Kamarajar University, 1986–1992.

———. *Islāmiyat Tamiḻilakkiya Nūl Vivarakkōvai.* Madurai: Madurai Kamarajar University, 1991.

Vaittiyanātaṉ, S. *Pirkālap Pulavarkaḷ.* Madras: Dr. U. Ve. Cāminātaiyar Nūlnilaiyam, 1986.

Vaittiyanāta Tēcikar. *Kamalālaya Ammaṉ Piḷḷaittamiḻ,* edited by Vī. Cokkaliṅkam. Srirangam: Śrī Vāṇi Vilāca Accakam, 1969.

Varatarājaṉ, Kaṇṇanūr Ponnumuttu. *Piḷḷaittamiḻ: Pāppā Pāṭalkaḷ.* Taccanvilai: By the Author, 1971.

Veṅkaṭacāmi Nāṭṭār, Na. Mu., com. *Tiruvilaiyāṭal Purāṇam.* Tirunelveli: SISS, 1965.

Vētarācaṉ, Ta. *Perumpāvalar Pārati Piḷḷaittamiḻ.* Nidamangalam: Valarthamizh Pathippagam, 1982.

English Sources

Abdul Rahim, M. "Islam in Negapatam." *Bulletin of the Institute of Traditional Cultures, Madras* (July–December 1974): 85–99.

Abu-Lughod, Lila, and Catherine Lutz. *Language and the Politics of Emotion.* Cambridge: Cambridge University Press, 1990.

Allchin, Raymond, trans. *Kavitāvalī.* London: George Allen and Unwin, 1964.

Appadurai, Arjun. "Topographies of the Self: Praise and Emotion in Hindu India." In *Language and the Politics of Emotion,* edited by Lila Abu-Lughod and Catherine Lutz. Cambridge: Cambridge University Press, 1990.

Asani, Ali. *Celebrating the Prophet: Images of the Prophet in Popular Muslim Poetry.* Columbia: University of South Carolina Press, 1995.

———, trans. "In Praise of Muhammad: Sindhi and Urdu Poems." In *Religions of India in Practice,* edited by Donald S. Lopez, Jr. Princeton: Princeton University Press, 1995.

Ate, Lynn Marie. "Periyāḻvār's *Tirumoḻi*—A Bāla Kṛṣṇa Text from the Devotional Period in Tamil Literature." Ph.D. diss., University of Wisconsin, Madison, 1978.

Baker, C. J., and D. A. Washbrook. *South India: Political Institutions and Political Change 1880–1940.* Delhi: Macmillan, 1975.

Barnett, Marguerite Ross. *The Politics of Cultural Nationalism in South India.* Princeton: Princeton University Press, 1976.

Bayly, Susan. *Saints, Goddesses and Kings: Muslims and Christians in South Asian Society.* Cambridge: Cambridge University Press, 1990.

Bennett, Peter. "In Nanda Baba's House: The Devotional Experience of Pushti Marg Temples." In *Divine Passions: The Social Construction of Emotion in India,* edited by Owen M. Lynch. Berkeley: University of California Press, 1990.

Blackburn, Stuart. *Inside the Drama-House: Rama Stories and Shadow Puppets in South India.* Berkeley: University of California Press, 1996.

Bryant, Kenneth. *Poems to the Child-God: Structures and Strategies in the Poetry of Sūrdās.* Berkeley: University of California Press, 1978.

Burrow, T., and M. B. Emeneau. *A Dravidian Etymological Dictionary.* Oxford: Clarendon Press, 1961.

Bynum, Caroline. *Holy Feast and Holy Fast: The Religious Significance of Food to Medieval Women.* Berkeley: University of California Press, 1987.

———. "Women's Stories, Women's Symbols: A Critique of Victor Turner's Theory of Liminality." In *Anthropology and the Study of Religion,* edited by Robert L. Moore and Frank E. Reynolds. Chicago: Center for the Scientific Study of Religion, 1984.

Chelebi, Suleyman. *The Mevlidi Sherif.* Translated by F. Lyman MacCallum. 1943. Reprint, London: John Murray, 1957.

Chellamuthu, K. C., T. Padmanaban, and P. V. Nagarajan, comp. *International Catalogue of Tamil Palmleaf Manuscripts.* Thanjavur: Tamil University, 1986.

Classified Catalogue of the Public Reference Library Consisting of Books Registered from 1867–1889 at the Office of the Registrar of Books, Old College, Madras. Madras: By the Superintendent, Government Press, 1894.

Clothey, Fred W. *The Many Faces of Murukan̲: The History and Meaning of a South Indian God.* The Hague: Mouton, 1978.

Crystal, David. *An Encyclopedic Dictionary of Language and Languages.* Oxford: Basil Blackwell, 1992.

Cutler, Norman. *Songs of Experience: The Poetics of Tamil Devotion.* Bloomington: Indiana University Press, 1987.

———. "The Fish-eyed Goddess Meets the Movie Star: An Eyewitness Account of the Fifth International Tamil Conference." In *Cultural Policy in India,* edited by Lloyd Rudolph. Delhi: Chanakya Publications, 1984.

———. *Consider Our Vow: An English Translation of Tiruppavai and Tiruvempavai.* Madurai: Muttu Patippakam, 1979.

Dimmitt, Cornelia. "Sītā: Fertility Goddess and Śakti." *Anima* 7 (1980): 19–30.

Dimmitt, Cornelia, and J. A. B. van Buitenen, trans. *Classical Hindu Mythology.* Philadelphia: Temple University Press, 1978.

Dimock, Edward C. "Doctrine and Practice Among the Vaiṣṇavas of Bengal." In *Krishna: Myths, Rites, and Attitudes,* edited by Milton Singer. Chicago: University of Chicago Press, 1966.

Dingwaney, Anuradha, and Carol Maier, eds. *Between Languages and Cultures: Translation and Cross-Cultural Texts.* Pittsburgh: University of Pittsburgh Press, 1995.

Doniger, Wendy, and Brian Smith, trans. *The Laws of Manu.* London: Penguin, 1991.

Edgerton, Franklin, and Eleanor Edgerton, trans. *Kalidāsa: The Cloud Messenger.* Ann Arbor: University of Michigan Press, 1968.

Encyclopedia of Islam, New Edition. Leiden: E. J. Brill, 1978.

Fabricius, J. P. *Tamil and English Dictionary.* Tranquebar: Lutheran Publishing House, 1972.

Fat-Ḥud-Dayyān Fi Fiqhi K̲h̲airil Adyān (A Compendium on Muslim Theology and Jurisprudence by Sayyid Muḥammad Ibn Aḥmad Lebbai ʿAlim Al-Qāhiri Al-Kirkari). Translated by Saifuddin J. Aniff-Doray. Colombo: The Fat-Ḥud-Dayyān Publication Committee, 1963.

Firestone, Reuven. *Journeys in Holy Lands: The Evolution of the Abraham-Ishmael Legends in Islamic Exegesis.* Albany: SUNY Press, 1990.

Gerow, Edwin. *A Glossary of Indian Figures of Speech.* The Hague: Mouton, 1971.

Guruswamy, Sridharam K. *A Poet's Poet: Mahavidwan Sri Meenakshisundaram Pillai of Tiruchirappalli.* Madras: Dr. U. V. Swaminatha Iyer Library, 1976.

Hardy, Friedhelm. *Virāha-Bhakti: The Early History of Kṛṣṇa Devotion in South India.* Delhi: Oxford University Press, 1983.

Hart, George L., and Hank Heifetz. *The Forest Book of the Ramāyana of Kampan̲.* Berkeley: University of California Press, 1989.

Hawley, John Stratton. "Images of Gender in the Poetry of Krishna." In *Gender and Religion,* edited by Caroline Bynum, Stevan Harrell, and Paula Richman, 231–256. Boston: Beacon Press, 1986.

———. *Krishna, The Butter Thief.* Princeton: Princeton University Press, 1983.

Hiltebeitel, Alf. *The Cult of Draupadī,* vol. 1: *Mythologies: From Gingee to Kurukṣetra.* Chicago: University of Chicago Press, 1988.

Hudson, Dennis. "Śiva, Mīn̲akṣī, Viṣṇu—Reflections on a Popular Myth in Madurai." *The Indian Economic and Social History Review* 14, no. 1 (January–March 1977): 107–118.

Index des mots de la litterature tamoule ancienne, 3 vols. Pondichery: Institut Français D'Indologie, 1970.

Indian National Bibliography. Calcutta: Central Reference Library, Ministry of Education and Social Welfare (Department of Culture), 1957–1978.

Jardine, Alice, and Paul Smith. *Men in Feminism.* London: Methuen, 1987.

Jeyechandrun, A. V. *The Madurai Temple Complex (with Special Reference to Literature and Legends).* Madurai: Madurai Kamaraj University, 1985.

Kakar, Sudhir. *Indian Childhood: Cultural Ideals and Social Reality.* Delhi: Oxford University Press, 1979.

Kangle, R. P. *The Kautiliya Arthaśāstra.* Bombay: University of Bombay, 1972.

Lakshmi, C. S. "Mother, Mother-Community and Mother-Politics in Tamil Nadu." *Economic and Political Weekly* (20–29 October 1990): WS 72–83.

Lewandowski, Susan J. "An Historical Analysis of Madurai and Madras." In *Economy and Society: Essays in Indian Economic and Social History,* edited by K. N. Chaudhuri and Clive J. Dewey, 299–329. Delhi: Oxford University Press, 1979.

Ludden, David. *Peasant History in South India.* Delhi: Oxford University Press, 1989.

Lutgendorf, Philip. "The Secret Life of Rāmchandra." In *Many Rāmāyaṇas: The Diversity of a Narrative Tradition in South Asia,* edited by Paula Richman. Berkeley: University of California Press, 1991.

Mahalingam, V. R. "Kulottungan Pillaittamil." M.A. thesis, University of Madras, 1956.

Mani, Vettam. *Puranic Encyclopedia: A Comprehensive Dictionary with Special Reference to the Epic and Purāṇic Literature.* Delhi: Motilal Banarsidass, 1979.

Mines, Mattison. *The Warrior Merchants: Textiles, Trade, and Territory in South India.* Cambridge: Cambridge University Press, 1984.

Moraes, Francis. "Dr. Swaminatha Aiyar, Editor and Writer." *Tamil Culture* 4, no. 1 (January 1955): 40–53.

Murdoch, John, comp. *Classified Catalogue of Tamil Printed Books with Introductory Notices.* Madras: Christian Vernacular Education Society, 1865.

Mutharasu, P. *Life and Works of Saint Kumara Gurupara Swamigal.* Srivaikuntam: Kumaraguruparan Sangam, 1973.

Natarajan, D. "Endowments in Early Tamil Nadu." *Bulletin of the Institute of Traditional Cultures, Madras* (July–December 1974): 101–118.

Olaganatha Pillay, L. *A Descriptive Catalogue of the Tamil Manuscripts in the Tanjore Maharaja Sarafoji Saraswathi Mahal Library, Thanjavoor,* 3 vols. 1925. Reprint, Tirucchirappali: Southern Printers, 1964.

Olsen, Tillie. *Silences.* New York: Delacourt Press, 1978.

Pandian, M. S., S. Anandhi, and A. R. Venkatachalapathy. "Of Maltova Mothers and Other Stories." *Economic and Political Weekly* (20 April 1991): 1059–1064.

Parker, Alan Michael, and Mark Willhardt. *Cross-Gendered Verse.* London: Routledge, 1966.

Parmar, Aradhana. *Technique of Statecraft: A Study of Kautilya's Arthaśāstra.* Delhi: Atma Ram and Sons, 1987.

Peterson, Indira Viswanathan. *Poems to Śiva: The Hymns of the Tamil Saints.* Princeton: Princeton University Press, 1989.

———. *The Play of the Fortune-teller and the Birdcatcher: Discourses of Identity in an Eighteenth Century South Indian Literary Genre.* Forthcoming.

Petievich, Carla. "The Feminine Voice in the Urdu Ghazal." *Indian Horizons: Indian Council for Cultural Relations* 39, nos. 1–2 (1990): 25–41.

Rajam, V. S. *A Reference Grammar of Classical Tamil Poetry,* vol. 1. Philadelphia: American Philosophical Society, 1992.

Ramachandra Dikshitar, V. R., trans. *The Cilappatikaram.* Tirunelveli: SISS, 1978.

Ramakrishna, G., N. Gayathri, and Debiprasad Chattopadhyaya. *An Encyclopedia of South Indian Culture.* Calcutta: K. P. Bagchi and Co., 1983.

Ramanujan, A. K. "Language and Social Change: The Tamil Example." In *Transition in South Asia: Problems in Modernization,* edited by Robert Crane, 61–84. Durham: Duke University, 1970.

———. "Where Mirrors are Windows: Toward an Anthology of Reflections." *History of Religions* 28, no. 3 (February 1989): 187–216.

———, trans. *The Interior Landscape: Love Poems from a Classical Tamil Anthology.* Bloomington: Indiana University Press, 1967.

———, trans. *Speaking of Śiva.* Baltimore: Penguin Books, 1973.

———, trans. *Poems of Love and War from the Eight Anthologies and the Ten Long Poems of Classical Tamil.* New York: Columbia University, 1985.

Ramaswamy, Sumathi. "En/gendering Language: The Poetics of Tamil Identity." *Comparative Studies in Society and History* 35, no. 3 (July 1993): 683–725.

Richman, Paula. "E. V. Ramasami's Reading of the *Rāmāyaṇa.*" In *Many Rāmāyaṇas: A Narrative Tradition in South Asia,* 175–201. Berkeley: University of California Press, 1991.

———. "Prospects for the Study of Islamic Tamil Literature." *Sri Lanka Studies: A Newsletter of the Sri Lanka Studies Group* (November 1994): 1–5.

Richman, Paula, and Norman Cutler, eds. *A Gift of Tamil: Translations from Tamil Literature.* New Delhi: Manohar and the American Institute of Indian Studies, 1992.

———. "A Gift of Tamil: On Compiling an Anthology of Translations from Tamil Literature." In *Between Languages and Cultures: Translation and Cross-Cultural Texts,* edited by Anuradha Dingwaney Needham and Carol Maier. Pittsburgh: University of Pittsburgh Press, 1996.

Schimmel, Annemarie. *And Muhammad is His Messenger: The Veneration of the Prophet in Islamic Piety.* Chapel Hill: University of North Carolina Press, 1985.

———. *The Triumphal Sun: A Study of the Works of Jalāloddin Rumi.* London: East-West Publications, 1980.

A Short History of the Thiruvavaduthurai Adheenam of Thirukkailya Parambarai. Publication Series No. 163. Thiruvavaduthurai: Adheenam Press, 1979.

Shulman, David Dean. *The Hungry God: Hindu Tales of Filicide and Devotion.* Chicago: University of Chicago Press, 1993.

———. *The King and the Clown in South Indian Myth and Poetry.* Princeton: Princeton University Press, 1985.

———. "Muslim Popular Literature in Tamil: The Tamīmaṉcāri Mālai." In *Islam in Asia,* vol. 1: *South Asia,* edited by Yohanan Friedmann. Boulder: Westview Press, 1984.

Subramanian, S. V., and N. Ghadigachalam, eds. *Tamil Writers Directory.* Madras: International Institute of Tamil Studies, 1981.

Tamil Lexicon. 7 vols. Madras: University of Madras, 1982.

Uwise, M. M. *Muslim Contribution to Tamil Literature.* Kandy: Tamil Manram Publishers, 1953.

Varadarajan, Mu. *A History of Tamil Literature.* New Delhi: Sahitya Akademi, 1980.

Woolf, Virginia. *A Room of One's Own.* New York: Harcourt, Brace, and World, 1965.

Yousuf Kokan, Muhammad. *Arabic and Persian in Carnatic, 1710–1960.* Madras: Ameera Press, 1974.

Zvelebil, Kamil Veith. *Companion Studies to the History of Tamil Literature,* vol. 2, fasc. 5, of *Handbuch der Orientalistik,* gen. ed. Jan Gonda. Leiden: E. J. Brill, 1992.

———. *Tamil Literature,* vol. 2, fasc. 1, of *Handbuch der Orientalistik,* gen. ed. Jan Gonda. Leiden: E. J. Brill, 1975.

———. *Tamil Literature,* vol. 10, fasc. 1, of *A History of Indian Literature,* gen. ed. Jan Gonda. Wiesbaden: Otto Harrassowitz, 1974.

INDEX

Tamil Names of Paruvams

Ammāṉai (girl's game like jacks), 12, 14, 233, 235
Ampuli (moon), 12–13, 26

Cappāṇi (clap), 12–13
Ceṅkīrai (sway to and fro), 12–13, 138, 232, 240–241 n. 18
Ciṟṟil (little house), 12–14, 162
Ciṟupaṟai (little drum), 10, 12–14
Ciṟutēr (little chariot), 12–14

Kaḻaṅku (alternative paruvam for girls), 235, 241 n. 21
Kāppu (protection), 12–13, 163, 230, 240 n. 17

Muttam (kiss), 10, 12–13, 59, 61–62, 97, 139, 248 n. 11

Nīrāṭal (bathing in the waters), 10, 12, 14

Tāla (tongue), 12–13, 71, 121, 162, 199, 244 n. 14

Ūcal (swinging), 12, 14

Vārāṉai. See *Varukai*
Varukai (coming), 12–13, 162

English Translations of Paruvam

Bathing in the waters (*nīrāṭal*), 10, 12, 14, 89, 110–111, 233

Clap (*cappāṇi*), 10, 12–13, 55, 72, 91, 104–106, 124, 137–139, 149, 170, 173–174, 184, 232, 239 n. 6, 241 n. 18
Come (*varukai* or *vārāṉai*), 6–7, 11–13, 30, 55, 74–75, 83–88, 97–98, 125–127, 151, 228, 232

Jacks (*ammāṉai*), 12, 14, 95–96, 109, 233

Kiss (*muttam*), 10, 12–13, 55, 59–61, 72–73, 97, 107, 137, 139–140, 150, 187, 195, 207, 232, 255 n. 6

Little Chariot (*ciṟutēr*), 12, 14, 55, 80, 143, 156–157, 204, 232, 263 n. 20
Little Drum (*ciṟupaṟai*), 10, 12, 14, 55, 76, 122, 153, 204, 217, 225, 232
Little House(s) (*ciṟṟil*), 12, 14, 17, 55, 61–65, 77–79, 128–129, 140–143, 154–155, 162, 177, 191, 203, 213–215, 217, 232, 242 n. 21, 264 n. 11
Lullaby (*tāla*), 12–13, 55, 71, 97, 105, 120–121, 148, 162, 181, 199, 232, 239 n. 6, 241 n. 19

Texts

Subject Index

Asceticism, 30, 125, 127, 154, 174, 195, 225
Ash (sacred, emblem of a Śaivite devotee), 54, 105, 120–121, 124, 139, 223
Astrologers, 27–28, 169, 191
Astronomy, 17, 28, 38
Aśvins, 94
Ate, Lynn, 239 n. 6
Atheist, 18, 27, 33–34, 49, 179, 190–191, 225, 227
Audience: and accessibility of pillaittamil poetry to modern readers, 135, 166–170; across and within religious boundaries, 3–4, 223–226; at a book-releasing ceremony, 210; as communities of sentiment, 221–223; for debut of pillaittamil, 82, 117; deity as, 82, 88, 209, 250 n. 13; and enhancement of bhakti, 210–212; and familiarity with poetic conventions, 10, 229; for Tamil poetry in translation, 18–19, 212–216, 263 n. 3; for vocal performance of pillaittamil, 97–98
Audiocassettes, of *MMPT*, 97
Auvaiyār, 186, 243 n. 2
Ayisha, 131, 255 n. 6

Baby: in cradle, 94–95; implications of God in the form of, 4–8, 66; Kṛṣṇa as, 239 n. 6, 264 n. 9; lullaby to, 29–30; protection for, 56–59; realistic depiction of, 214–216, 228; tradition of Jesus as, 158, 160, 162, 166–167. *See also* child
Bamboo, 59–61, 77, 127, 211
Banares, 248
Barnett, Marguerite, 261 n. 3
Bethlehem, 259 n. 8
Bhairava, 106
Bhakti, 4–5, 230, 238 n. 5, 239 n. 6, 251 n. 3. *See also* devotion
Bharati, 178, 186, 260 n. 2
Bharatidasan, 186
Bhāva, 4, 220
Bheda (Tamil, *pētam*), 47, 246 n. 26
Bhūdevī, 35–36
Biblical references, 167, 169, 173, 176–177
Birth: of E. V. Ramasami, 189–190; of Jesus, 160, 167, 169; of Mīṉāṭci, 90, 104–105; of monastic leaders, 252 n. 8; of Muhammad, 131, 135, 143, 256 n. 7; of the universe, 78
Birthday: of Jesus, 166–167; monastic celebrations of, 116, 120; of the Prophet, 131, 135
Bishop, 159, 258 n. 1, 259 n. 7
Blackburn, Stuart, 244 n. 7
Blood, shed in battle, 20–23, 184, 187, 196
Body: as subject of philosophical debate, 125; bathing, dressing, and nursing the child, 7–8, 105; child learning to move limbs, 12–13; construction of female, 216; in danger (in moon paruvam), 188, 196; dead, 19–25, 262 n. 19, 242 n. 23; demon's, 28–29, 40; fragrance of, 156; half male, half female (Śiva), 37–38; pollution from, 193; resurrection of, 168–169
Book-releasing ceremony, 161, 259 n. 7
Boy, paruvams for, 10, 14, 216, 231–232, 235
Brahmā, 57–58, 63, 66, 71, 94, 100, 104, 127, 233–234
Brahmanical ideology and power, 34, 139, 178, 188–192, 198–199, 202
Breast(s): as burden for waist, 63–64; erotic, 6–7, 140–143; of gopīs, 80; maternal, 6–7, 105, 216; of Muhammad, 147, 216; as sign of attaining puberty, 62; three, of Mīṉāṭci, 90–91, 107; of Vaḷḷi, 6–7, 68, 74
Bryant, Kenneth, 239 n. 6, 265 n. 20
Buddhists, 122
Business, (protection of), 134, 137
Bynum, Caroline, 264 n. 13, 265 n. 16

Caitu. *See* Sayyid
Cakravāka (bird), 28, 41–42
Cakravāla Mountain, 8, 70, 104

Hands: beating drum, 153; folded in veneration, 31, 191, 197; sore from sifting sand, 63–64, 69, 79, 154. *See also* clap paruvam
Hanumān, 264 n. 9
Hardy, Friedhelm, 239 n. 6
Hare (or rabbit) in moon, 28, 30, 34, 152, 169
Hart, George L., III, 249 n. 7
Hawley, John Stratton, 239 n. 6, 243 n. 6, 265 n. 15
Heaven(s), 8, 40, 65, 69, 76, 90, 100–101, 123, 138, 144, 146–147, 150, 156, 172, 175, 200–202, 257 n. 19, 264 n. 9
Hieronymus, Reverend, 160, 166
Hillwoman (Vaḷḷi, wife of Murukaṉ), 7–8, 31–32, 74
Himalaya Mountains, 9, 68, 84, 88, 101, 106, 111
Hindi, 135; literature, 29, 239 n. 6; Tamilian opposition to, 187, 192, 196, 198, 202, 217, 223
Hindu, 4–9, 16, 31–32, 37–40, 43–44, 53–129, 163, 190–191, 208, 220, 222–226, 234, 238 n. 3, 268 n. 26
Hindustani, 248 n. 2
Honor(s): earned through sacrifice, 123, 126; given to patrons, 124; given to Tamil poets, 114, 116–120, 159, 262 n. 19; for Prophet Muhammad, 132–133, 138; of a royal lineage, 35–36, 184–85; shown to books, 161, 259 n. 6
Houris, 138, 146, 157
Housework, 8–9, 64–65, 220
Hunger, 74–75, 102, 214
Husband, 7–8, 28, 37, 65, 69, 74, 90–91, 95, 108, 232
Hydroelectric power, 16, 165

Icon(s), 37, 58–59, 92–94, 97, 119, 124, 223
Icumāyīl, 137, 145
Ideology, 27, 33–34, 55, 178, 187–188, 190, 194, 208, 223–224, 260 n. 11, 262 n. 13
Ilakkaṇam, 234, 266 n. 1, 268 n. 22
Ilakkiyam, 229, 237 n. 3, 240 n. 12, 243 n. 2, 247 n. 9, 266 n. 3
Indra, 21–22, 40, 44, 57, 63–65, 69–70, 72, 76–77, 90, 101, 110–111, 129, 233, 242 n. 24
Industrialism, 193, 204, 223, 262 n. 18
Infantilized, 217
Initiation into a pillaittamil, 55–59, 226. *See also* protection paruvam
Insults to moon, 17, 38–39, 47, 216
Interview(s), 18, 159–171, 188–194, 224, 226, 255 n. 6, 258 n. 2, 262 n. 15
Invention (poetic), 4, 10, 14, 25, 227
Inventions (scientific), 26, 48, 165
Invocation to a deity (or equivalent), 11–12, 55–59, 68, 94, 97, 136, 190, 207, 230, 233, 235, 268 n. 26
Ipūṟahīm (Abraham), 145
Ishmael, (also spelled Ismail and Icumāyīl) 137, 145
Islam: among Tamil-speaking poets, 15–16, 130–136, 254 n. 1, 257 n. 18; history in Tamil country, 130–136, 255 nn. 2, 3, 4, 5; Qu'ranic passages, 131, 256 n. 17; traditions about the Prophet, 29, 42, 132–133, 139–152, 156, 257 n. 27

Jain, 121–122, 128, 186, 225, 242 n. 22, 246 n. 1
Janaki, S. (vocalist), 97–98
Jesus, 16, 27, 45, 49, 158–163, 166–172, 174, 177, 217, 222–223, 226, 258 n. 1, 259 n. 8
Jewels, 7, 56, 60, 66, 71–72, 79, 103, 122, 125, 138, 144, 146, 151, 170, 199, 232, 249; anklet, 66, 68, 71, 78, 80, 151, 170, 185; earrings, 56, 66, 71, 74, 103, 105
Jeyechandrun, A. V., 248–250
Jinns, 138, 146
Juxtaposition of adult's and child's deeds, 4–8, 24, 66

Ka'ba, 138–139, 149, 222
Kailasam, Saundara, 181
Kakar, Sudhir, 216–217, 263 n. 7

Mṛdangam, 69
Muhammad, 29, 41–42, 130–158, 217, 222, 224, 226, 238 n. 3, 243 n. 4, 256 n. 7, 257 n. 18
Murukaṉ, 6–8, 11, 19–25, 31–32, 43–44, 54–81, 100, 105, 113, 170, 210–212, 217, 223, 233, 246 n. 5, 247 n. 6, 248 n. 15, 263 n. 2
Music: and *MMPT*, 81, 93, 97–98; musicians, 76, 114, 116; of sonorous poetry, 83–88, 102, 120–121
Muslim: communities in South India, 82, 189, 255 n. 2, 256 nn. 11, 12, 13; pillaittamils, 48, 133–157, 208, 224, 235, 238 n. 3, 255 nn. 5, 6, 256 n. 14, 257 n. 18; poets, 16, 130–133, 186, 195, 212, 224, 238 n. 3, 254 n. 1, 255 nn. 3, 7; religious tenets, 41, 131–133, 136, 141
Muttalib, Abdul, 154
Mutturācaṉ, Ku., 238 n. 4, 243 n. 2, 247 n. 9
Mysore, 237 n. 2
Myths, Hindu, 26, 48–49, 116; about the nature of the cosmos, 8; churn ing of the ocean, 28, 69, 243 n. 5; descent of the Ganges, 37–38; DK attack on, 192, 227; in the moon paruvam, 17. *See also* Mīṉāṭci

Nācciyappaṉ, Nārā., 183–185
Nagarajan, P. V., 246 n. 6
Nagerkoil, 29
Nandi, 106
Nathar Wali, 135, 255 n. 5
Nāyaṉārs, 251 n. 3
Niches, in protection paruvam, 56–59, 94, 98, 136–137, 163, 190, 209, 226, 233–235, 253 n. 11, 257 n. 18
Nīli, 126, 233–234
Non-brahmin, 34, 122, 183, 188, 199, 227
Nursemaid(s), 5, 64, 79, 181

Olsen, Tillie, 5, 239 n. 11
Orphan, Muhammad as, 139
Orthodoxy: in Hinduism, 191, 197; in Islam, 131, 134
Oṭṭakkūttar, 35–37, 242 n. 22, 244 n. 14, 245 n. 24
Ōtuvār, 97, 250 n. 17

Paddy (rice), 59, 73, 122, 128, 254 n. 16
Padmanaban, T., 246 n. 6
Pakaḻikūttar, 43–44, 53–54, 56–62, 67, 118, 140, 210, 224, 240 n. 13, 245 n. 24, 247 n. 7
Pakistan, 131, 189
Pakuttaṟivu, 263 n. 20. *See also* Rationalism
Palaiyanur. *See* Nīli
Pallava lineage, 129
Palmleaf manuscripts, 113, 115, 117, 246 n. 6, 256 n. 11
Pandian, M. S. S., 264 n. 8
Pandiyan lineage, 82, 88, 93, 99–102, 185, 187, 249 n. 6
Paṇpāṭu, 183–184, 261 n. 7
Parañcōti Muṉivar, 234, 268 n. 21
Paraṇi (literary genre), 242 n. 23, 267 n. 5
Parmar, Aradhana, 47, 246 n. 27
Parrot, 93, 96, 99, 109, 250 n. 16
Paruvam Structure, 9–14, 17–18, 25–27, 48, 53–55, 67, 98, 130, 143, 163, 167, 181, 187, 194, 207–209, 212, 227–228. *See also* individual paruvam entries
Pārvatī, 58, 66, 68, 71, 78, 88, 106, 217, 233
Patronage of poets, 4, 82, 117–118, 122–123, 134–137, 160, 183–184, 186, 195, 252 n. 5, 253 n. 9
Pāttimā, Ci., 238 n. 3, 256 n. 14
Pāṭṭiyal(s), 56–59, 62, 190, 229–235, 247 n. 9, 248 n. 14, 267 nn. 9, 10, 268 nn. 20, 21, 22, 26
Peacock, 41–42, 44, 60, 65–66, 70, 72, 75, 99, 170–171, 173
Pearls, 170, 173; in the ammāṉai paruvam, 95, 109; as a divinely-bestowed gift, 36, 59, 63, 83, 92; imagery associated with the seaside,

Publication of pillaittamils: by a Catholic seminary, 160; by the Fifth International Tamil Conference, 179–181; of *NNPT,* 133–137, 224; as part of monastic celebrations, 15, 54, 119, 123, 247 n. 6, 252 n. 7; role of Tamil savants in, 118
Pulamaippittaṉ, 187
Pun(s), 6, 31, 59–61, 139–140, 143, 169–170
Punishment (in moon paruvam), 26, 43–47, 187–188, 192–193, 245 n. 20, 246 n. 26
Puṉṉaivaṉanāta Mutaliyār, Ci., 240, 247 n. 6, 250 nn. 19, 20
Puṟam, 161
Pūvainilai, 244 n. 13

Quraishi (lineage of Muhammad), 41, 149, 152, 222–223
Qur'an, 131, 139, 222–223, 257 n. 27
quṭb (Arabic "pole"), 152

Rabbit (or Hare) in moon, 28, 30, 34, 152, 169
Raga, 10
Rāhu, 28, 39–42. *See also* eclipse
Rain, 121, 126, 138, 144, 149, 164, 170, 172–173, 190, 200, 233–234
Rajagopalachari, C., 178, 260 n. 2
Rajam, V. S., 227, 249 nn. 11, 12, 263 n. 1
Ram, Sadhu, 42–43
Rāma, 216, 241 n. 19
Ramanujan, A. K., 3, 97, 224, 239 n. 9, 243 n. 25, 248 n. 12, 251 n. 1, 264 n. 14
Ramasami, E. V., 18, 33–34, 178–179, 188–194, 200–204, 222, 225, 227, 262 nn. 14, 18
Ramaswamy, Sumathi, 182, 185, 261–262
Ramnad, 53
Rationalism, 179, 190–193, 197, 200–201, 203, 263 n. 20
Ravat, 135
Rāvuttar, 29, 134–135, 256 n. 20
Rawther. *See* Rāvuttar
Recitation, 15, 88, 209–212, 256 n. 14; by Cellatturai, 159–160; by Mīṉāṭcicuntaram Piḷḷai, 113, 116–118, 209–210, 222; of *MMPT,* 82–83, 92, 97
Refrain, of pillaittamil, 7–8, 10–13, 18, 21–25, 34, 40, 59, 64–66, 88, 90–91, 121–122, 136, 141–142, 185, 187, 193–194, 223, 225, 241 n. 19, 243 n. 25, 255 n. 6
Regional identity, 135, 137, 178–179, 186, 220–227
Rice, 30, 65, 77, 120–121, 177, 232, 242 n. 21
Richman, Paula, 259 n. 6, 262 n. 14, 263 n. 4, 265 n. 15
Ritual, 15, 260 n. 1; attacks on Hindu, 178, 190; book releasing, 161, 210, 259 n. 6; monastic, 116–117, 121, 123, 252 n. 8
Rockets, 165, 167
Rūdras, 94
Rut (of an elephant), 35, 59, 68, 73, 153

Śacī (wife of Indra), 57
Sacrifice: of Ishmael, 136–137, 145, 256 n. 17; to maintain honor, 123, 126, 184–185; Vedic, 121, 234
Saiva Siddhanta: conferences on *ciṟṟilakkiyam,* 237 n. 3; reprinting of pillaittamils, 54, 247 n. 6
Śaivite tradition, 98, 186, 208, 217; devotees, 81–82, 97; iconography, 29, 37–38, 48, 59, 233, 254 n. 19; monasteries, 54, 112–122, 252 n. 8; pillaittamils, 53–129; saints, 120–129, 223, 253 n. 11, 268 n. 26. *See also* Śiva
Sandalpaste, 7, 57, 68, 74, 102, 151
Sangam, 45, 104, 159, 161, 183, 185, 215, 223, 225, 230–231. *See also* Tamil literature, classical
Sanskrit: language, 68, 81, 158, 189, 114–116; terms, 43, 125, 229, 240 n. 15, 245 n. 26, 257 n. 4,

266 n. 1; texts, 4, 190, 250 n. 16, 265 n. 19
Sarasvatī, 69, 93–94, 99, 111, 183, 233
Sāsta, 233
Sayyid, 133, 145
Scepter of kingship, 127, 177
Schimmel, Annemarie, 132–133, 139, 243 n. 4, 256 n. 16, 257 n. 19
Science: referred to by Cellatturai, 42, 158–159, 163–165; in the thought of E. V. Ramasami, 191–193, 198, 262 n. 18
Sculpture based on pillatittamils, 92–96, 98
Seaside: bringing forth pearls, 59, 73, 248 n. 11; building little houses at, 14, 61–62; shrine of Murukan̲, 7, 16, 54, 223
Secular, 113, 167, 178, 227, 260 n. 1
Self-respect Movement, 188–194, 199, 203, 217, 227
Sentiments. *See* Devotional, Maternal
Servant mode of relating to the child, 64, 79, 80, 141, 155, 257 n. 23
Śeṣa, 66, 69–70, 258 n. 27
Sesame seed: image of poetic texts, 229, 266 n. 2; image of tininess, 74, 174
Seyyitu An̲apiyyā Pulavar. *See* An̲apiyyā Pulavar, Seyyitu
Shahul Hamid (of Nagore), 255 n. 5
Sherīf, Mu., 255 n. 6
Shoulders, 57, 60–61, 72, 74, 78, 102, 108, 120, 151, 154
Shrine, 193; of Amutāmpikai, 37; of Mīn̲āṭci, 92, 97, 221; of monastery, 118–119; of Murukan̲, 7, 16, 54–80, 211
Shudra, 34, 189
Shulman, David, 122, 242 n. 23, 246 n. 28, 249 n. 8, 254 n. 16, 267 n. 5
Sifting: girls in sand, 63–64, 79, 154; Sarasvatī, 93, 99
Similarity (strategy in moon paruvam), 26, 30–35, 47, 167, 215, 246 n. 26
Sindhi, 131, 255 n. 7
Singaravelu, Mu., 33–34, 178–179, 188–194, 198, 225, 227, 244 n. 12, 262 nn. 15, 18
Sitā, 244 n. 15, 265 n. 16
Sītakkāti, 195, 262 n. 19
Śiva: 126, 254 n. 19; as father of Murukan̲, 6, 54, 57, 71, 78; as husband or consort, 8–9, 81, 96, 124, 217, 249 n. 4; iconography of, 29, 31–32, 37–38, 107, 109, 125; matted hair of, 32, 37–38, 58, 68, 108, 124–125; in protection paruvam, 58, 68–69, 233–235; salvific deeds, 89–90, 95, 101, 118–119, 123; as warrior and destroyer, 104, 106, 108. *See also* Śaivite
Skanda (name for Murukan̲), 32, 69, 71, 211–212
Skandhas, 122, 125
Sky: as element of the heavens, 8, 44–45, 148, 152–153, 175; filled with rain clouds, 173, 203; filled with vultures, 21–24; from which the Ganges flowed, 32, 58; moon in the (*See also* Moon), 14, 29, 168–169, 187, 196
Slave(s): lower castes treated as, 197, 199, 203; relating to God as a, 79
Sleep, putting child to, 66, 71, 105
Śleṣa, 244 n. 10
Smile, of the child, 19–25, 71, 74, 103, 138, 175
Snake, 38, 42, 44, 68, 70, 75, 104
Son, 29, 71, 257 n. 24; of Abraham, 138, 145; of Amina (*See also* Muhammad), 41; An̲appiyā as, 133–134; of God (*See also* Jesus), 163–64, 166, 172, 175–177; in-law, 101; of Konguland (*See also* Ramasami, E. V.), 194, 204; Murukan̲ as, 6, 8, 31, 54, 71, 100, 113, 217; in *pāṭṭiyals*, 232
Songs, 29–30, 76, 84, 88, 97–98, 122, 164, 181, 195, 239 n. 7
Sonority in Tamil poetry, 83–88, 102, 113, 121, 160

Spear of Murukan̲, 7–8, 19–23, 44, 70, 72
Śrīdevī, 35–36
Sri Lanka, 54, 135–136, 237 n. 2, 263 n. 4
Srivaikuntham, 81
Strategies, four; in *Arthaśāstra*, 46–48, 245 n. 26, 246 n. 28; in moon paruvam, 14, 17, 26–46, 209, 192–193, 215; to save little houses 61–65
Stylus in Islamic poetry, 138, 146
Subramanian, S. V., 230, 267 n. 7
Subverting pillaittamil norms, 213, 220
Sugarcane, 129, 150
Sun, 8, 20–23, 30, 75, 100–101; as an eye of Śiva, 29; from which moon gets reflected light, 168, 201; in protection paruvam, 190, 233–234; riding in its chariot, 138; in sky, 65, 70, 146, 148, 153
Sunni Islam, 133
Superiority (in difference strategy of moon paruvam), 26, 35, 175
Supernatural, 190, 260 n. 1
Superstition, according to E. V. Ramasami, 49, 189–194, 200
Suras (of Qu'ran), 131, 139, 257 n. 27
Sūrdās, 29, 239 n. 6, 243 n. 6

Tablet in Islamic poetry, 138, 146
Talatu (lullaby), 241 n. 19
Tālēlō, 12–14, 71, 121, 123, 148, 199, 241 n. 19
Talib, Abu, 154
Tamil̲aracu (magazine), 181, 261 n. 2
Tamil language, 3, 19–24, 33, 45, 83–88, 114, 121, 130, 158–159, 163–165, 185, 188–189, 212, 228, 237 n. 2, 243 n. 25, 245 n. 26, 261 n. 7. (*See also* transliteration)
Tamil literature: classical (*See also* Sangam), 5, 18, 61–62, 64, 99, 159, 161, 177, 179, 183–185, 217, 219, 223, 225–226, 231, 244 n. 13, 259 n. 5; commentaries and poetics, (see *pāṭṭiyals*); conferences as celebrations of, 178–187, 194, 224, 227, 237 n. 3, 261 n. 5; medieval genres, (see *cir̲r̲ilakkiyam*). *See also* Vaiṣṇavite tradition, Śaivite tradition
Tamilnadu, 3, 29–30, 54, 130–131, 134–135, 159–160, 162, 166–167, 178–179, 186–189, 217, 227, 237 n. 2, 244 n. 8, 248 n. 15, 253 n. 8, 254 n. 1, 255 n. 2, 260 n. 2
Tamil Tay, 45, 178–188, 195–196, 217
Tamraparni River, 79, 100, 107, 111
tān̲am (Sanskrit *dāna*), 26, 191, 246 n. 26
Tan̲ittamil̲ Iyakkam, 159. *See also* Tamil Only Movement
Tanjore. *See* Thanjavur
Tuṇṭum (Sanskrit *daṇḍa*), 107, 193
Technology, 158, 163, 165
Telugu, 82, 188
Temple(s), 18; to Mīn̲ātci, 81–112, 221, 248 n. 3; pilgrimage to, 113, 116–118
Thangaraj, Thomas, 258 n. 2
Thanjavur, 54, 119, 187
Thenmozhi, 159
Theology, 117, 219, 226; of the birth of Jesus, 166–167; Islamic, 130, 132, 226; of protection paruvam, 136, 163
Thirty-three deities (Vedic gods), 94–95, 101, 233, 234
Thiruvavaduthurai. *See* Tiruvavatuturai
Threat (to moon), 26, 42–43, 46–47, 187–188
Tiger, 187, 196; emblem of Chola dynasty, 36, 187, 195; of paruvams, 26, 48–49, 167
Tilak (auspicious forehead mark), 6–7, 111, 166, 193, 199
Tinnevelly. *See* Tirunelveli
Tīrtaṅkiras, 242 n. 22
Tiruccentur, 7, 44, 53–81, 193, 223, 246 n. 5
Tirucchirappalli, 112–113, 118, 135
Tirumalai Nāyakkar (ruler of Madurai), 81–83, 221, 249 nn. 3, 4
Tirunelveli, 54, 81–82, 134, 158, 160, 244
Tiruppanandal, 248 n. 2

Tiruvaḷḷuvar, 186, 190
Tiruvavatuturai, 112, 114, 118–119, 252 nn. 4, 7, 253 n. 8
Toṭukkum kaṭavuḷ (first phrase of *MMPT* 61), 83, 85, 87
Trade, in the protection paruvam, 134–135, 137, 255 n. 2
Translation of pillaittamils, 207–208; criteria for selection of poetry, 15–18, 242 n. 22; for a dual audience, 212–216; English scientific terms in, 158–159, 163, 262 n. 20; formal qualities in Tamil, 17, 83–87, 120–121, 249 nn. 11, 12; grammatical complexities of, 19–21, 250 n. 13; of Persio-Arabic terms, 133–137, 144–149, 152, 212, 222, 226, 257 nn. 23, 24; sample in stages, 19–24, 243 n. 25; from a single paruvam, 30–45; verse and paruvam structures in (*See also* refrain), xiii, 9–24, 212
Transliteration, xii, 17, 85–87, 165; of Persio-Arabic terms, 133, 152, 226, 256 n. 13, 257 n. 23; of Sanskrit terms, 244 n. 10, 245 n. 26, 266 n. 1
Tribute paid by defeated kings, 35–36, 66, 70, 95, 100
Trichy. *See* Tirucchirappalli
Tulsidas, 243 n. 6
Tyagaraja, Chettiyar, 192

Ulā, 211, 161, 267 n. 5
Ulama, 257 n. 18
Umā, 58, 68–69, 74, 124
Umaṟuppulavar, 255 n. 4
Ūmatam flower (worn by Śiva), 9, 38, 104
Universe, 8–9, 34–36, 70, 80, 103–104, 123, 138, 147, 152, 220; in the little house paruvam, 63–65; in protection paruvam, 57, 197, 233
Upāyams. *See* strategies
Urdu, 189, 255 n. 7, 264 n. 7
Uwise, M. M. (Ma. Mu. Uvaicu), 254 n. 1

Vadakarai, 134, 256 n. 12
Vaigai, 39–40, 90, 100, 111, 223
Vaiṣṇava tradition, 53, 186, 208, 217, 264 n. 9
Vaiṣṇavi Devī, 42–43, 245 n. 19
Vāli, 44
Vaḷḷi (wife of Murukaṉ), 7, 31, 69, 74
Vasūki, 44
Vāsus (Vedic deities), 94
Vātsalya bhakti, 4, 220, 239 n. 6
Vaṭukaṉ, 233
Vedanayaka Sastri, 259 n. 8
Vedic rites and deities, 76, 94, 101, 120–121, 233–234
Veḷḷāḷas, 81, 112–113, 120, 122–123, 126, 223, 225–226, 254 n. 16
Venkatachalapathy, A. R., 264 n. 8
Vessels, washing of, 8–9
Victories: on the battlefield, 20–25, 35–36, 132, 142–143, 156, 181, 212; in intellectual, moral, or spiritual battles, 124, 126, 191, 197, 225
Vijayanagar Empire, 82
Vināyakar, 97–98, 252 n. 7. *See also* Gaṇeśa
Vindhya Mountains, 20, 22–23
Vīrarākavaṉ, Antakavi, 210–212, 263 n. 2
Virgin: Mary, 168, 177, 258 n. 27, 264 n. 9; Mīṉāṭci, 100; Tamil Land, 202; Tamil Tay, 184–185, 196
Viruttam, aciriya (meter), 83
Viṣṇu, 28, 66, 70, 100, 104, 127, 190; identified with Tamil kings, 35–36, 244 n. 13, 260 n. 1; in protection paruvam, 56–58, 98, 190, 233–235; in *trimūrti*, 63, 94
Vocative, 84–85, 88, 250 n. 13
Voice: of little girls, 14, 61, 141; maternal, 5, 160, 181, 208, 217–220, 228, 233, 264 n. 12
Vowels in poetic prescriptions, 86
Vṛṣabhadeva, 242 n. 22
Vultures, 20–23

Wafer (Christian communion), 168–169